Classroom Management for Middle and High School Teachers

Classroom Management for Middle and High School Teachers

SEVENTH EDITION

Edmund T. Emmer
The University of Texas, Austin

Carolyn M. Evertson
Peabody College, Vanderbilt University

Murray E. Worsham
Northeast Independent School District, San Antonio, Texas (retired)

Boston   New York   San Francisco
Mexico City   Montreal   Toronto   London   Madrid   Munich   Paris
Hong Kong   Singapore   Tokyo   Cape Town   Sydney

Senior Editor: *Arnis E. Burvikovs*
Editorial Assistant: *Kelly Hopkins*
Marketing Manager: *Tara Kelly*
Editorial-Production Service: *Matrix Productions Inc.*
Composition and Prepress Buyer: *Linda Cox*
Manufacturing Buyer: *Andrew Turso*
Cover Administrator: *Kristina Mose-Libon*
Interior Designer: *Ellen Pettengell*
Cover Designer: *Suzanne Harbison*
Photo Researcher: *Katharine S. Cook; Larissa Tierney*
Electronic Composition: *Omegatype Typography, Inc.*

Photo Credits: p. 1: Will Faller; **p. 17:** Will Hart; **p. 41:** Roy Morsch/Corbis/Bettmann; **p. 57:** Dick Blume/The Image Works; **p. 87:** Jim Cummins/CORBIS-NY; **p. 111:** Bonnie Kamin/PhotoEdit; **p. 131:** Will Hart/PhotoEdit; **p. 147:** Will Hart; **p. 169:** Tom Lindfors Photography; **p. 195:** Tom Lindfors Photography.

Library of Congress Cataloging-in-Publication Data

Emmer, Edmund T.
    Classroom management for middle and high school teachers / Edmund T. Emmer, Carolyn M. Evertson, Murray E. Worsham.—7th ed.
       p. cm.
    Rev. ed. of: Classroom management for secondary teachers. 6th ed. c2003.
    Includes bibliographical references and index.
    ISBN 0-205-45534-4
    1. Classroom management. 2. Education, Secondary. I. Evertson, Carolyn M., 1935– II. Worsham, Murray E. III. Emmer, Edmund T. Classroom management for secondary teachers. IV. Title.

    LB3013.C53 2005
    373.1102'4—dc22

                  2004062320

Printed in the United States of America

10 9 8 7 6 5 4 3   09 08 07 06

To the many teachers who have taught us about classroom management

E.T.E.
C.M.E.
M.E.W.

Contents

3

Managing Student Work 41

4

Getting Off to a Good Start 57

5

Planning and Conducting Instruction 87

6

Managing Cooperative Learning Groups 111

7

Maintaining Appropriate Student Behavior 131

10

Managing Special Groups 195

APPENDIX

Answer Keys for Chapter Activities 225

Preface

Public scrutiny of our schools has never been more intense than it is today. This attention has prompted demands on schools and teachers for accountability and more student testing; it has increased media coverage of school violence at the same time that most scholarly studies report that violence has actually decreased; and it has led to the call for "better schools" as a means of furthering a variety of political agendas. These societal pressures might give the impression that schools and classrooms are fundamentally different and that the task of managing a classroom has changed markedly. In fact, the basic principles for creating an effective learning environment remain the same. What teachers must do is adapt these core ideas to the settings in which they now teach, a problem that every generation of teachers has had to address and solve as they encounter changing social and demographic conditions.

Students entering the nation's schools come with such widely diverse backgrounds, capabilities, interests, and skills that meeting their needs and finding appropriate learning activities require a great deal of care and skill. Because one of the first and most basic tasks for the teacher is to develop a smoothly running classroom community where students are highly involved in worthwhile activities that support their learning, establishing an effective classroom management system is a first priority. Teachers who have developed such systems have taught us a great deal about the essential features of their classrooms and how they work to establish them.

What we have learned is that well-managed classrooms exist because teachers have clear ideas of the types of classroom conditions and student behaviors necessary for a healthy learning environment. They not only have clear ideas, but they also work very hard to create these conditions. This book describes what you can do to create a well-managed classroom. The process is described as teachers encounter it: first by planning in several key areas before the school year begins, then by implementing the plan and establishing good management at the beginning of the year, and finally by maintaining the management procedures throughout the year.

We have tried to make the materials useful and practical by providing checklists to help you organize your planning. Several case studies and problem-solving scenarios are also provided that focus on critical areas for managing students and the curriculum. We hope you will find much here that is helpful as you plan and organize your own classroom.

The book retains the same structure and many of the same topics as past editions. We have, however, made additions and revisions to reflect current research and practice. This edition retains the chapter on Managing Cooperative Learning Groups (Chapter 6), which describes background research and practical strategies for using cooperative groups to support students' learning.

This edition contains numerous new references and the addition of many websites that contain useful classroom management content. We added new activities to many of the chapters and increased our coverage of working with students with diverse backgrounds, needs, and skills. New sections on bullying and the Think Time strategy have been added. The title of the book was changed to include both middle and high school teaching to make explicit that its contents apply to both levels. We have indicated in numerous places how recommendations should be adapted to take into account age and grade differences.

A classroom management video that illustrates procedures, planning, communication, and managing classroom behavioral issues accompanies this edition. Taken from actual classroom footage, this video shows real teaching examples and challenges new teachers to respond to various problem situations. Also, new to this edition is an **Instructor's Manual/Test Bank** that is available electronically by contacting your local sales representative.

Our own experiences as teachers continue to inform the foundation of this text. However, much of our knowledge about systematic classroom management comes from our own and others' classroom research. We have also drawn on recent experiences in providing research-based findings and support to new teachers through COMP: Creating Conditions for Learning at Peabody College, Vanderbilt University (www.comp.org). As always, we appreciate the contributions of the many observers, school administrators, and other researchers who have both assisted and enlightened us, and we gratefully acknowledge our debt to the teachers who have allowed us to learn from them.

We also extend thanks to the following reviewers whose suggestions guided this revision: Scott Grubbs, Valdosta State University; Virgiana Hamm, Athens State University; Thelma Isaacs, Marshall University; and Mark Ryan, National University.

Classroom Management for Middle and High School Teachers

1

Organizing Your Classroom and Materials

A logical starting point for classroom management is arranging the physical setting for teaching because it is a task that you must complete before the school year begins. Many teachers find it easier to plan other aspects of classroom management after they have a clear idea of how the physical features of their classroom will be organized.

Good room arrangement can help you cope with the complex demands of teaching twenty-five to thirty or more students at a time for five or more periods a day. During any given period, students will come and go, many activities will occur, and you and your class will use a variety of materials, texts, reference books, equipment, and supplies. Appropriate room preparation and arrangement of materials help activities proceed smoothly and conserve class time for learning, while inadequate planning interferes with instruction by causing interruptions, delays, and dead time.

When you arrange the classroom, you will need to make many decisions. Should desks be set out in rows or clusters? Where should your desk be? What areas of the room will you use for presentations? What equipment will you use, and how will you and your students gain access to it? Do your classes include any students with special needs that must be considered? How will you and the students obtain materials and supplies, and where will these be stored? This chapter helps you make these and other decisions about room arrangement. Each component is described along with guidelines and examples to help you plan. In addition, a checklist for organizing your classroom, supplies, and equipment is provided. Use it to focus your efforts and to be certain that your classroom is ready for the beginning of school.

Five Keys to Good Room Arrangement

Remember that the classroom is the learning environment for both you and your students. Although it may hold as many as thirty or more students each period, it is not a very large space. Your students will be participating in a variety of activities and using different areas of the room, and they will need to enter and leave the room rapidly when classes change. You will get better results if you arrange your room to permit orderly movement, few distractions, and efficient use of available space. The following five keys will be helpful as guidelines when you make decisions about arranging your room.

1. **Use a room arrangement consistent with your instructional goals and activities.** You will need to think about the main types of instructional activities that will take place in your classes and then organize the seating, materials, and equipment compatibly. Thus, if your main activities will be teacher-led recitations, demonstrations, and presentations, students should be seated so that they can easily see the main instructional area, and you will need nearby storage space and sur-

face for materials. If you plan to use small work groups, however, you may need to arrange student seating and access to supplies quite differently.

2. **Keep high traffic areas free of congestion.** High traffic areas include group work areas, the space around the pencil sharpener and wastebasket, doorways, computers, certain bookshelves and supply areas, student desks, and the teacher's desk. High traffic areas should be separated and easily accessible.

3. **Be sure students are easily seen by the teacher.** Careful monitoring of students is a major management task. If the teacher cannot see all students, it will be difficult to determine when a student needs assistance or to prevent task avoidance or disruption. Therefore, clear lines of sight must be maintained between areas of the room that the teacher will frequent and student work areas.

4. **Keep frequently used teaching materials and student supplies readily accessible.** Easy access to and efficient storage of such materials and supplies will aid classroom management by allowing activities to begin and end promptly and by minimizing time spent getting ready and cleaning up.

5. **Be certain students can easily see instructional presentations and displays.** Be sure that the seating arrangements will allow all students to see the overhead projector screen or chalkboard without moving their chairs, turning their desks around, or craning their necks. Don't put your instructional area in a far corner of the room, away from a substantial number of students. Such conditions do not encourage students to pay attention, and they make it more difficult for students to take notes or copy material.

Applying the five keys will help produce good room arrangement. Some specific suggestions for achieving this goal are described in the next section. By attending to these areas, you will address all the important aspects of room preparation. You can then be confident that you have designed a physical setting conducive to good management.

Suggestions for Arranging Your Classroom

Bulletin Boards and Walls

Wall space and bulletin boards provide areas to display student work, instructionally relevant material, decorative items, assignments, rules, schedules, a clock, and other items of interest. Ceiling space can be used to hang mobiles and other decorations. The following points should be considered when preparing these areas.

1. At the start of school, you should have at least the following displays for walls and chalkboards: a place for listing daily assignments and some decorative display to catch your students' interest such as a bulletin board with a "Welcome Back to School" motif or a display organized around a school-spirit theme ("Go Hippos!").

2. If you are teaching in a middle school or if you are teaching ninth graders in a high school, you should also reserve some wall or bulletin board space for posting classroom rules (at higher grade levels, you might also post rules, or you might handle the communication of expectations orally and/or via a handout—see Chapters 2 and 4).

3. Other displays that many teachers find useful include an example of the correct paper heading to be used in your class and a content-relevant display such as one highlighting a topic that will soon be taught.

4. Covering large bulletin board areas with colored paper is an easy way to brighten your classroom. This paper comes on large rolls and is often kept in the school office or in a supply room. You can also trim the bulletin boards with an edging or border of corrugated paper. If you can't find these items in your supply room, consider spending a few dollars for them at a school supply center or variety store. You can also find books of bulletin board ideas as well as posters, cardboard punchout letters, stencils, and other graphics for sale at such stores.

5. If you need ideas for decorating your room or for setting up displays, borrow some from other teachers. A look in some other rooms will probably give you several new ideas. Also, your departmental supply room may contain some instructionally relevant display material. Ask your department chairperson for assistance if necessary.

6. Don't spend a lot of time decorating your room. You will have many other, more important things to do to get ready for the beginning of school. A few bare bulletin boards won't bother anybody. Leave one or two empty; you can add displays later or allow your homeroom/advisory students to decorate a blank space for an art project. You can also reward a "class of the month" with the privilege of redecorating a bulletin board. Finally, don't overdecorate your classroom. Wall space that is too filled up with detail can be distracting, and it makes a room seem smaller. It will seem small enough when all your students are in it.

Floor Space

Arrange your furniture and equipment so that you can easily observe students from all areas in which you will work. Students should be able to see you as well as the overhead projector screen, the main chalkboard, and any other area that will be used to give presentations to the whole class. Of course, you will have to adjust to whatever constraints exist in your assigned classroom. A classroom may be too small or have inadequate or poorly located chalkboard space or electrical outlets. You should assess your space and determine whether any changes can be made to accommodate whatever constraints exist. For example, if the classroom is small, be sure to remove unnecessary student desks or extra furniture or equipment; if you have inadequate storage, perhaps you can locate an extra file or supply cabinet.

A good starting point for your floor plan is to decide where you will conduct whole-class instruction. Examine the room and identify where you will stand or work when you address the entire class to conduct lessons or give instructions. You can usually identify this area of the room by the location of a large chalkboard and the placement of the overhead projector screen or TV monitor with computer display connection. This area should also have space for a table or desk where you can place items needed in presentations and an electrical outlet for the overhead projector. Once you have located this area, you are ready to begin planning floor space.

As you read the following items, refer to Figure 1.1, which shows a well-designed floor plan for a secondary school classroom in which whole-class instruction and individual seatwork are the main types of activities. Note how each item is addressed in this floor plan. Of course, this is just one of many possibilities. Consider how you might need to alter this floor plan to accommodate additional computer workstations, for example. Note that moving or removing the table on the right side of the room would open up space. The location of desks, work areas, and other physical features of the classroom depends on the size and shape of the room and how different parts of the room will be used.

ARRANGEMENT OF STUDENT DESKS

Many different arrangements of student desks are possible, but be sure to arrange them so that all students can look at the whole-group instruction area without having to get out of their seats. Also, avoid having students sit with their backs to the area. Try to minimize having students face potential sources of distraction such as windows, the doorway, an area where small groups of students will work, or eye-catching displays. Even if other arrangements are to be used later in the year, you might start the year with desks in rows facing the major instructional area. In such an arrangement, students are less likely to distract each other than if their desks are arranged in groups with students facing one another. In the example presented in Figure 1.1, the desks are arranged in rows, and no student is seated with his or her back to the major instructional area. Thus, if the teacher puts a display on the

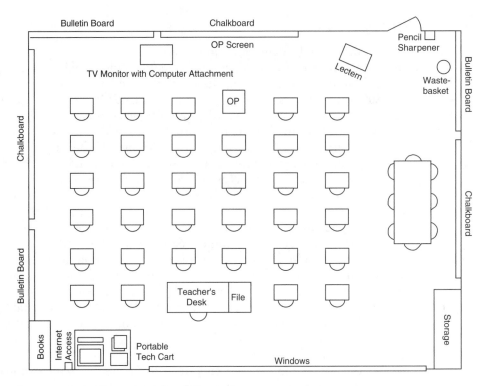

Figure 1.1 An Example of Good Room Arrangement
for Whole-Class Instruction

overhead projector screen, all students can see it easily and take notes when necessary. The following items may also be of concern:

- Because it is important to keep high traffic areas clear, don't put desks or other furniture in front of doors, computers, the pencil sharpener, sinks, and so on.
- Be sure to leave ample room around student desks so that you can easily approach students when you are monitoring seatwork activities.
- Count the desks or chairs and make sure you have enough.
- Replace damaged furniture or have it repaired.

THE TEACHER'S DESK, FILING CABINET, OVERHEAD PROJECTOR, AND OTHER EQUIPMENT

Your desk needs to be placed where it is functional. If you intend to keep at your desk instructional materials used during presentations, the desk should be adjacent to the main instructional area or areas. If you plan to work at your desk at any

"Miss Marpole, I need to talk to you about your seating arrangement."
Reprinted by permission of George Abbott/*Phi Delta Kappan.*

time during the day, you will need to locate your desk to facilitate monitoring: Sit facing the students and be sure you can observe all of them from your seat. However, it is not necessary that students be able to see you from their seats, and some teachers prefer placing their desks at the back of the room rather than at the front (see Figure 1.1). If you plan to work with individual students at your desk, you will also have to consider traffic patterns. Student desks should not be so close to yours that students will be distracted by other students approaching your desk or working with you there.

Other furniture, such as the filing cabinet and storage bins, needs a functional location. A cabinet used for storing seldom-used supplies can be safely tucked away in a corner or hidden from view. Supplies that will be used frequently during class should be located near the area in which they will be used. All electrical equipment must, of course, be placed near an outlet and covered or otherwise secured.

COMPUTER WORKSTATIONS

Many classrooms are equipped with computers for student use. Their location may be limited because of the need for wall outlets and a phone line or Ethernet connection, so consider placing the computer workstation first and then arranging other activity areas. Place the computer(s) in an area away from chalk dust, liquids, and magnets. When arranging your room, make sure that you are able to monitor the entire room while standing by the computer to help a student. You will also need space for storing paper, printer cartridges, software manuals, and other computer supplies.

If you have three or four computers for student use, you may have to move some furniture out of your room to have suitable space and avoid overcrowding around the computer area. Visit some other teachers' classrooms to get ideas for configurations that might work in your class.

Large groups of students around a computer can create a disturbance and get off-task easily. Limit the number of students working on a computer to no more than three or four, and establish a policy that students who are using the computer have a purpose and a time limit so that the resource can be shared fairly. Teach students to save their work so that they will not lose it if they are unable to finish it in a session.

BOOKCASES

These should be placed where they will neither prevent your monitoring students nor obstruct students' ability to see chalkboards or relevant displays. If a bookcase contains items that are to be used frequently, such as dictionaries or supplemental texts, it needs to be conveniently located and easily monitored. If a bookcase is used to store seldom-used items, an out-of-the-way place is best. If you have only one bookcase, store unneeded items in a cabinet so that the single bookcase can be used for materials in frequent use.

WORK AREAS

In many subjects, such as science, industrial arts, homemaking, or art, students may spend part of their time in a laboratory, shop, or other work area. With these or other subjects, students may spend time at computer stations or a computer lab. The area may be in the same room or in another room adjacent to the classroom. Students may work individually or in groups. Students may also work in small groups for discussion activities or for special projects in other subject areas as well. When arranging group work or lab areas, follow the same principles you used when positioning student desks. Be sure you can see all students, keep traffic lanes clear, and avoid congested areas, especially near supply and cleanup areas. Provide clear lines of sight between students and any area of the room from which you will conduct instruction while students are in the work area.

CENTERS

A center is an area where a few students come to work on a special activity or to study some topic. Often, a center will have special equipment, such as a tape recorder with headphones, for individual students. Other centers may be organized around a special study topic or around skill areas in a particular subject. In the latter case, the teacher might have a box of activity cards that students use to progress through a series of objectives as part of enrichment or remediation programs. Some teachers like to arrange a more informal area in their classroom. This area might include, for example, an area rug, bookcases, a small table, and some comfortable seating. Such an area adds a homey, personal touch to the setting, and it may make your room more appealing to some students. Students might be allowed to use the area for special projects, group work, or during free reading activities. (You will need to develop procedures for when and how the area will be used; see Chapter 2.) If you do plan to use such a center, plan its location so that it won't interfere with or distract from other activities. Because this type of center requires quite a lot of floor space, you'll have to weigh its advantages against the loss of space for other activities and the crowding that will result, especially if you have a small room or large classes. If and when you do use a center, be sure to place it in a location where you can monitor students easily. Also, be certain that all necessary materials and equipment are available at the center and work properly.

PETS, PLANTS, AQUARIUMS, AND SPECIAL ITEMS

These can add interest and individuality to a room. However, the first week of school is already quite exciting for students, so it is not necessary to introduce these special features immediately. When you do bring in such items, place them where they won't be distracting, especially during whole-class activities. Of course, they should not impede movement about the room or interfere with students' work.

Storage Space and Supplies

Once you have decided on your wall and bulletin board displays and have organized space within the classroom, you can concentrate on obtaining supplies and providing for storage. Some supplies will be used frequently and thus will need to be readily accessible. Other items will be seasonal or used infrequently and can go into deeper storage.

TEXTBOOKS AND OTHER INSTRUCTIONAL MATERIALS

You should identify the textbooks and supplemental materials (dictionaries, reference books, additional reading materials) that will be used in your class. Determine which books students are expected to keep in their possession and which must remain in the room. Then find easily accessible shelves in a bookcase for those everyday books and materials that will not be kept by students. If you do not know what supplemental materials are available or what the school policies are regarding these items, check with your department chairperson, with the librarian, or with another teacher. Also, find out what system is used for obtaining textbooks; often, it is first come, first served. If so, get in line early to ensure that you obtain the books you need. Further information is provided in Chapter 4 concerning textbooks that are checked out to students.

FREQUENTLY USED CLASSROOM MATERIALS

These are supplies that you and your students will use; the necessary items will depend somewhat on the subject you teach. A basic set includes paper in varying sizes and colors, overhead projector pens, rulers, scissors, chalk and erasers, transparent tape and masking tape, stapler, and glue. Other than the chalk kept in the chalk trays, these and any other supplies you need on a daily basis should be kept in a readily accessible place, such as on a worktable or shelf. Usually, students are expected to supply certain materials, including pencils, erasers, pens, and notebook paper or spiral notebooks. Because you cannot expect all students to bring these materials at the beginning of the year, you should make sure you have an ample supply of items needed by students. It is also a good idea to give parents a list of supplies that students will need in your class.

TEACHER'S SUPPLIES

You will receive some materials from the school office for your own use. These items, which usually should be stored in your desk, include pencils and pens, paper, extra chalk, overhead transparency sheets, scissors, ruler, stapler, file folders, paper clips, and thumbtacks. In addition, you should receive a grade book, a lesson plan book, teacher's editions for all textbooks, and any school forms or tablets needed for attendance reports and for handling money. Set up a filing system that allows you to separate the notes, forms, papers, and other materials used in each class. Use different file folders for different periods, and color code them for added efficiency. For each period, keep frequently needed materials and forms separate from those needed only occasionally.

OTHER MATERIALS

In addition to the items supplied by the school, a number of other supplies will come in handy. If your room does not have a clock and a calendar, obtain these now. Both should be large enough to be seen from all areas of the room. You may wish to buy a desk bell or a timer if you are going to use these as signals for starting or stopping activities. You might also add the following items: tissues, rags or paper towels, a bar of soap, bandages, scouring powder or liquid cleanser, and a small plastic bucket. Some teachers like to keep a few basic tools such as a hammer, pliers, and a screwdriver in case a minor repair needs to be made. Store all these items where they are accessible to you but not to your students.

EQUIPMENT

Check all equipment, including the overhead projector, computers, calculators, tape recorder, headphones, pencil sharpener, and so on, to make sure they are in working order. Get any necessary extension cords or adapter plugs, and store them either with the equipment or in a handy place.

SEASONAL OR INFREQUENTLY USED ITEMS

This category includes Halloween, Thanksgiving, Christmas, and other holiday and seasonal decorations, bulletin board displays, or special project materials. Also included are instructional materials that are used only on some occasions—for example, compasses and protractors, templates, special art materials, science equipment, and so on. Because you don't need to have ready access to these materials, you can store them at the backs of closets, in boxes on top of cabinets, or even out of the room if you have access to outside storage space. Check with your department chairperson about using a storeroom.

SPECIAL PROJECT MATERIALS

In a few subject areas, such as industrial arts, homemaking, or art, students may regularly work on projects. Occasionally, these projects may become too bulky or awkward to store in lockers and must remain in the room. You will need to provide special storage areas to which you can control access to safeguard the materials. You will be wise to avoid beginning such projects until you have arranged for adequate storage. Chemicals or potentially hazardous materials should be stored according to district or state standards.

If You Have to "Float"

At some time in their careers, many teachers have to share classrooms with other teachers. Sometimes teachers who are new to a school find that they have no classroom that they can call their own but instead have to "float," conducting their classes in several rooms during the day. Obviously, such a situation presents some problems for classroom organization and management. If this is the situation you face, your ability to arrange and organize your classroom space the way you would like will be very limited. However, there are some things you can and should do before school begins.

First, confer with the other teachers whose classrooms you will be using. Inspect each room carefully so that you will know where everything is when school begins. In each room, try to arrange for the following:

- An overhead projector in place for daily use. This is practically a must. You will not have the time—and you may not have the space—to put lessons, assignments, notices, and so on, on the chalkboards each period. You can save yourself much effort by preparing ahead of time transparencies to use in each of your classes. Also, you can use blank transparency sheets to write on as you would a chalkboard during lesson presentations. (Another advantage of using transparencies instead of chalkboards in borrowed classrooms is that they provide you with a record of what you presented to your students.)
- A regular space on the chalkboard or on a bulletin board where you can post assignments or announcements for your class and leave them up for several weeks.
- One shelf, cabinet, or table, especially if your course requires a classroom set of materials that you cannot carry around with you all day.
- A sufficient number of desks.

Either plan to carry all essential teaching supplies with you each day or store them in one desk drawer or in a box in each room. Don't depend on other teachers for supplies. You will probably need transparency sheets and markers, water and paper towels, chalk, extra pens and pencils, paper, paper clips, and tissues. File folders, large manila envelopes, and rubber bands will be useful for organizing and carrying student papers. Color coding folders for each class will also help.

If all of your classes are on one floor, try to obtain a rolling audiovisual cart. A large sheet of tagboard taped to the front will provide bulletin board space and also a little bit of privacy for your belongings. Think about assigning early arriving students the task of preparing the room (e.g., erasing boards, arranging chairs, or positioning the projector). Request access to a computer for your use as needed for preparing materials. If you share a computer with another teacher, you will need to set up your own folder for storing your documents, and you should back up this information on disk.

Further Reading

Butin, D. (2000). *Classrooms.* ERIC Report number ED446421. Washington, DC: National Clearinghouse for Educational Facilities. Available at www.edfacilities.org/pubs/classrooms.html

The author discusses classroom design. Trends in classroom design principles and major issues in the use of classroom space are summarized. The website www.edfacilities.org also has articles dealing with classroom design in content areas as well as links to many related websites.

Evertson, C. M., & Poole, I. R. (2004). *Effective room arrangement.* IRIS Center for Faculty Enhancement. Nashville, TN: Peabody College, Vanderbilt University.

http://iris.peabody.vanderbilt.edu/casestudies.html.

This website contains activities and case studies for accommodating special needs students in the classroom. Click on "Effective Room Arrangement" for the cases.

Fraser, B. J., & Walberg, H. J. (Eds.) (1991). *Educational environments: Evaluation, antecedents and consequences.* Oxford: Pergamon.

Classroom environments are much more than physical arrangements; they include organizational, instructional, and interpersonal dimensions. Their effects, moreover, depend substantially on how students perceive or experience the environments. This book thoroughly explores many aspects of learning environments, connecting them to a variety of social, institutional, and personal factors.

Jones, R. A. (1995). *The child-school interface: Environment and behavior.* London: Cassell.

Jones presents an analysis of how children's behaviors are influenced by the various environments they encounter at school. The author's point of view is ecological, incorporating the physical setting of the classroom as one of the contributors to children's behavior, along with social and organizational factors.

Lambert, N. M. (1994). Seating arrangements in classrooms. *The International Encyclopedia of Education* (2nd ed.), vol. 9, 5355–5359.

This article provides a summary of research on classroom seating arrangements. Although it is only one factor, the way the teacher arranges student seating can have an important influence on a variety of student behaviors.

Rosenfield, P., Lambert, N. M., & Black, A. (1985). Desk arrangement effects on pupil classroom behavior. *Journal of Educational Psychology, 77,* 101–108.

The authors conducted an experiment comparing student behavior during discussion activities, using different seating arrangements. Circle and cluster formations promoted more on-task behavior during discussions than did seating students in rows. The results suggest the importance of considering instructional and behavioral goals when planning the classroom's organization.

Suggested Activities

The following activities will help you plan and organize your classroom space. Do as many of them as you have time for.

1. Figure 1.2 shows a classroom with quite a few problems. See how many you can find, and consider how each problem might be corrected. (A key for this activity is found in the Appendix.)

2. Two other room diagrams are shown in Figure 1.3. Discuss their advantages and disadvantages for different types of classes. With which keys are they consistent or inconsistent? Would any rearrangements be helpful?

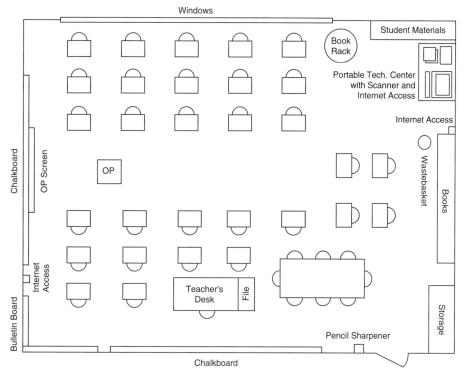

Figure 1.2 A Room Arrangement with Problems

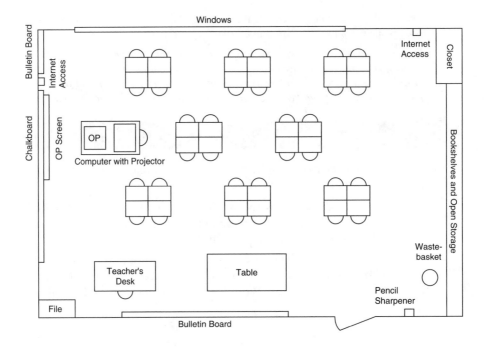

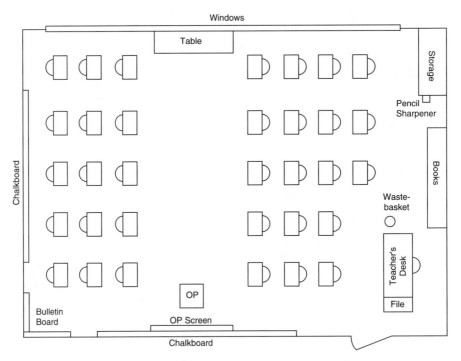

Figure 1.3 Two Room Arrangements for Discussion

3. Make a scale drawing of your room, as in Figures 1.1 and 1.2. A classroom set-up tool is available at http://teacher.scholastic.com. You can now experiment on paper or computer with different furniture arrangements and the organization of space—a much simpler task than pushing the furniture around yourself. Try to evaluate your arrangement using the five keys to successful room arrangement presented earlier in the chapter.

4. Visit some other teachers' classrooms and examine their room arrangements. Use the items in Checklist 1 at the end of the chapter and the five keys to room arrangement to guide your observation and analysis. If you are having a specific problem, ask several teachers for suggestions and see how they may have coped with the same problem.

5. After you have arranged the furniture in your room, test the traffic patterns, keeping in mind the recommendations in this chapter.

   a. Go to each instructional area and check it for your ability to observe all students wherever they may be during the instructional activity in that portion of the room. Also, be sure that needed materials are readily accessible.

   b. Now pretend you are a student. Enter the room; go to several desks; check for visibility, ease of movement to other parts of the room, and possible distractions. Alter the arrangement if you detect problems.

 ## Checklist 1

To organize and keep track of your activities as you arrange your room and get supplies and equipment ready, you will find it helpful to use Checklist 1. Each aspect of room arrangement has been listed, and space has been provided for noting things to be done and for checking off the area once you have it ready.

Room Preparation

Check When Complete	Subject	Notes
☐	A. Bulletin boards and walls	_____
☐	B. Floor space	
☐	1. Student desks/tables	_____
☐	2. Teacher's desks and equipment	_____
☐	3. Computer workstations	_____
☐	4. Bookcases	_____

(continued)

Check When Complete	Subject	Notes
☐	5. Work areas	_____
☐	6. Centers	_____
☐	7. Pets and plants	_____
☐	C. Storage space and supplies	
☐	1. Textbooks	_____
☐	2. Frequently used instrructional materials	_____
☐	3. Teacher's supplies	_____
☐	4. Other materials	_____
☐	5. Equipment	_____
☐	6. Seasonal items	_____
☐	7. Special project materials	_____

2

Choosing Rules
and Procedures

Good classroom management is based on students' understanding of the behaviors expected of them. A carefully planned system of rules and procedures makes it easier for you to communicate your expectations to students. It also helps ensure that the procedures you set up will be workable and appropriate. The goal of this chapter is to help you identify a good system of rules and procedures for your classes.

Why Rules and Procedures Are Needed

Rules and procedures vary in different classrooms, but all effectively managed classrooms have them. It is not possible for a teacher to conduct instruction or for students to work productively if they have no guidelines for how to behave or when to move about the room or if they frequently interrupt the teacher and one another. Furthermore, inefficient procedures and the absence of routines for common aspects of classroom life, such as taking and reporting attendance, participating in discussions, turning in materials, or checking work, can waste large amounts of time and cause students' attention and interest to wane. Here is a brief example of a classroom with major problems in the area of rules and procedures.

> When the tardy bell rang, only a few of Mr. Smith's third-period students took their seats. Two played catch with the erasers, while others congregated in small groups and chatted noisily. Mr. Smith had to shout over the din to be heard: "Get to your seats. I need to take roll." Some students moved to sit down, while others vied for places at back-row desks. After much prompting, most of the students were seated, and Mr. Smith began taking roll. Loud talking continued, abating only momentarily after Mr. Smith called repeatedly for silence. After ten minutes, roll call was finally completed. Mr. Smith then asked students to get out their books and homework assignment. Loud protests ensued as students insisted that no assignment had been given. Furthermore, many students did not have their textbooks with them. Rather than allow a large number of students to go out into the hallways to retrieve their books from their lockers, Mr. Smith decided to conduct a recitation on the assigned lesson. By then, however, three students had already left the classroom to retrieve their texts. Attempting to get the recitation under way, Mr. Smith called in vain for silence. He finally began to ask questions, but before he could select a student to respond, several others called out the answer. A chorus of comments greeted the responses. Mr. Smith tried to continue asking questions, but the noise from students' social talk made it difficult to hear. Soon paper airplanes began to drift through the air. . . .

Observers of this classroom might criticize Mr. Smith for allowing students to get away with so much misbehavior. "Be stricter," they might say. "Punish the misbehaving students." Or "Develop more interesting lessons to capture student interest." Some might even suggest that Mr. Smith set up a reward system to encourage good behavior. While these suggestions could be helpful under some circumstances, they do not address the fundamental problem in this classroom: The students have not learned the behaviors that are expected of them. These students almost certainly know that many of their behaviors would not be allowed in other classrooms, but the problem is that Mr. Smith has not taught the students how to behave in his class. Areas in which this is evident in this example include (1) what to do upon entering the room, (2) behavior during roll call, (3) bringing materials for class, (4) completing assignments, (5) out-of-room policies, (6) talking during discussions, (7) responding to questions, and (8) seating assignments.

Of course, the fact that students know what is appropriate does not mean that they will behave that way. (For that reason, this book will not end with the present chapter!) However, a clear set of expectations of what constitutes appropriate behavior will be a major start toward establishing a well-managed classroom environment.

Finally, remember that the unique setting created by middle and high school organization makes it essential that you establish a clear set of rules and procedures for your classroom. You will need to work with five or more groups of twenty-five to thirty or more students every day. Generally, you will be confined to a single room with limited space and materials; you will be responsible for teaching many cognitive skills to a diverse population of students; and at the same time, you will have to handle administrative tasks, arrange for appropriate materials and supplies, and evaluate students. To do these things well, you need an orderly environment with minimal disruption and wasted time, leaving everyone free to concentrate on the critical tasks of learning. Carefully planned procedures help create this environment.

Definitions

Rules and *procedures* refer to stated expectations regarding behavior. A rule identifies general expectations or standards. For example, the rule "Respect other persons and their property" covers a large set of behaviors that should always be practiced. Rules sometimes indicate behavior that is not acceptable, although teachers occasionally manage to write only rules that are positively stated (e.g., "You may talk when given permission"). In such instances, the unacceptable behavior is implied (i.e., "Don't talk without permission"). In addition to general rules, many teachers will have a rule or two governing a specific behavior they anticipate being an issue or that they want to prevent (e.g., "No profanity" or "Gum chewing is not allowed").

Classroom rules are used by secondary teachers to help communicate expectations for appropriate behavior. Based on interviews with high school students serving detention for school infractions, Thorson (2003) recommends that rules should be positively worded, limited to a small number (three to five), and clearly stated. Similar suggestions have been made by many other researchers (e.g., Malone & Tietjens 2000; Bicard 2000; Brophy 1998; Evertson 1994; Boonstrum 1991), who have also noted that student acceptance of the rules will be strengthened if they are presented positively and if their usefulness for maintaining a classroom environment conducive to participation and learning is emphasized.

Procedures also communicate expectations for behavior. Also called *routines,* they usually apply to a specific activity, and they are usually directed at accomplishing something rather than at prohibiting some behavior or defining a general standard. For example, you will set up procedures or routines with your students for collecting assignments, turning in late work, participating in class discussions, leaving the room to go to lockers or the bathroom, and so on. Some procedures, such as safety practices for equipment use or student notebook requirements, may be sufficiently complex or critical that you should provide duplicate copies of guidelines for students to retain, or you may have students copy the procedures into their notebooks. However, many procedures are not written because they are very simple or because their specificity and frequency of use allow students to learn them rapidly.

Identifying School Rules and Procedures

In most schools, teachers are expected to enforce school rules. It is to your advantage to do so. A set of rules applied consistently in all classes and areas of the building is easy for students to learn. The rules also acquire more legitimacy in the eyes of some students because the rules are everyone's rules. In addition to rules and procedures that regulate student behavior, all schools have certain administrative procedures that must be followed by every teacher (e.g., keeping attendance records). You need to find out about your school's rules and procedures before the year begins so that you can also incorporate them into your own classroom procedures. You can find out about school rules for students and administrative procedures for teachers at a school orientation meeting or from a teacher's handbook, a building administrator, or another teacher. Pay careful attention to the following:

1. Behaviors that are specifically forbidden (e.g., running in the halls, possession of particular items) or required (e.g., being in possession of a hall permit when out of the classroom during class time, bringing a note for absence).

2. Consequences of rule violations. In particular, you should note the responsibility you have for carrying out the consequences, such as reporting the student to the school office. If the school does not have a policy for dealing with certain rule violations, check with other teachers to learn about school norms. For example, if it is up to the teacher to deal with the issue of coming late to class, you must be ready with a system.

3. Administrative procedures that must be handled during class time. These procedures include beginning-of-year tasks, such as assigning textbooks to students, collecting fees, and checking class rosters. Fee collection may go on all year, so you'll need some system of recordkeeping and a safe place to keep the money until you can turn it in to the school office. Some administrative tasks will have to be conducted each class period. These include taking and recording class attendance in your grade book, handling previously absent students, and reporting attendance to the office via a computer-based system or a paper or card form. You will also

That's Miss Clamhouse. She runs a tight ship.
Reprinted by permission of Tony Saltzman

need a procedure for tardy students and for allowing students to leave the room once the period begins (not that you'll encourage it). Procedures in these areas usually are schoolwide. If uniform procedures have not been adopted in some area, talking with experienced teachers about their procedures should be helpful.

Planning Your Classroom Rules

Once you have information about school rules and procedures, you will be ready to begin planning for your own classroom. Guidelines for rules will be presented separately from procedures. Note that some teachers prefer to call their rules *policies* or *guidelines*.

Many different rules are possible, but a set of around five should be sufficient to cover most important areas of behavior. Six general rules that encompass many classroom behaviors are listed below. These or similar rules are often found in well-managed classrooms, although we do not present them as a definitive list. You may decide to use other rules (e.g., a rule prohibiting a specific behavior) or different wording. For some teachers, these rules might be too general, and these teachers might like to have more rules with greater specificity. After each rule are examples of behaviors related to the rule. When presenting general rules to students, it is important to discuss your specific expectations relevant to each rule.

During the discussion of the rules and related behaviors, it is best to emphasize the positive "do" parts of the rules rather than only their negative counterparts. When you do the former, you help students learn how to behave appropriately. You will have to be explicit about behaviors that are not acceptable when such behaviors might occur frequently (e.g., chewing gum, leaving one's seat, calling out). These may be incorporated into your set of rules or discussed when presenting procedures associated with specific activities. However, there is no need to recite a long list of forbidden behaviors during your initial discussion of rules.

The set of rules you choose will be used later in several ways. First, you will discuss these rules with your students on the first day or two of class. If you teach at the middle school level, you will also post the rules in the room and/or make certain that students have their own copies. You might also send a copy home to be returned with parents' signatures. A posted set of rules allows you to focus student attention on and create a strong expectation about behaviors that are very important to you. If you teach in a senior high school, posting rules is not mandatory, although it is definitely recommended for ninth-grade classes; these students will be less aware than older students of what behaviors are appropriate for the high school setting. At higher grade levels, you can provide students with a handout describing class rules, along with other information about the class. There is also some difference in how you should present the classroom rules to younger and older students, but this will be described in Chapter 4. Finally, you may refer to specific rules as needed to remind students of appropriate behavior during the year. It should be noted that your posted rules need not (and cannot) cover all aspects of behavior in detail. Procedures for specific activities and perhaps some ad hoc rules will be needed. For instance, you may wish to keep your policies regarding student work separate from rules about general conduct. Examples of some commonly used, basic rules follow.

RULE 1. BRING ALL NEEDED MATERIALS TO CLASS. This rule can be helpful because it emphasizes that students must be prepared for each class period. It is important for students to know exactly what they are expected to bring to class for this rule to be followed. Thus, students should know whether to bring a pen or pencil, paper, notebook or folder, and if more than one textbook is used in the class, which textbook. If the materials vary (e.g., a notebook being required on one day but not another), some system will be needed to signal this to students. If possible in such cases, the teacher should develop a routine, such as having students bring certain materials on particular days of the week (e.g., spelling books on Thursday) or having students copy into their notebooks on Monday a list of materials needed for each day that week.

RULE 2. BE IN YOUR SEAT AND READY TO WORK WHEN THE BELL RINGS. Included under this rule may be procedures such as (a) pencils should be sharpened before the bell rings; (b) paper and pens should be out and ready for work (including heading); and (c) warmups or other opening activities are to be started as soon as possible after entering the room.

RULE 3. RESPECT AND BE POLITE TO ALL PEOPLE. Included under this rule are listening carefully when the teacher or a student is speaking and behaving properly for a substitute teacher. Some "don'ts" include fighting, name calling, bothering, and so on.

RULE 4. LISTEN AND STAY SEATED WHEN SOMEONE IS TALKING. This rule addresses two student behaviors that, if unregulated, can become sources of widespread misconduct. Rule 4 is actually a more specific but less inclusive variation of Rule 3. Because it is clearly stated, the rule requires little interpretation for students to understand it.

RULE 5. RESPECT OTHER PEOPLE'S PROPERTY. This rule encompasses behaviors and guidelines such as (a) keep the room clean and neat; (b) pick up litter; (c) return borrowed property; (d) do not write on the desks; and (e) get permission before using another person's materials.

RULE 6. OBEY ALL SCHOOL RULES. This is a useful rule to include because it reminds students that school rules apply in your classroom as well as outside it. It also suggests that you will monitor behavior in the areas covered by the school rules. Finally, including it in your rules gives you an opportunity to discuss whatever school rules are pertinent to your classroom.

Student Participation in Rule Setting

Some teachers involve students in rule setting to promote student ownership of the rules and more student responsibility for their own behavior. Student involvement can take many forms, such as a discussion of reasons for having rules and clarifying the rationale for and the meaning of particular rules. For example, a discussion might begin with the teacher making an analogy between society's laws and classroom rules and asking students what purpose these laws serve. Depending on the age level and sophistication of the students, typical responses might include ideas about protecting individuals and group rights, preventing violence or destructive behavior, and permitting normal activities to take place. After this initial discussion, rules can be presented one at a time. The teacher may first clarify the rule by describing (or asking students to describe) the area of behavior it covers. Students can usually supply concrete examples, although they will tend to give negative instances (e.g., "Respecting property means not breaking things or not stealing"). Consequently, you should be prepared to encourage students to state some positive examples. The discussion of individual rules should also include a rationale for those rules whose justification is not obvious.

Another way of involving students in rule setting is to allow them to share in the decision-making process for specific rules. This is sometimes done at a school level by having student representatives or student council members participate in the identification of school rules. However, shared decision making is not commonplace in secondary classrooms for several reasons. First, the domain in which student participation is acceptable is limited. Schoolwide rules must be accepted as they are. Also, policies that are essential to managing instruction cannot be left to student discretion. Finally, it must be remembered that secondary school teachers instruct five or more classes. If each class generates different rules, posting them may be a problem and remembering which rules are associated with which class may become cumbersome.

Some teachers permit student choice in particular activities or behaviors. For example, if chewing gum is not prohibited by a school rule, and if you do not find it objectionable, you could give your students a choice. It would be a rare class that decided to prohibit it. Another area in which an option may be available concerns whether seatwork is to be done silently or whether quiet talking is acceptable. When students are given such choices, you must also make them aware of their responsibility for making the chosen procedure or rule work and remind them that they will lose the privilege if their behavior warrants it.

It is important to note that many effective managers do not provide for student choice in rule setting. Instead, they clearly present their rules and procedures to students and provide explanations of the need for such rules. These teachers strive to be reasonable and fair in their rules and procedures: Teachers who act autocratically invite challenges from adolescents. However, a teacher who is authoritative, who establishes reasonable rules and procedures, who provides an understandable rationale for them, and who enforces them consistently will find the great majority of students willing to abide by them.

 FOR REFLECTION

As you plan your routines and rules, consider what roles students will play in their selection and implementation. Some teachers prefer that students participate extensively, such as by helping formulate rules, discussing their rationale, and offering alternative procedures in some areas. Other teachers prefer a more traditional, teacher-directed system of rules and procedures. Still others prefer a blend of teacher specification and student participation. Whichever you prefer, consider your rationale and the concerns you have regarding alternative approaches.

Consequences for Rule Violations

You should give careful consideration to consequences for violations of your rules. One type of consequence is usually prescribed by school policy, such as consequences for tardiness and unexcused absences. Other consequences are often specified for fighting, classroom use of profanity, damage to property, and loss of books. You will have to familiarize yourself with these policies so that you can do your part in following through if rules violations occur and to be sure that your own classroom policies are consistent with the school's. You must also consider what other consequences you will use to deal with classroom rules that aren't covered by school policy. For example, what will you do if a student ignores your rule for respecting others and chooses to interrupt your lessons by walking around the room to visit with friends? What consequence will you use if a student turns in an incomplete assignment? Planning consequences ahead of time is a good idea because it helps you use them consistently, and you will be more confident about using them. Also, you will be better able to communicate them to students. Ideas for consequences, including many alternatives applicable to different types of problems, can be found in Chapters 8 and 9, so we do not elaborate on the topic at this time.

Planning Classroom Procedures

If you have never analyzed the specific behaviors required of students in a typical secondary school classroom, you are going to be surprised by the complexity and detail in the following sections. Do not hurry through them, even though some of the items may appear trivial. These bits and pieces will combine to form the mosaic of your management system. Four categories of procedures are described: general procedures needed each class period, procedures for teacher-led instruction and seatwork activities, procedures for student group work, and miscellaneous procedures. The greatest emphasis is on the first two areas, although the third is very important should you plan to use such activities. A fifth area, keeping students accountable for work, is presented in Chapter 3. As you read the sections that follow, you can note ideas for procedures on Checklist 2 at the end of this chapter.

 ## General Procedures

Beginning-of-Period Procedures

On five or more occasions every day, you will need to begin a class period. It is important to conduct this activity efficiently so that you will be able to begin content activities quickly. The following five items cover the things most frequently involved in getting the period under way.

ATTENDANCE CHECK

In most schools, teachers are expected to file an attendance report during the initial part of every class period. To do so efficiently, prepare a seating chart for each class and use it to check attendance. Keep your seating chart along with attendance material such as tardy slips and attendance report forms at the location from which you will take attendance. This location should provide an unobstructed view of all students. (Note: You may wish to call roll for the first few days of class and then use a seating chart once your class enrollment stabilizes and your students' seating arrangements are reasonably final.) If your school uses computerized attendance reporting, you'll simply click on the names of students who are absent. If your school uses a paper-based reporting system, you'll list or check off names of absent/tardy students on an attendance slip or card and post it outside your door or place it in some other designated location for pickup.

Even though the attendance report is sent to the school office or attendance clerk, you will likely maintain your own record of student attendance. This can be done on your computer or in a grade book. Having your own record will be useful in identifying assignments that are missing or turned in late because of absence, for having at hand during parent conferences, and for a backup record.

STUDENTS ABSENT THE PREVIOUS DAY

As these students enter the room, they can leave their absence slips at the location where you check attendance. You can sign and return the absence slip while you are checking roll, immediately after, or during the first seatwork activity. To facilitate these students' getting the handouts they might have missed, use a system of writing the absent students' names and the date on each copy and putting them in an absentee file. Direct returning students to the absentee folder for missed papers.

An alternative procedure for assisting returning students is the use of student helpers or assistants. You can use volunteers, who take responsibility for keeping a set of handouts for each absent student, along with a list of missed assignments. The task can be rotated among several volunteers on a weekly or monthly basis.

TARDY STUDENTS

Most schools have a policy in this area; if yours does, be sure to follow it consistently. Teachers who begin to deviate from tardiness policies (e.g., letting students slip into the classroom if they are only a few seconds late) will soon find that the rate of student tardiness will increase and that their beginning-of-class procedures will break down. Tardiness to class can become a nagging management problem if you allow it. If there is no specific school policy or norm, you will have to develop a procedure of your own. Some teachers assign detention before or after school each time students are tardy without a valid excuse. Other teachers give a warning for the first incident and then provide detention or some other penalty beginning with the second occurrence of tardiness.

If your school does not provide you with a computer-based record of absent and tardy students, then you will need to maintain your own record. You should keep track of tardy students just as you keep a record of absences. A simple system is to mark a t in the grade book each time a student is tardy, just as you might record a for absence. Another system is to put a spiral tablet or a clipboard on a table or attach it somewhere near the door. When the tardy students enter the room, they sign in before taking their seats. This preserves a record of tardy students and allows you to continue your instruction without interruption. You can then check tardiness permits at a convenient time.

BEHAVIOR EXPECTED OF ALL STUDENTS

Students should be told what they are expected to do at the beginning of the period, while you are handling the administrative tasks. They should know that they are expected to be in the room (some teachers require that they also be seated at their desks) when the bell rings, or else they will be counted as tardy. Once the bell rings, socializing should stop. Good managers often handle the beginning-of-class activity in one of two ways. Students may be given a regular activity that they are expected to perform at the beginning of every period. Some teachers use a warmup in which several problems, a question, or some very brief assignment is displayed on the chalkboard or on the overhead projector screen. The question or problems may review the preceding day's assignments. An alternative to a work assignment is for the teacher to display an outline of activities for the class period. Students are expected to copy this in their notebook or on an assignment sheet. Another way to begin class is to tell students to use the time to get out any needed materials (headings on papers if needed, homework papers, textbooks, project materials, etc.) and to remain seated with no talking until you finish your administrative duties. This will work only as long as you handle these matters quickly and do not leave students in dead time for very long.

LEAVING THE ROOM

Occasionally, students will need to leave your room during the period—for example, to use the bathroom, to get a drink of water, to take medication, or to go to the library, the school office, or another area of the building. Schools usually have policies for handling these matters, typically requiring the use of a hall pass signed by the teacher or by office personnel. Most effective managers discourage trips to the bathroom or water fountain except for emergencies. Sometimes keeping a record of requests will deter overuse. Unfortunately, lax policies in this area frequently result in classroom (and school) management problems.

A second area that is sometimes troublesome concerns whether students are allowed to return to their lockers to retrieve materials during the class period. Frequently, teachers do not allow this at all and require that the students sit in class without materials or look at another student's text. In such a case, the student might receive reduced credit for work not brought to class. Another procedure is to allow the student to return to the locker to obtain the necessary materials but to impose a mild penalty or count the student as tardy. Whatever policies you establish, the overriding considerations are to minimize the number of students who go out of the room for noninstructional purposes and to follow your procedures consistently.

Use of Materials and Equipment

Your classroom will have a variety of materials and equipment. Identify those things that you expect students to use, and indicate how these items should be operated and under what conditions. This should be done as soon as students are expected to use the equipment. There may also be a number of items in the room that you do not want students to use or handle. Identify these to the students and explain your rationale for keeping them off-limits.

EQUIPMENT AND MATERIALS FOR STUDENTS

These items include the pencil sharpener, student desks, tables, special equipment such as computers, microscopes, globes, encyclopedias, dictionaries, and other room materials. You should establish procedures for the use of whatever items you have in your room. A common procedure for the pencil sharpener is to request that students sharpen pencils before the tardy bell rings, not during activities in which the teacher is presenting or instructing the whole class. If students need to sharpen their pencils during seatwork, a common procedure is to allow only one student at a time at the pencil sharpener. If students have access to storage cabinets, bookshelves, or equipment in different parts of the room, you should identify how and when these different areas and materials may be used. Consider posting directions for the use of these areas or equipment if they aren't obvious. Procedures concerning computer and media equipment may include such matters as the timing of their use, the number of students permitted in the area at the same time, and provisions for appropriate Internet use or e-mail access.

TEACHER MATERIALS AND EQUIPMENT

Included here are your desk, storage areas, filing cabinet, and closet, as well as your own personal possessions. You should make it clear to students that they are not to take things from your desk or use your supplies without permission. Older, more mature senior high students generally do not need to be told this procedure unless, of course, you observe students taking liberties with your materials. However, you should state the expectation to younger students, especially to middle school classes. Be pleasant when you explain it; the rationale for the procedure is so obvious that you need not dwell on it.

Ending the Period

Just as procedures are needed to begin a period, so too are routines helpful at its close. Two items are of general concern: getting students and the room ready for the end of the period and dismissing class. Any room equipment or materials used during instructional activities must be returned to their storage spaces. Cleanup of materials and equipment should be completed before the end-of-period bell. Finally, you may wish to remind students of particular items needed for the next day or for future activities. Consequently, you need to leave sufficient time at the end of the period for whatever cleanup and announcements are required. If students have been engaged in seatwork with their own materials, only a short time (less than half a minute or so) may be needed to put materials away. You will have to judge the time needed and signal the students when to begin cleaning up. Sometimes students will stop work and get ready to go well in advance of the bell. If you tell students that you will let them know when they should begin to clean up or to put their materials away, they will be less likely to develop this habit. Be conscientious about giving students sufficient time before the bell rings. They have a limited amount of time to get to their next class, and it is not fair to them or to their next teacher to cause them to be tardy.

The second item of concern in ending the class is the signal for dismissal. Many teachers prefer to dismiss the students themselves rather than allow the end-of-period bell to be the students' signal. This allows the teacher to hold the students in their seats if the room is not yet properly cleaned up or if an announcement remains to be given. If you wish to use this procedure, you will need to tell students that you—rather than the bell—will dismiss them and that they should remain in their seats until you give a signal indicating that it is appropriate to leave. If you use this procedure, some students are sure to test it by leaving their seats when the bell rings. In such a case, you must be prepared to call them back to their seats. You might then dismiss all the students except those who left their seats early. These students leave last.

Procedures during Seatwork and Teacher-Led Instruction

Good procedures for these activities are especially important because it is during these times that much instruction and learning take place. Good procedures will prevent or reduce the interruptions or distractions that can slow down content development activities or interfere with student work.

Student Attention during Presentations

It is helpful to consider how students should behave when you or another student is presenting information to the class or while you are conducting a discussion or recitation. Students are typically expected to listen attentively to the presenter and to other students. (In fact, teachers often translate this expectation into a general classroom rule, such as, "Show respect by listening carefully to speakers.") Teachers also expect that students should neither engage in social conversation with each other during such activities nor read unrelated materials or work on other assignments. The simplest way to enforce the latter requirement is to require that only books or other materials needed for the lesson be on the students' desks. You may also want students to take notes during your presentations. If so, you must state explicitly that this is desired, and you will have to teach your students how to do it. Initially, many students may be unable to abstract key points from your presentations, so you will have to help them by telling them what they should record in their notes or by providing an outline on the chalkboard or overhead. You could also provide students with a partially filled-in outline, with directions to complete it after the presentation. If note taking is expected, you should show them how you expect their notebooks to be organized. This can be done by presenting an example of a properly organized notebook and periodically inspecting student notebooks.

Student Participation

You will have to identify some procedure by which students can ask a question, contribute to a discussion, or receive help without interrupting you or other students during whole-class activities. During presentations and discussions, the simplest procedure is to require that students raise their hands and wait to be called on. (Some teachers occasionally have students call on the next contributor to avoid having all interactions channeled through the teacher.) Do not limit class participation only to volunteers. Call on all students and be sure that everyone has a response opportunity. In most circumstances, it is not a good idea to allow students to call out comments or answers without raising their hands. Undesirable consequences of allowing call-outs include domination of participation by a few students, frequent inappropriate comments, and interruptions of discussions and presentations. Teachers who rely on call-outs may get an inaccurate impression of overall understanding. Requiring that students raise their hands before commenting or asking questions gives all students an opportunity to participate.

Two exceptions to the "no call-out" procedure are reasonable. The first occurs when teachers want students to provide a choral response—that is, a whole-class response to a question. This can be handled by telling students at the beginning of the activity that they do not have to raise their hands. Also, many teachers use a nonverbal signal for a choral response—such as cupping one hand behind an ear—or a verbal signal—such as prefacing the question with a cue word such as, "Everyone, . . ." A second exception may occur during activities in which hand raising might slow down or interfere with a class discussion. Again, students can be told that it is not necessary to raise hands during that particular activity. It is worth noting that such variations from a standard procedure generally should not be used early in the school year. Instead, follow a simple routine for several weeks until you are certain that students understand it. Then, if you choose to depart from the procedure, clearly communicate the difference to the students at the beginning of the activity.

Procedures for Seatwork

In many subject areas, students are frequently given assignments to work on in class. During such activities, the teacher usually circulates around the room, monitoring students and providing individual feedback. A number of procedural areas should be planned so that you will be able to direct student efforts while they engage in this activity.

TALK AMONG STUDENTS

Some effective managers do not allow any student talk during seatwork activities. They require that students work on their own, that they neither seek nor provide help to other students, and that they refrain from social conversation. Other effective managers allow quiet talking among students when such talk is content related. You will have to decide what your policy will be. The "no talking" rule is easier to monitor, and you may want to start with this procedure during the first month or two of the school year and then try allowing students to help each other on a trial basis. If you decide to allow students to talk to one another or to work together during seatwork activities, you will have to establish guidelines. For example, you might say that during certain activities quiet talking is allowed, but if it gets too loud, the privilege will be lost. Be specific about what you mean by "quiet talking"—for example, whispering, low-volume natural talking, or talk that can be heard no more than two feet away.

OBTAINING HELP

When students are working at their seats and need help, you should have them raise their hands. You may then go to them or have them come to you one at a time. This procedure will avoid the formation of long lines of chatty students at your desk. It will also allow you to control where you give individual assistance. If you help students at a location other than their desks, choose one that allows you an unobstructed view of the rest of the class. Moving among students allows you to monitor their progress and helps keep them on task, so it's best not to rely on giving help from a single location for long periods of time.

OUT-OF-SEAT PROCEDURES

To eliminate unnecessary wandering around the room during seatwork, you can indicate when students are allowed to leave their seats. For example, students may sharpen pencils, turn in papers, get supplies, and so forth only when necessary. Trash can be kept at each student's desk and discarded at the end of the period. A one-at-a-time rule often works well for movement during seatwork.

WHEN SEATWORK HAS BEEN COMPLETED

Sometimes one or several students will finish their seatwork before the end of the period or before the next scheduled activity. This circumstance is frequently handled either by having students complete an additional, enrichment assignment for extra credit or by allowing such students to use the remaining time for free reading or to work on assignments from other classes. If you have enrichment activities that involve additional materials not in the students' possession, you must specify when these materials may be used, where they are kept, and what the procedures are for returning the materials to their proper place. Note that if many students frequently complete their work early, this is evidence of insufficient assignments or spending too much time in seatwork activities rather than content development.

Procedures for Student Group Work

Some teachers use groups extensively for a variety of tasks, such as short- or long-term projects, peer explanation and other assistance, and review of content learned in other formats. Other examples include laboratory assignments in science classes, the preparation of group reports or projects in social studies and English, home-making labs, and study groups organized to accomplish specific learning objectives or to prepare for an exam. To whatever extent groups are used, it is important for the teacher to develop efficient routines that support the learning objectives.

Routines are typically introduced to the students whenever groups are first used, and they are reinforced thereafter until the groups are working well. It is important that students learn appropriate group behavior, especially if the teacher intends to use groups extensively. Although the teacher can monitor group work, the fact that six or seven groups may be working simultaneously at varying paces using a variety of resources precludes the teacher from closely directing all group activities. Therefore, the procedures implemented for group work must be carefully chosen to encourage groups to work more or less independently toward the instructional goals, to promote desirable interaction among students in the group, and to support efficient use of time.

Johnson and Johnson (1999) recommend giving careful attention to teaching social skills to students who are going to work extensively in groups. First, students should be engaged in a discussion about the importance of each skill. Some common types of desirable group behaviors include staying on-task, frequent participation, listening carefully, and sharing and helping. Each skill needs to be carefully described. The Johnsons recommend discussing with students both what each behavior "looks like" and what it "sounds like" so that students have cues in several modalities.

In addition, it may be especially helpful to middle school students if the teacher makes simple wall charts listing the desired behaviors. Besides communicating an expectation for these behaviors, teachers can give students feedback about their performance of the behaviors—for example, by engaging the whole class in a discussion about how well the groups are working and what could be done to improve them. It is helpful to stress each student's responsibility toward the common good. A recommended strategy is to ask students to critique their own group's performance—for example, "What are three things my group is doing well, and what is one thing that we need to improve?" To provide practice of various desired behaviors, teachers can ask students to take various roles. Roles should be rotated to give each student an opportunity to practice all behaviors. A number of procedures that can help small-group activities proceed smoothly are described below.

Use of Materials and Supplies

Small-group activities, particularly those that are run as part of a laboratory, frequently require the use of a variety of materials and equipment. To avoid traffic jams, you must plan distribution stations carefully and use more than one if necessary. When possible, save time by placing some or all needed materials on students' desks or worktables before class starts. Be sure to check equipment for proper functioning ahead of time and have replacements on hand for use when needed. Student helpers may be assigned to distribute supplies and materials, to monitor supply stations, and to clean up work areas. If students need to bring special materials for group or project work, they should be told far enough in advance so that they can obtain them, and you may have to locate safe places for materials to be stored while work is in progress. If any of the equipment poses a potential hazard to students or can be easily damaged by careless use, you must identify safety routines and plan appropriate demonstrations.

Assignment of Students to Groups

This topic is important for several reasons. First, students who do not work well together should probably not be placed in the same work group. Also, a group composed mainly of poorly motivated students is not likely to accomplish much. If each person's grade is based partly on the individual's accomplishments and partly on the group's accomplishments, everyone in the group has a stake in what everyone else does, and the chances for a successful experience are increased. To obtain groups that are well balanced, to discourage excessive social talk during the assignment, and to save time in forming groups and getting started on the task, assignment of individual students to groups should be determined ahead of time by the teacher.

Student Goals and Participation

Students should be told what they are supposed to accomplish in their small-group work and taught how to go about the task. It is a good idea to assign specific roles and to discuss with students ahead of time the different roles they will take in the group work (e.g., reader, recorder, reporter, etc.). Preparing a list of steps that should be followed and displaying it on a chalkboard, on an overhead projector transparency, or on a handout can help students monitor their own progress. You might even discuss or suggest time allotments for accomplishing each step.

Other areas of behavior such as out-of-seat movement, contacting the teacher, and so on can be managed using the same procedures identified for seatwork activities. Obviously, quiet talk should be permitted, but the noise level may become a problem. Impress students with the importance of keeping talk focused on the task. During the activity, monitor the groups carefully and stop inappropriate behavior quickly at the individual or group level before it spreads to the whole class. You may want to identify a signal you will use to warn the class if the noise level gets too high.

Cooperative Learning

An instructional method that makes extensive use of groups is called *learning teams* or *cooperative learning groups*. (Johnson & Johnson 1999; Slavin, Karweit, &

Wasik 1994). This method has been applied widely in many subjects and grade levels. Typical practices are for teams to be formed heterogeneously and to work on academic tasks requiring interdependent action. Evaluation criteria reward the group for individual achievement, thus encouraging cooperation; teams may compete against each other and be rewarded on the basis of group performance. Procedures for learning teams incorporate many of the factors described in the preceding sections on the use of small groups, but they also have some unique characteristics. Suggestions for the management of cooperative learning groups are presented in Chapter 6. If you plan to make extensive use of this instructional method or if you are going to introduce groups early in the school year, you should find the material in Chapter 6 helpful.

Miscellaneous Procedures

A few other procedures merit mention. Although not all of these will be of concern to you, some may be helpful to consider.

Signals

A signal is some action, behavior, or physical prop that is used to obtain student attention or to indicate that some procedure or behavior is called for. If you always begin instruction by moving to a specific location in the room where you stand facing students, they will learn that you are giving them a signal that instruction is about to begin. Some teachers like to have a readily identifiable signal to notify students that seatwork or group-work activity is about to end and that another activity will soon begin. Examples of such signals include turning the lights off momentarily, ringing a bell, or turning on the overhead projector. Any signals that you intend to use should be explained to the students. The class should not have to guess what you are trying to accomplish.

Public Address (PA) Announcements and Other Interruptions

It is important that you and your students be able to hear PA announcements. Therefore, you should explain that during such announcements there is to be no talking, and students should not attempt to ask you questions or leave their desks. You should also listen during these announcements. This shows respect for your own rules. Other interruptions, such as visitors, office workers seeking information or forms, loud noises in the hall, and so forth, may be a frequent distraction in your school. You can reduce their effects by teaching your students a procedure to handle interruptions. A simple one is to indicate that whenever you are interrupted, students should sit quietly with no talking if they have no assignment, read a book, or continue working if they already have an assignment. Be sure to have at least one set of handouts ready as a backup assignment in case the interruption is very long.

Special Equipment and Materials

If you have special equipment or materials that are likely to capture students' immediate interest (e.g., computers or live animals), decide on policies for access and use, and communicate them to students right away. For most special equipment, learning centers, and special materials, however, wait until the first time they are actually used to give a demonstration and instructions. You can also post a list of specific instructions.

Fire and Disaster Drills

Find out what procedures are used in your building. Because most secondary students know the basic procedures, a few timely sentences during the first week about the procedure for leaving the room (e.g., by row) and where to go will be sufficient. You may want to post a map showing where students are supposed to go. Eventually, a schoolwide rehearsal will be held.

Split Lunch Period

Tell students whether they should clear their desks or leave their work out when they are dismissed for lunch. Tell them whether it is safe to leave personal belongings in the room. Show or tell the class what route they should take from your room to the cafeteria, and remind them of school areas that are off-limits and of proper hallway behavior. Be specific as to the time class will resume and stick to it; otherwise, you will find students wasting five or more minutes every day.

Further Reading

Bicard, D. F. (2000). Using classroom rules to construct behavior. *Middle School Journal, 31*(5), 37–45.

This article does a good job of describing how rules are part of a comprehensive plan for establishing and maintaining appropriate behavior. Implementation involves teaching, monitoring, praising, and correcting.

Evertson, C. M. (1994). Classroom rules and routines. *International Encyclopedia of Education* (2nd ed.). Oxford: Pergamon Press.

This article contains key ideas about choosing and implementing rules and routines. Their role in supporting learning goals is emphasized, along with the need for careful planning, implementation, monitoring, and revision when needed.

Fenwick, D. T. (1998). Managing space, energy, and self: Junior high teachers' experiences of classroom management. *Teaching and Teacher Education, 14,* 619–631.

This study found that teachers think about their work in terms of classroom management, with three dominant aspects: managing classroom space and objects within it, managing persons and teaching practices, and managing themselves. Teachers organize space and behavior using routines that provide structure and help them manage student activity and energy.

Good, T. L., & Brophy, J. E. (2000). *Looking in classrooms* (8th ed.). New York: Longman.

Research-based and informative, this book offers many insights and suggestions about classroom teaching. Several chapters provide a good foundation for planning important classroom procedures, activities, and routines.

Leinhardt, G., Weidman, C., & Hammond, K. M. (1987). Introduction and integration of classroom routines by expert teachers. *Curriculum Inquiry, 17*(2), 135–176.

Data from the classrooms of successful teachers show the importance of establishing and practicing routines from the beginning of school. Three types of routines are identified: management, instructional support, and teacher-student exchange. The authors point out that teachers build on simple routines to support more elaborate ones.

Suggested Activities

1. Identify the schoolwide rules and procedures you and your students are expected to observe. Be sure these are incorporated into your own classroom rules and procedures where appropriate.

2. Conduct an Internet search using the descriptors "classroom rules and procedures" or similar terms. You'll find many websites developed by teachers who have posted their classroom systems. Review some of these and consider which ones can be useful for your classroom.

3. Read Case Studies 2.1 and 2.2 on the following pages. They illustrate classroom procedures and rules for most major areas, and they will be helpful as you develop your own system of management.

4. Use Checklist 2 at the end of the chapter to help organize your planning of classroom procedures. Be sure you think through your expectations for student behavior in each of the general areas as well as in instructional areas that you will be using. Then develop a set of procedures that will communicate your expectations to your students.

5. Develop a list of four to eight classroom rules. Be sure they emphasize areas of classroom behavior that are important to you and to the functioning of your classroom.

6. After you have developed a set of rules and procedures, review them with an administrator or with another teacher in your subject area. If you do not know whom to choose, ask several teachers or a counselor for nominations.

CASE STUDY 2.1

RULES AND PROCEDURES IN AN EIGHTH-GRADE CLASS

The classroom rules in Ms. Ashley's English class were simple: Be prompt, be prepared, and be polite. When the tardy bell rang each day, students were expected to be in their seats copying the plan of the day from the overhead transparency. This plan usually included the topic, objectives, and materials for the day's lesson and the assignment for homework. Thus, the beginning class routine consisted of putting away their books, getting out their spiral notebooks, recording the date, and copying a daily plan. While students did this, the teacher checked roll. If students were tardy to class, they immediately signed a tardy roster on a table by the door and took their seats. The penalty for unexcused tardiness was thirty minutes of detention after school. Students who had a valid excuse checked the "Please excuse" column on the tardy roster and left their "tardy excuse form" in a tray next to the roster.

The "be prepared" rule required that students bring their materials and completed homework assignments to class each day. Students were not allowed to return to their lockers. Late papers were not accepted, but incomplete work was accepted for partial credit.

The "be polite" rule required that students not interrupt the teacher or other students when they were speaking to the class. To avoid interruptions and to give everyone an opportunity to speak during whole-class discussions or instruction, students were required to raise their hands to get permission to speak. However, the teacher did not limit questioning only to volunteers; any student could be called on at any time. This rule also covered listening carefully when the teacher or another student was addressing the class. Students were not to use the pencil sharpener or do other distracting things during these times. Students were expected to treat other students with consideration.

Students in Ms. Ashley's class were expected to use quiet voices during activities in which talking was permitted. These included small-group or class-discussion activities or when the teacher had given special permission. Students were not allowed to talk among themselves during individual seatwork activities.

Ms. Ashley's students were allowed to leave their seats to turn in work at designated trays or get supplies of materials from shelves without permission from the teacher, but if individuals wandered and bothered other students, they lost their privilege and had to raise their hands for permission. When seatwork began, the teacher circulated among students, checked progress, and gave individual feedback and/or instruction. She later sat at a worktable from which she could monitor the class easily while she helped individuals or small groups. Students raised their hands for permission to come to the table. Sometimes the table was used for peer tutoring, which the teacher arranged.

Consequences of breaking class rules or not following procedures were related to a schoolwide system of demerits. Demerits resulted in detention after school and in contacting parents. Ms. Ashley emphasized communication with parents about student behavior and work. She called students' parents with good news as well as bad, and each grading term she presented awards to two groups of students: those with very good attendance and behavior records and those who did outstanding work or improved their work during the term.

Each day, Ms. Ashley used the last few minutes of class for cleanup and announcements. If students were working on seatwork, she had them stop, get their supplies ready to go, return materials to shelves, and check around their desks for papers and trash. Then she made announcements of upcoming events and reminded students of any unusual supplies they would need to bring the following day. After the bell rang, she dismissed her students.

PROCEDURES FOR SMALL-GROUP WORK/LABORATORY ACTIVITIES

The day before her science class had its first laboratory assignment, Ms. Davis discussed procedures and rules for group work and use of the laboratory facilities. The rules and procedures she discussed included the following guidelines:

1. Work with your assigned partner(s). Participate, do your share of the work, and be polite and considerate.

2. Raise your hand for assistance from the teacher. Don't call out.

3. All talk should be quiet and work related.

4. Stay at your group work stations unless it is necessary to get supplies. Don't wander or return to your desk until the teacher tells you to.

5. Read instructions on the board, overhead transparency, and worksheet, and listen to the teacher's instructions.

6. When you finish work, check over your worksheet to be sure it is complete and neat. If there is extra time, ask the teacher for more lab instructions. If there are none, read the references listed for the day's lesson.

7. The teacher dismisses the class. The class will not be dismissed until the laboratory area is clean.

8. Report broken equipment quietly and quickly to the teacher.

9. Obey laboratory safety rules: Never turn on gas jets unless instructed to do so; never put anything in electrical outlets; never drink from laboratory faucets; stay out of the laboratory storeroom; keep your hands away from your mouth and eyes; wash your hands after laboratory activities; no horseplay.

Students in this class worked in pairs for most laboratory activities. Partner assignments were changed several times during the year, not at every lab session. On the day of a lab, Ms. Davis began activities by quickly going over the objectives of the lesson, the grading criteria, and the procedures listed on the lab worksheet. If the laboratory activities consisted of several major parts, she suggested time allotments for each part to help students pace themselves. The teacher also had a list of some references in the text and from other sources in the room for students to read for background when completing the worksheet, studying for a quiz, or as an enrichment activity in case a student completed all assigned work early. New words or terms used on the worksheet were defined. All this information was already listed on the blackboard or on an overhead transparency to save time. If the laboratory work involved many procedures, the teacher helped students divide the work. For example, jobs for Partner A and for Partner B were listed separately, either on the chalkboard or overhead. Two separate supply stations were often used to avoid congestion.

During lab activities, the teacher circulated and answered questions of students who raised their hands. Ms. Davis gave several reminders about time, providing a ten-minute, a five-minute, and a two-minute warning before cleanup. She allowed plenty of time for cleanup (usually at least five minutes before the end of the period). To make sure the class did not run overtime, she used a kitchen timer. Immediately after cleanup, the teacher had all students return to their desks. There she discussed any common procedural or academic problems. This information was helpful to students in future lab sessions and in filling out or correcting their worksheet for the day.

Sometimes Ms. Davis used work groups for discussions, problem-solving sessions, or test review. For these activities, she decided on group assignments ahead of time and listed names of students in each group on an overhead transparency. On the transparency, she would also indicate specific responsibilities within groups (e.g., discussion leader, recorder, reporter, supplier). Tables and/or groups of desks were numbered before students arrived, and students were told to sit in the group indicated on the overhead transparency. In arranging seating beforehand, the teacher spread these groups as far apart as possible in the classroom. Then, as soon as class began, Ms. Davis went over the objectives, procedures, and grading criteria for the activity before letting students begin work. Especially at the beginning of the year, she reminded students of the classroom rules for group work. As students worked in groups, she carried a clipboard so that she could note participation easily. At the end of group discussion activities, students always filled out self-evaluations on how well their group had met the objectives of the lesson, how well they had followed the small-group activity rules, and how well they, individually, had met their responsibilities to their group.

Checklist 2

Rules and Procedures

Check When Complete	Area	What Is Your Procedure in This Area?
	General Procedures	
☐	A. Beginning-of-period	_____
	1. Attendance check	_____
	2. Previously absent students	_____
	3. Tardy students	_____
	4. Expected student behavior	_____
☐	B. Out-of-room policies	_____
☐	C. Materials and equipment	_____
	1. What to bring to class	_____
	2. Pencil sharpener	_____
	3. Other room equipment	_____
	4. Student contact with teacher's desk, storage, other materials	_____
☐	D. Ending the period	_____

(continued)

Check When Complete	Area	What Is Your Procedure in This Area?

Seatwork and Instruction Procedures

☐ A. Student attention _____

☐ B. Student participation _____

☐ C. Seatwork procedures _____

    1. Talk among students _____

    2. Obtaining help _____

    3. Out-of-seat _____

    4. When seatwork has been completed _____

Student Group Work

☐ A. Use of materials and supplies _____

☐ B. Assignment of students to groups _____

☐ C. Student participation and behavior _____

Miscellaneous

☐ A. Signals _____

☐ B. Behavior during interruptions _____

☐ C. Special equipment _____

☐ D. Fire and disaster drills _____

☐ E. Split lunch period _____

3
Managing Student Work

When we presented a set of procedures for establishing an orderly class-room setting in Chapter 2, we also indicated that additional proce-dures would be needed to help manage student work and learning. In this chapter, we describe the additional procedures that are aimed at encourag-ing students to complete assignments and to engage in other learning activities. Ul-timately, the goal of a system for managing student work is to help students become independent learners; thus, your procedures should give as much responsibility as possible to the students themselves rather than depend on either you or parents to see that assignments are completed.

As we discuss student work procedures, it is easy to focus on the products stu-dents will create: completed assignments, test scores, and so on. After all, these are the tangible, measurable outcomes of the activities you will engage in with students each day. It is important, nevertheless, not to lose sight of your goal as a teacher: to facilitate student learning. Your system for managing student work should lead you and your students to examine their learning and the learning process in which they are engaged.

In all of the academic core subjects and in many of the others, students are given assignments or projects frequently, perhaps even daily. Projects, written as-signments, problem sets, and a variety of other academic tasks are typical of the secondary school curriculum. Sometimes these assignments are done in class, at other times they are given as homework, or perhaps both. These assignments are important for learning and retention because they provide systematic practice, ap-plication, and repeated exposure to concepts. Consequently, your management sys-tem supports learning when it supports consistent and successful engagement in these assignments. However, when procedures for managing student work are not working well or when students are not held accountable for their performance and learning, many problems can occur. Consider the following example.

> Toward the end of the first grading period, Ms. Peters noticed several disturbing signs of lack of student interest in completing written work in her social studies classes. The deadline had passed for students to turn in their first major project of the year, a report on their state's water resources, and fewer than half the students had met the deadline. Ms. Peters then extended the due date by one week. But even with the extension, one quarter of the reports were not turned in. Those re-ports that were completed were disappointing because many consisted mainly of pictures of water scenes clipped from magazines or downloaded from a website and a short discussion taken from an encyclopedia reference that Ms. Peters had suggested as one resource—not as the sole source of information. Many of the re-ports looked as though they had been thrown together the night before they were due. With a sinking feeling, Ms. Peters realized that if she graded strictly, many stu-dents would do poorly. Because she had intended to use the report for a major por-tion of the grade, many students were in danger of failing. To make matters worse, numerous students had not been completing recent shorter assignments, and many of those that were completed were of poor quality. These had not been de-manding assignments, and they were well within most students' capabilities. The activities included completing worksheets and answering questions listed at the

end of the text chapters. Ms. Peters typically had students do two or three of these assignments each week and place them in their notebooks. She collected them every three weeks and assigned a grade to the notebook. Of the students who did complete all assignments, quite a few did them poorly, with very sloppy or partially completed work. Ms. Peters felt herself caught in a dilemma. If she graded strictly (or just fairly), many students would fail, and she might face great resistance from both students and their parents. However, if she relaxed her grading standards, students would learn that they could get away with not doing their work.

It is safe to say that many students in Ms. Peters's classes do not feel accountable for completing work carefully or on time. The basis for the lack of student cooperation can be determined from answers to the following questions.

- Do students know how each assignment contributes to their overall grade?
- Are requirements for assignments clear with respect to standards for quality, amount of work, and due dates?
- Is student progress being monitored frequently enough?
- What kinds of feedback do students receive about their progress as well as about their completed work? How immediate is the feedback?

In each area, Ms. Peters could have done several things to encourage students to complete assignments promptly and correctly. This chapter focuses on aspects of classroom procedures that communicate the importance of work assignments, enable students to understand what is expected of them, and help them make desired progress. Critical procedures for which you must plan include your grading system, monitoring and feedback, and communicating assignments and work requirements. Each of these areas is discussed in this chapter. Checklist 3 is provided to help organize your planning in these areas. In addition, some case studies are provided at the end of the chapter.

FOR REFLECTION

Consider the purposes of your procedures and routines for managing student work. As a teacher, you need ways to keep from being swamped by paperwork and grading, and you must provide a fair, documented basis for grading. But think beyond how keeping students accountable helps *you*. What do *students* learn from an effective work management system? One example might be organizational skills. What are some others?

Your Grading System and Record Keeping

At the end of each grading period, you will have to record a report card grade for each student. How you determine this grade has important implications for classroom management. Grades are very important to most students (and to their parents) because they are tangible evidence of student accomplishment. It is therefore important that your grading system accurately reflects the quality of student work. In addition, you will want to use your grading system to help ensure that students complete their assignments by the due dates.

The first thing you should do before deciding on a grading system is to determine whether your department, school, or district has any policies that you must follow. Usually, a school or district will have established a numerical standard for grades (e.g., 90–100 = A, 80–89 = B, etc.). If so, you will have to become familiar with the policy and adapt your grading system to it.

After determining the relevant school policies, you should identify the components of your grading system. Most secondary teachers use several factors in grading students. Academic achievement is the most important one, of course, but effort, participation, homework, and improvement are also given weight by many teachers (McMillan 2001). High school teachers are more likely to use major exams than are middle school teachers.

Remember that the most accurate assessment of performance generally will be based on frequent evaluation of all aspects of student work, not on a few test scores or a major project grade. A system incorporating a daily grade that contributes significantly to an overall grade allows for frequent evaluation and feedback and keeps students accountable for their everyday work; it is an important aid to the academic success of many students. In subjects that have individual projects extending over several days or weeks (for example, industrial arts, home economics, or writing projects in English), a teacher can still examine student work daily and record a grade or note "satisfactory" or "unsatisfactory" progress. In addition to daily assignments, other frequently used components of grading systems are tests, papers, projects, workbooks, quizzes, performance, quality of participation (as in discussions), and extra-credit work. Many teachers include student notebook grades in their grading system. Students are required to keep all their work organized in a notebook, which is graded periodically for completeness and neatness. Often, students must make corrections on all graded work before putting it in their notebooks. If you want students to keep notebooks, be explicit about what should be placed in the notebook and how it should be organized. It is a good idea to include this information in a course syllabus. In addition, the notebook should include a table of contents and/or a list of assignments. Also, a sample notebook can be displayed so that students can see what is required. These practices encourage students to be organized and help them keep track of materials they need to study for exams. In planning your grading system, be sure that you can manage the bookkeeping aspects, and remember that you will have to evaluate twenty-five to thirty or more students in each class.

After you have identified the components of your grading system, decide what percentage of a student's grade each component will represent. Once you have established your system, you can prepare a handout for students explaining the basis for grading, and you can have them take this home to be signed by a parent. This procedure has several virtues. For one thing, it makes very clear to students what criteria will be used to determine the grade. It also informs the parents, who

Reprinted with special permission of King Features Syndicate.

may then be of some assistance in monitoring progress or assisting their child. Having sent this information to the parents, you may find it helpful later in the year to refer to it when discussing their child's progress in your class.

If your grading system contains any unusual features, the recommendations in the preceding paragraph are especially important. Providing the information in written form helps signal its importance, and it might prompt students to seek clarification if they don't understand some aspect. Also, parents apprised of your system may be more supportive than those who learn of it only after some problem has occurred.

You should also set up your grade book so that important information can be entered into it. You will find it most convenient if you record all relevant information for each student in the grade book rather than keeping separate lists of student numbers and book numbers, absences, project grades, and so on. Leave an extra line between student names to provide space for the additonal information. You can use the top line for each student to record a daily grade or homework score and to note absences or tardiness (write *a* or *t* in the upper right corner of the space, using pencil in case the absent student arrives late). Use the other spaces to record any other information (e.g., quiz or project grades) that might be collected on the same day. Some teachers like to use pens of different colors to highlight different components of their grading system. Using more than one line per student might require that you use a second page for a larger class, and thus you might run out of pages before the year is over. Get a second grade book if necessary. To enable you to turn quickly to the appropriate page, place small index clips (paper clips will do if necessary) or color-coded plastic tabs on the appropriate page for each class.

Computer programs are available to store and calculate grades according to the weighting you designate. Because the information you input into this type of a program is confidential, be sure that you use grading programs securely and prohibit student access to the computer files generated.

Your school may provide software that will allow you to record student performance data and calculate report card grades. If not, you may purchase such software or even download freeware from the net. Well-written programs contain features that construct seating charts and compute grades based on various weighting methods. These features can make grade calculation more efficient, but data entry can be time-consuming if the grading system includes daily grades or other multiple components that are frequently recorded. Teachers who have such systems often choose to maintain a traditional grade book for daily grades and attendance information, and transfer a summary score into the computer for use in calculating a report card grade. Because the information entered into such programs is confidential, the program needs to be used securely with password-protected access. A backup copy of the files is essential to prevent possible loss of student grade information.

Feedback and Monitoring Procedures

In conjunction with a system for recording and assigning grades, you should have other procedures for giving students feedback about their performance. Regular feedback is more desirable than sporadic feedback because it offers students more information and reduces the amount of time they practice making errors if their performance is incorrect. If you give daily assignments, you will almost certainly wish to involve students in checking them because your time will be too limited to check 125 to 150 assignments every day. Of course, you cannot expect students to check complex assignments calling for advanced levels of knowledge (e.g., essay scoring). However, many daily assignments are of a more routine nature and can be checked by students. The following procedures will be helpful to keep in mind:

1. Students can be allowed to check some of their own assignments. You can reduce the temptation to be dishonest by requiring that a different color pen (or pencil) be used for checking. When students do check and correct their own work, you must monitor them closely and then collect and spot-check the papers yourself.
2. Describe and model to students how you want the checking done; for example, mark or circle incorrect answers, put "graded by" and their name in a specified place on the paper, put the number missed or correct or the grade at the top of the first page, and so on.
3. Hold students responsible for accurate checking. If a student feels that his or her paper was marked incorrectly by another student, a simple system is to have the student write a note to that effect on a designated part of the paper. You can then verify the work when you examine the papers.
4. We do not recommend the practice of recording grades by having students call them out. If you do not wish to collect an assignment after checking, a simple procedure is to have students leave the work on their desks so that you can record grades as you move from student to student. This can be done during a later seatwork or classwork activity to avoid leaving students in dead time while you record their grades.

Another type of feedback includes having students keep their own record of daily grades, quizzes, and so on. Some teachers have students calculate a weekly or

biweekly average from this record during a few minutes of class time. This type of self-monitoring keeps students informed about how they are progressing and makes obvious the effects of failure to complete or turn in assignments.

When you have students working on long-term projects, it is important to help them make satisfactory progress. Break the assignment into smaller parts or checkpoints and then set deadlines and goals for each part. A term paper, for example, might have intermediate checkpoints established for (1) a description of the topic and thesis statement, (2) a list of sources and an outline, and (3) a rough draft. It is not necessary (or efficient) to collect the interim products; instead, circulate around the room to check each student's work and give feedback. You might assign a letter grade for satisfactory progress at some major checkpoint, though most teachers who use checkpoints assign a simpler "satisfactory/unsatisfactory" assessment. For a construction project, a plan or description of the project or major stages in its completion can be evaluated as an intermediate check.

Some teachers utilize peer review of first drafts of written products or project plans. Peer feedback from such reviews can stimulate new learning and promote student reflection, thus improving the quality of student products. Peer review is usually done in a small-group format (e.g., pairs), so the teacher should prepare students for the activity by, for example, conducting a discussion of the types of feedback and comments that are desirable and most likely to be helpful.

Monitoring Student Work in Progress

After you have given students an assignment, you should give careful attention to student work. Group seatwork needs a guided beginning. If you immediately begin work at your desk or go to help one student without first checking to see that all are working, some students may not even begin, and others may proceed incorrectly. Two simple strategies will help avoid this situation. First, you can assure a smooth transition into seatwork by beginning it as a whole-class activity; that is, have everyone take out papers, worksheets, or other materials, and then answer the first question or two or work the first few problems together as a group, just as you would conduct a recitation. For example, ask the first question, solicit an answer, discuss it, and have students record it on their papers. Not only will this procedure ensure that all students begin working, but immediate problems with the assignment can also be solved. A second way to monitor student involvement in the assignment is to circulate around the room and check each student's progress periodically. This allows corrective feedback to be given when needed and helps keep students responsible for appropriate progress. Avoid going only to students who raise their hands seeking assistance, or else you will never note the progress of other students who may be unwilling to ask for help.

Long-Range Monitoring

Be sure to use your grade-book records to monitor completion rates and performance levels on assignments. The first time a student fails to turn in an assignment, talk with him or her about it. If the student needs help, give help, but require that the work be done. If the student neglects two assignments consecutively or begins a pattern of skipping occasional assignments, call the parent(s) or send a note home immediately. Be friendly and encouraging, but insist that the work be done. Don't delay making contacts with the home, and above all, don't rely on using only the grade at the end of the grading period to communicate that a student's performance is below par. By then, a pattern of poor performance may have developed, and both you and the student will find it difficult to recoup.

Communicating Assignments and Work Requirements

Students need a clear idea of what their assignments are and what is expected of them. This means that the teacher must explain all requirements and features of the assignments. However, that alone will not be enough: Not all students will listen carefully, some students may be absent when the assignment and requirements are discussed, and the assignment itself may be very complex. In addition, there is more to completing assignments than doing the work accurately; standards for neatness, legibility, and form should be considered. Although we do not want to encourage an overemphasis on form to the detriment of the content objectives, some standards in these areas must be set. After all, good work habits, neatness, and careful attention to detail are valued attributes in most occupations. The following three areas should be considered.

Instructions for Assignments

In addition to an oral explanation of the assignment requirements, you should post the assignment and important instructions on a chalkboard in a place marked "Do not erase." Use the routine of requiring that students copy the assignment into a notebook or onto an assignment sheet. It is a good idea to record each day's as-

"Oh no, not homework again."

signment for a whole week (or more) somewhere in the classroom. This is helpful to students who have been absent.

The grading criteria and requirements for each assignment should be clear. Be sure you explain these to the students. If the instructions are complex, as for a long-term project or portfolio, it is best to duplicate the instructions and requirements or have students copy the instructions into their notebooks. If in-class performance is to be evaluated, as in a home economics class or science lab, tell students exactly what you will be rating (e.g., following correct laboratory procedures, working quietly and cooperatively, cleaning up) and how much weight (or how many points) each factor will carry. Be realistic in your grading criteria and systematic in following through with your evaluation.

Standards for Form, Neatness, and Due Dates

You'll have to decide whether students may use pencil or pen and what color or colors of ink are acceptable. If students may complete written work on a word processor, what size and style of font is acceptable? Also communicate to students what type of paper and notebook are to be used in class and whether students should write on the backs of pages. A policy for neatness should also be determined. Students need to know whether you will accept paper torn from a spiral notebook, how to treat errors (e.g., draw a line through them, circle them, erase), and how stringent you are about legibility. You should also think about the consequences for students in this area if they do not complete work properly. For example, will you deduct points or reduce the grade on the assignment? Because some students may turn in incomplete work, you must decide whether you will accept it and grade only what is done, subtracting the part not done from the grade, or whether you will accept papers only when complete and assess a late penalty.

Decide on a heading for students to use on their papers. Post a sample heading, have students make copies to keep in their notebooks, and go over it with students the first time they are to use it. You may have to remind them of this heading several times during the early weeks of school.

Finally, due dates must be reasonable and clear; exceptions should not be made without good cause. Classwork should be turned in before students leave class. Accept late homework only with a written excuse from parents, or impose a penalty such as reduction in grade. The reason underlying this firmness is that many middle and high school students still require active help to develop good work habits and to avoid procrastination.

Procedures for Absent Students

When students are absent from classes, they miss instruction, directions for assignments, and assistance they may need in getting work underway. Establishing routines for handling make-up work can be very helpful to returning students. Routines will also help prevent these students from milling around your desk asking questions about missed assignments and from interrupting you to obtain directions for makeup work. The following items should be considered:

1. As mentioned earlier, either post weekly assignment lists on a bulletin board or keep a folder with lists of assignments in an accessible place so that absent students can determine what work they missed without interrupting you. Keep an "absentee" folder for each class and place in it copies of handouts.
2. Decide how much time will be allowed for making up work.
3. Set up a place where students can turn in make-up work and where they can pick it up after it has been checked (e.g., baskets or trays labeled "Absent In" and "Graded"). The "Graded" basket will also provide a place where students can pick up any graded work that was distributed while they were absent.
4. Establish a regular time, such as thirty minutes before or after school, when you will be available to assist students with make-up work. Also, you can designate class helpers who will be available at particular times of the class period (usually during seatwork) to help students with make-up work.
5. Determine how students who have missed group work will make it up. Assist groups in planning for the inclusion of absent members and in helping those members catch up when they return.

Further Reading

Burns, M. (1995). The eight most important lessons I've learned about organizing my teaching year. *Instructor, 105*(2), 86–88.

Many of the ideas in this article focus on planning for instruction. Their implementation would be a big step toward managing student work and are well worth consideration by new or experienced teachers.

Eilam, B. (2001). Primary strategies for promoting homework performance. *American Educational Research Journal, 38,* 691–725.

This study provides details about reasons some students experience great difficulty completing homework satisfactorily, including not keeping track of assignments, not organizing their work, and limited understanding of the task. The research highlights the importance of teaching students to record assignments, be able to locate the record, set deadlines, organize their work, and know how to proceed with the task on their own.

Guskey, Thomas R. (Ed.) (1996). *Communicating student learning.* Alexandria, VA: Association for Supervision and Curriculum Development.

This ASCD Yearbook contains chapters on many aspects of communicating student learning, including grading of students with special needs, reporting methods for different grade levels, alternatives to traditional grading, and the use of technology.

Suggested Activities

1. Identify a subject and grade you will teach; then use Checklist 3 at the end of the chapter to organize your plan for managing student work. Note areas in which you are not certain of your procedures and then seek advice.

2. You can obtain additional ideas for managing student work at the website www.atozteacherstuff.com. Click on the link for "Tips." As part of a group discussion activity, compare your procedures to those developed by other group members.

3. Reread the case study used to introduce this chapter. Suggest some procedures or actions this teacher might have taken to prevent the problems she is facing.

4. Read Case Studies 3.1, 3.2, and 3.3, noting positive examples and ideas you might apply to your own classroom. Then read Case Study 3.4 and suggest ways the teacher might revise her procedures to manage her class better.

5. In Activity 1, you assumed a particular grade or age level of the students. Now assume that you will teach a class several grades above or below that level. How would such a change affect the nature of academic work and the procedures you use to manage it? Discuss the rationale for any changes in your plans.

AN ACCOUNTABILITY SYSTEM IN AN ENGLISH CLASS

Ms. Clark posted a weekly chart listing daily activities and showing the maximum number of points students could earn for each activity (a possible 100 points for daily work and tests per week). In addition, the students kept a copy of the weekly chart in their notebooks, recorded the points they earned beside each assignment, and had the sheet signed by their parents each week. Also on the chart was a list of books and materials to bring to class each day.

In addition to the weekly chart, the teacher listed daily activities in detail on the front chalkboard. Her lessons followed the order on the list, and several times during each class period, she pointed out to students their progress on the list. When describing seatwork assignments, she told students how much time they would have to complete each assignment; she then actively monitored students as they worked, circulating and providing assistance. During class discussions, she made sure that all students participated by calling on non-volunteers as well as volunteers at least once and by keeping a checklist to be sure everyone responded.

Students who had been absent were responsible for finding their assignments on the weekly list, conferring with the teacher before or after school, and filing make-up work in a special folder. Students picked up papers that were handed back in their absence from an "Absent" basket. The first few times the teacher placed an absent student's paper into this basket, she reminded the class whose responsibility it was to get the paper.

Ms. Clark was consistent in her procedures for checking student work. She had students check their own work with red pen or pencil. She always collected papers afterward. Sometimes she had students turn papers in for checking and grading. Students recorded their points on their weekly assignment sheets when the papers were handed back. All papers for the week were handed back by the end of class on Friday. Students were expected to record their grades on their assignment sheets and have them signed by a parent.

MANAGING STUDENT WORK IN A MATH CLASS

An important tool in Mr. Richard's accountability system was a notebook he required that his students maintain. On the first day of class, he introduced it by showing a sample notebook. In addition to daily assignments and tests, the notebook included a grade sheet that was sectioned for recording homework grades, test grades, pop quiz scores, and a notebook score. Students recorded their grades on this page each marking period, calculated an average, and compared their computations with the teacher's to verify their grades. Major tests were put in the notebooks after having been signed by parents. The notebook also had a section for the class notes that students regularly took during presentations. Mr. Richard collected and assigned a grade to student notebooks a week before the end of the grading period. The notebook grade was given a weight equal to a major test grade in determining the student's course grade. Although he did not collect the notebooks until late in the grading period, Mr. Richard circulated around the room to check notebooks several times before collecting them. The first time he checked the notebooks, shortly after the beginning of the first grading period, Mr. Richard simply looked for correct form and made sure that each student had begun using a notebook. Several weeks later, he verified that the students were including the appropriate material and continuing to follow correct procedures.

Each day's assignment was written on the front board. Beginning on the fourth day of school, students did warmup problems immediately on entering the room. These problems were displayed on the overhead projector screen, and students handed in their work when the teacher finished checking roll. These daily exercises were always graded and returned to the students either at the end of the period or on the following day.

Homework was always checked and had to be completed on time. Mr. Richard explained to students that it would not be fair to those who completed their homework promptly for others to have more time or perhaps the opportunity to copy answers from another student's completed paper. When students were taught how to average their grades, Mr. Richard also demonstrated the effect a zero would have on their homework average.

When grading a homework assignment, students were given explicit instructions on how to mark it. When work was checked by students, Mr. Richard frequently asked who had missed a particular problem. If many students had difficulty, he explained the problem to them in detail. After the papers were checked, he told students how to determine the grade. Points were deducted if a student failed to use pencil or did not write out each problem.

At least once a week, Mr. Richard collected students' homework papers and checked them himself. After recording grades during class, or when he returned papers to students, he reminded them to record their grades on their grade sheet in their notebook.

CASE STUDY 3.3

MANAGING LONG-TERM ASSIGNMENTS

In Ms. Curry's science class, students completed two multimedia research projects during the year. Ms. Curry had carefully planned the procedures to help students achieve success on these assignments. For the first multimedia project, she assigned topics rather than allowing students to choose their own. An assigned topic made it easier for students to begin quickly and allowed the teacher to make some adjustments in the difficulty of the assignment for different ability levels of students. When she introduced the first project, Ms. Curry gave her students two handouts describing requirements. On one page was a description of the topic and a list of cards or slide categories the computer presentation should include. The other handout was the same for all students. This outlined general requirements for the project, a calendar of checkpoints, due dates, and information about how the project would be graded.

Following an initial multimedia presentation she had prepared as an example, Ms. Curry reviewed all of the directions and requirements with the students, using slides from her presentation as examples. One requirement was appropriate color selections of backgrounds and text to ensure that the presentation could be read by an audience when displayed. These standards were defined in detail and included information about the final appearance of the project. Additionally, Ms. Curry included a written admonition for students to save their work frequently and in two places: both to the school network and to a personal disk. Another requirement concerned references and the bibliography, including sample citations for both text and Web-based references. Students were to use at least four references, with one of those being Web based. There was a specific requirement for the minimum number of cards or slides in the presentation, and at least one of the cards or slides had to include a sound or movie file rather than written text.

Ms. Curry provided a printout of her example presentation with notations for transitions and actions she had included. She also indicated the days the class would be scheduled to work in the library and computer lab and provided a sign-up sheet for using the classroom computers during classwork time or study hall.

The checkpoints for the multimedia research project included an initial approval of the list of references identified by each student. Ms. Curry also examined the students' notes or sketches. At both of these checkpoints, she gave students feedback about the appropriateness of their sources or work. Ms. Curry gave two grades: one based on the project and the other based on the oral presentation of the project to the class. Before the multimedia project was due, students received a checkoff sheet that they could use to determine whether they had met all of the requirements before submitting their disks. Before the oral presentations, Ms. Curry gave students copies of the check sheet she used to evaluate each presentation. She discussed with students each item on the evaluation check sheet.

CASE STUDY 3.4

POOR WORK AND STUDY HABITS IN MATHEMATICS

Ms. Wood's mathematics classes are free of serious disruptions, and for the most part, students pay attention to her presentations. In her first-year and second-year algebra classes, in which most of the students are very conscious of report card grades and seem serious about doing well in school, conduct problems are limited to isolated cases. In the three sections of general mathematics that Ms. Wood teaches, students are less task oriented and more inclined to misbehave. Nonetheless, students usually observe major class rules and procedures, with most of the inappropriate behavior limited to off-task socializing or inattentiveness.

Ms. Wood's classes are not without problems, however; numerous students are falling behind in their work and are receiving low grades as a result of their poor performance on chapter tests. These tests are used as 75 percent of the report card grade, with the remaining 25 percent based on a score assigned to each student's notebook, which is turned in at the end of the grading period. At the beginning of the year, students were told to keep all classwork and homework assignments in the notebook along with any daily notes they might take. Their notebook grade is based on an overall score assigned by the teacher one week before the end of the grading period. "After you check each assignment in class, be certain to place it in the notebook so that it will be there when I determine notebook grades," Ms. Wood told her students. "Otherwise, you will not receive credit for doing your assignments." About once a week, Ms. Wood collects daily work and checks it herself; however, several students do not turn in completed homework assignments. The students in the algebra classes have followed the instructions for notebooks reasonably well, although several in each class have presented incomplete notebooks at grading time. In the general math classes, more of the student notebooks are poorly done, with many assignments missing and contents sloppily assembled. A handful of students in each class have not bothered to turn in notebooks at all. Ms. Wood found herself becoming annoyed a few days before the notebooks were due, when many students asked what was supposed to be in them. As a result of the confusion over the contents, Ms. Wood allowed an extra several days for students to turn in the notebooks, and she told students to listen more carefully the next time she explained a course requirement.

During presentations to classes, Ms. Wood holds students' attention well because she presents new concepts and procedures clearly. She always explains each type of problem that students are likely to encounter, and she demonstrates solutions and a rationale, using several examples. Ms. Wood generally works at her desk while students do seatwork, although she allows them to come up to her desk for assistance when they encounter difficulty or when they need to determine what work they have missed while they were absent. As the year has progressed, Ms. Wood has observed more and more students doing poorly on their exams, presenting incomplete or sloppy notebooks, and receiving low grades.

 ## Checklist 3

Accountability Procedures

Check When Complete	Area	Notes
	Grading System	
☐	A. Does your school have a policy in this area?	_____
☐	B. What components will your grading system have?	_____
☐	C. Weight or percentage for each component?	_____
☐	D. How will you organize your grade book?	_____
	Feedback and Monitoring	
☐	A. What checking procedures will you use?	_____
☐	B. What records of their work will students keep?	_____

(continued)

Check When Complete	Area	Notes
☐	C. When and how will you monitor classwork?	_____
☐	D. When and how will you monitor projects or longer assignments?	_____
	Communicating Assignments	
☐	A. How will assignments be posted or otherwise communicated?	_____
☐	B. What grading criteria and other requirements will be described?	_____
☐	C. What standards for form and neatness will you have?	_____
☐	1. Pencil, color of pen	_____
☐	2. Type of paper	_____
☐	3. Incomplete work	_____
☐	4. Late work	_____
☐	5. Heading	_____
☐	D. What procedures will you establish for make-up work?	_____
☐	1. Assignment list	_____
☐	2. Handouts	_____
☐	3. Time for completion	_____
☐	4. Where to turn in	_____
☐	5. Help for absentees	_____

4
Getting Off to a Good Start

The first few weeks of school are especially important for classroom management because during this time your students will learn behaviors and procedures needed throughout the year. Your major classroom management goal for the beginning of the year is to obtain student cooperation in two key areas: following your rules and procedures and successfully engaging in all learning activities. Attaining this goal will establish a classroom climate that supports learning, and it will help your students acquire good work habits and attitudes toward your subject.

Getting off to a good start requires careful attention to how you will communicate your expectations to your classes, introduce your course to the students, plan lessons and assignments, and decide on the sequence and amounts of time for various activities. This chapter addresses these topics and considers some special problems encountered during the first week or so of classes. In addition, three case studies of beginning-of-year activities in secondary school classrooms are presented along with a checklist that will help organize your planning for the first weeks of school.

Perspectives on the Beginning of the Year

Several principles described below should guide your planning for the beginning-of-year classroom activities.

1. **Resolve student uncertainties.** When your students arrive on the first day, they will not be sure of your expectations for behavior or of your course requirements. Although previous experiences in other teachers' classrooms will have given them general expectations about what constitutes acceptable or unacceptable behaviors in school, they will not know what *you* expect in your classroom. For example, should they raise their hands if they want to comment or ask a question? May they leave their seats without permission? May they speak to each other during seatwork or at other times? Moreover, the students do not know how consistently you will enforce your procedures and rules or what the consequences will be if they do not follow them. In addition, they will be unfamiliar with your system for grading and other accountability procedures. Because of these uncertainties, you will be in a very good position at the beginning of the year to help students learn appropriate behavior by providing a specific, concrete description of your expectations for behavior, course requirements, and standards for work. If you do not take advantage of this opportunity, however, students may begin to behave in ways that interfere with good instruction and learning. You will then face the more difficult task of eliminating unacceptable behavior and replacing it with more appropriate behavior.

Take the necessary time during the first few days of classes to describe carefully your expectations for behavior and work. Do not be in such a hurry to get started on content activities that you neglect to teach good behavior. Rather, combine learning about procedures, rules, and course requirements with your initial content activities to build the foundation for the whole semester's or year's program.

2. **Help students be successful by planning uncomplicated lessons.** Your content activities and assignments during the first week should be selected and designed to ensure maximum success by students; students should feel secure and optimistic about their ability to do well in your class.

3. **Keep a whole-class focus.** You should plan activities for the first week or so that keep a whole-class focus. This means that your instruction and directions will be made to the entire class at the same time and that students will work on the same tasks or assignments. You might still plan for group work during this time, but the groups should work on the same task or assignment, and you should give initial instructions to all students at once. Unless it is necessary, you should not individualize instruction or assignments during the first week or so, nor should you have groups engage in activities or projects that require you to work extensively with individuals or a group while the rest of the class waits. You might wish to prepare some extra-credit, enrichment assignments, problems, questions, and so on to challenge students who complete seatwork assignments early.

One reason for emphasizing a whole-class focus is that it will keep your classroom procedures simpler and therefore easier to implement with a new group of students. Another reason is that more complex activities are often more difficult to monitor; thus, inappropriate behavior will be more likely to go uncorrected, giving it a chance to take root. After your classes are running smoothly and students have learned correct behavior, you can use more complex activities.

4. **Be available, visible, and in charge.** It's important that students learn to look to you for information about procedures and behaviors. Even if you're careful to state your expectations clearly during the first several days, questions will arise regarding appropriate behavior in domains that weren't explicitly covered. Students will experience uncertainty because guidelines or rules are often general and require a context to be understood. Moreover, students may have learned that teachers don't always follow through, and they will check your limits to see how much "give" is in your system and to establish the boundaries between acceptable and unacceptable behaviors.

Make yourself available during seatwork time or group-work activities rather than retreat to your desk to finish paperwork. Circulate around the room, monitoring student progress and providing assistance when needed. Your physical proximity to students will encourage appropriate behavior and work habits. Try to make eye contact with students as much as possible during whole-class activities. For example, use an overhead projector rather than the chalkboard. Avoid becoming so involved with one or a few students that you lose contact with the rest of the class.

Planning for a Good Beginning

Before you plan classroom activities for the first week, you need to have your room and materials ready and to have identified your rules, procedures, and consequences. If you have used the checklists and suggestions in Chapters 1 through 3, you are ready to consider a few final items.

"Good morning class. My name is Miss Applegate. One false
move and I'll kill you."

© Leo Cullum 1998. Reprinted by permission of Leo Cullum.

Procedures for Obtaining Books and Checking Them Out to Students

Identify the procedures teachers use in your school to obtain books and have on
hand any needed forms to record book numbers and names of students. If there is
no special form, you can record book numbers in your grade book. Be sure to wait
until students have been assigned their lockers before you check out textbooks.
If you are teaching in a school district in which students are expected to cover
district-issued books, have an adequate supply of covers on hand.

Some teachers prefer not to enter student names into their grade book until
sections have been leveled and enrollment stabilizes. If you choose to wait, you
can record book numbers on the class roster sheet instead of the grade book and
transfer them to the grade book later.

Many teachers check out textbooks by the second or third day of classes and
do so during a content activity. A common procedure is to distribute the textbooks
to students at the beginning of the activity, indicating whether the books need to
be covered and providing any other relevant information, such as the cost of the
book if lost. Later, after students have begun the seatwork portion of the lesson,
they can be called to the teacher's desk one or two at a time so that the teacher can
record their book numbers and note any damage to used books. An alternative pro-

cedure is to move from student to student while they cover their books, recording book numbers and noting prior damage if any. Using a name stamp to record the teacher's name on the inside front cover facilitates the process and increases the likelihood that lost books will be returned. If you don't have a name stamp, have the students print your name legibly.

Required Paperwork

Have all forms on hand. If you have a homeroom or advisory class, there may be forms specific to that period. Examples of forms for one or all classes include book cards, office passes and hall permits, parental consent forms for field trips, health and emergency care forms, statements of having read the student handbook, computer use agreement, parking permit requests, locker release forms, and forms for recording collected money. Use file folders and desk drawer compartments to keep these materials separate and organized.

Class Rosters

Be sure you have these organized by period. Note any special students who have disabling conditions that must be taken into account in seating or who require medication. You will probably be told whether you have any such students by a special education teacher or counselor. These professionals are also a useful source of suggestions for working with such students in your classes.

Besides using roster printouts, another way to keep records until classes stabilize is to use a set of three-by-five-inch cards for each class. Have one card for each student and record on it the student's name, book number, and attendance and grades for the first two weeks. This not only makes it easier to move student records from period to period as schedules are finalized, but it also provides a set of name cards for use throughout the year to make sure all students are called on. Some teachers have students write their own names, parents' names, telephone numbers, and other useful information on these cards.

Seating Assignments

Plan to assign seats during the first week of classes. Assigned desks allow you to make a seating chart from which you can learn student names and also check attendance quickly. There is little point in assigning seats on the first day of classes unless you are quite sure that very few changes in your class rosters will occur. By the second or third day, however, class rolls may stabilize enough for permanent seating.

To avoid recopying your seating chart each time a change is made during the first several days of classes, you can use the following procedure. For each class, use small sticky notes to attach student names to a heavy sheet of 8½-by-11-inch paper in an approximation of the seating arrangement. Rearrange the sticky notes whenever you change student seating. You can use colored dots or other notation to identify special students or other needed information. Slip each page into a clear plastic sleeve or folder to prevent the stickies from inadvertently detaching. If you use grading software that prints out seating charts, changes in your class rosters and seating charts can be made easily with a few clicks of the mouse.

Some differences in seating assignment practices are observed between middle schools and senior high schools. It is more common at the middle school level for teachers to assign seats, often alphabetically. (An advantage of alphabetical seating is that assignments can be collected in the same order that you will record them in your grade book, thus saving you some time. Multiplied by five classes, the gain in efficiency is significant.) At the senior high level, some teachers assign seats, whereas other teachers allow students to choose their seats. In the latter case, the chosen seat is the permanent one; that is, students usually are not allowed to move around at will. Also, teachers reserve the right to reassign students to different seats if necessary. Whatever the grade level, you can change seating arrangements later in the year to accommodate work groups, to move students who need close supervision to more accessible seats, or just to provide a change.

First-Week Bell Schedule

Find out how much time is available for each period during the first week. Some class periods may be shortened to accommodate extra long advisory or homeroom periods. If so, find out which periods are affected and how much time will be available for each class.

Tardiness during the First Days of Classes

Most teachers do not attempt to enforce their tardiness policies during the first two days of classes; students are still trying to find classrooms, and the time for passing between periods is not always predictable. By the third class day, however, it is usually reasonable to expect all students to arrive at your classroom on time. Tell them the day before that you will begin to count students tardy unless they are in your room before the bell begins to ring (or whatever your policy is). Then enforce the policy the next day and thereafter.

Administrative Tasks

If you have not already done so as part of Chapter 2 activities, be sure you know what special administrative tasks are required during the first week. If you have a homeroom or advisory class, be sure to keep its forms and materials in separate file folders.

Rules

Discuss your expectations for behavior with your students on the first day you meet with them and as many times thereafter as needed. You can list rules or guidelines on a large chart and post it on a bulletin board or a wall, or you can include them in a course syllabus. You can also distribute copies of rules or display them on the chalkboard or overhead projector screen and have students copy them into their notebooks. If you have not yet decided on classroom rules, you should review the relevant section in Chapter 2.

Course Requirements

You will need to discuss course requirements with your students during the first week. You should outline the major requirements, such as tests, pop quizzes, a notebook, projects, and homework, indicating how they contribute to the students' grades. You do not have to list each requirement in great detail, but you should indicate the major features. It is a good practice to provide students with a copy of your requirements—perhaps on the same sheet as your classroom rules. Some teachers have students take it home for parents to sign.

A Beginning-of-Class Routine

Decide what standard routine you will use to open each period. The routine should enable students to make the transition into your classroom in an orderly manner, ready for instruction. It also will allow you to check attendance and perform other administrative tasks quickly and without interruption. If you have not yet decided on a beginning-of-period routine, you should review the relevant section in Chapter 2. Whatever your opening routine, it is reasonable to expect students to complete it without talking and to remain seated and quiet until you are ready to begin instruction.

Time Fillers

It is a good idea to prepare interesting academic activities for occasions when extra minutes are available and students have nothing to do. This is especially likely to occur during the first week or two of classes, when the bell schedule may be altered unexpectedly. Examples of time fillers include worksheets, puzzles, and logic problems related to your subject. You may find books containing such fillers among the supplementary materials in your department's storeroom, in a bookstore, or in a teachers' supply store. You may also order them from teachers' supply catalogs. Search for filler ideas on websites, such as www.education-world.com and www.712educators.about.com. A section of enrichment or supplemental exercises, questions, or problems might be found in the teacher's edition of your text and can be used either as a seatwork assignment or as a whole-class recitation topic. You might also allow individuals who complete work early to have free reading time while they are waiting for the next activity to begin. You can keep a shelf of books and magazines for such times. We don't recommend that you give students access to computers or special equipment as time fillers during the first week or so. You probably won't have had time to establish procedures for their use this early in the semester; you can add these later, if appropriate, after you've established more basic routines in your room.

⊙⊙ Activities on the First Day of Classes

For class periods of normal or nearly normal length, your first-day activities will generally include administrative tasks, introducing your course to students, communicating your course requirements and expectations for student conduct, and an initial content activity. For shortened class periods, some of the discussion of course requirements can be postponed, and the content activity can be shortened or eliminated. First-day activities are described below in a commonly used sequence. Where significant variations in the activity or sequence may occur, they are noted in the discussion.

Before Class Begins

Before the bell rings, stand near or immediately outside the door. Help students find the correct room, and prevent groups of students from congregating nearby and blocking your doorway. Students will have an easier time finding your room if you post a sign with your name outside the door. Usually, students enter quickly and quietly on the first day; however, should some students enter in an unacceptable manner, you can have them repeat their entrance properly or tell them that they are expected to enter quietly and without commotion in the future.

Greet students pleasantly, smile and make eye contact, but do not start long conversations. Tell students that they may choose their seats for the day, and when most students have arrived, enter the room. When in the room, help students with seating, stay in prominent view, and monitor student behavior. When the bell rings, tell students your name and the course title (this information should also be listed ahead of time on the chalkboard), and ask students to check their schedules to be sure they are in the correct room. Look around the room frequently, making eye contact with all students.

Administrative Tasks

Have all necessary materials close at hand so that you can begin quickly. You will first need to check attendance. When you do, have students raise their hands (rather than call out) when you call their names so that you can begin to associate names with faces. Using this procedure conveys the idea that hand raising is more desirable than call-outs. Pronunciations and preferred names can be noted on the class roster at this time. If students must complete forms or class cards, or if you must take care of other administrative matters at this time, tell students what needs to be done and what behavior is expected of them; for example, "After you fill in the class cards, hold them at your seat until I call for them to be passed in." To facilitate the completion of class cards or other forms, write the needed information on the chalkboard or display it on the overhead projector.

Introductions

Take a position "front and center" in the classroom. Look around while speaking and make eye contact with students. Smile and try to present a friendly, confident, businesslike demeanor. Tell students your name and something about yourself, such as your interests, hobbies, family, or why you enjoy teaching your subject. If many students do not know each other, you can use a brief get-acquainted activity. You can also have students complete a short questionnaire identifying interests, hobbies, or experiences related to your subject. Afterward, give students an introduction to your course, including an overview of topics to be covered. Try to emphasize the course's importance, interest, challenges, and applications. Mention some activities that will be of interest to the students so that they can begin the year looking forward to taking the course.

Discussion of Class Rules

During this activity, you will discuss your expectations for student conduct. Refer to the rules (some teachers prefer to call them *guidelines*) you have posted, displayed on the overhead projector, or made available on a handout. Read each rule and explain it, giving examples when needed. Describe the rationale for each rule and any penalties associated with breaking it. You can involve students in this discussion by asking them for examples or reasons for particular rules. Because students are often reserved in their class behavior on the first day or two of school, don't expect eager participation in this discussion. If you intend to use special incentives, you can introduce them now, or you might save this discussion for later in the week. If your rules do not already incorporate major procedures, you should discuss your expectations in these areas at this time. Students should understand what is acceptable with respect to student talk, how to contact the teacher for help, when movement about the room is permitted, and how to ask questions or volunteer an answer or comment. In addition, your procedures for tardy students and beginning the period should be explained. Do not go over procedures that will not be needed soon; you can discuss them when they are needed. Unless particular school rules are relevant for your classroom, you do not have to include these in your discussion; they probably will be discussed by a building administrator on the public address system or in a general assembly, or teachers may cover them during a homeroom or advisory period. Of course, if such a presentation has not occurred, you should go over the rules briefly during your first-period class for the benefit of students new to the building.

Some senior high teachers, particularly in the upper grades, prefer a less explicit approach to class rules. They do not identify expectations as "rules," nor do they post or otherwise provide copies of rules. They limit their discussions of expectations for conduct to a few major areas, such as tardiness and student talk. This does not mean that such teachers have no expectations in other areas of behavior—they are quick to give feedback when students' behavior is not acceptable. For example, if such a teacher is presenting material to the class and students leave their seats, the teacher will use the incident to tell the class that students should remain in their seats during presentations. The advantage of this approach is that it invites cooperation by recognizing that many older senior high students are well acquainted with prevailing school norms and will behave acceptably with no prompting. The disadvantage of this approach is that it places a considerable burden on the teacher's ability to monitor students' behavior so that initial deviations from expectations can be detected. If they are not detected and corrected, students may believe that the behavior is acceptable; consequently, more inappropriate behavior may occur. Note that the less explicit approach to rules is the practice of only some senior high teachers. Other good managers at this level are more systematic in their presentation of expectations for student conduct. Finally, we note that the less explicit approach should not be used at the middle school level or for ninth graders; these students benefit from the structure provided by an explicit set of rules and expectations for major procedures.

When you present and discuss your rules and procedures with students, you should set a positive tone, emphasizing the benefits to all: "These rules are intended to help us have a class atmosphere that is appropriate for learning. We all know that a classroom will work better when everyone's rights are respected." Or, "An orderly class helps everyone by giving students a good chance to listen and learn and to do their work without being bothered or interfered with." If some procedure or rule will be difficult to follow, you might acknowledge the students' feelings as you discuss it: "I know it isn't easy to remember to raise your hands before speaking during a discussion, but doing so will give everyone a chance to participate". Or, "It will be hard not to start using the new equipment right away, but we need to wait for directions so no one is injured." Such expressions of empathy when presenting rules that may appear arbitrary have been found to help students later exhibit more self-control.

Presentation of Course Requirements

Describe briefly the major course requirements and indicate how these will contribute to the course grade. It is not necessary to go into great detail about grading procedures or other course requirements unless some aspect of them will be used immediately. For example, you do not have to go over test or homework procedures at this time, but you should list on the board or display on the overhead projector screen those materials that students should bring to class each day. If you plan to give students a handout listing rules and major procedures, you can also include on it a list of materials and major course requirements.

When periods have been shortened, or to conserve time for a content activity, you may limit discussion of course requirements to the absolute essentials and wait until later in the week to fill out the picture.

An Initial Content Activity

Choose an activity that students can complete successfully with little or no assistance. This will leave you free to handle other matters and to monitor students. The activity should be an interesting one that will involve your students. Look in the teacher's edition of your textbook for ideas. Some possibilities include a review worksheet based on content from earlier grades, a subject-related puzzle, or a worksheet activity. You could also conduct a short demonstration or present an experiment, essay, story, description of an event, and so on, which you might then use as the basis for a short discussion. This could be followed by questions for which students write answers. Available time is a critical factor, so use an activity that can be continued the next day if the period ends before the activity. It is probably best to collect unfinished classwork at the end of the activity rather than to assign it as homework on the first day. You can then return it to students to be finished on the second day rather than relying on students to return it themselves—they may not yet have lockers, and some students will probably not have notebooks or other containers for papers on the first day.

Use the initial content activity for teaching important procedures. Begin the activity by stating what procedures students should follow. For example, if the activity is a presentation or a discussion, let students know what to do if they want to speak; for a seatwork assignment, inform students how to contact you to get help. Teachers who allow students to work together on seatwork assignments usually wait a week or more before beginning the procedure. Doing so allows the teacher to become better acquainted with students' work habits and to judge how much responsibility students can be given.

When you introduce a procedure for the first time, follow these steps: Explain the procedure by telling students exactly what they are expected to do, use the overhead projector or chalkboard to list the steps in the procedure if it is complex, and demonstrate the procedure whenever possible. Then, the first time students are expected to use the procedure, watch them carefully and give corrective feedback about their performance. For example, you will probably have students use a specific heading on written assignments. To teach this procedure, introduce it when the first assignment is given. Put a sample heading on the board, go over its parts, and then have students head their own papers. You could either check the students' headings at that time or wait until you circulate around the room after the seatwork assignment has been given.

In general, on the first day, avoid using small groups, projects, individualized instruction, or any other format that requires complicated procedures, extensive student movement, or materials that students may not have with them and that you cannot supply. Help your students learn whole-class and seatwork procedures before you try more complex activities.

Ending the Period

You should establish an end-of-period routine that helps your students get ready to leave the room as they found it and in an orderly manner. Make every effort to dismiss the class promptly to enable them to be on time for the next class. Shortly before the dismissal bell (the amount of time depends on how much cleanup needs to be done), signal your students that it is time to clean around their desks and put their materials away. If you consistently give students ample warning, you can prevent their stopping work too early.

Some teachers prefer to dismiss the students themselves, so they tell students, "Please do not leave your seats when the bell rings, because I may have an announcement to make, or I may need to give you materials before you leave the class. I will tell you when you can leave the room." Such a procedure allows the teacher to wrap up any unfinished business at the end of the period as well as to hold students until they have cleaned up the room properly. Some students may challenge this procedure by getting out of their seats as soon as the bell rings, so be prepared to call them back and have them wait.

⊙⊚ The Second Day of Classes

If your first day's class periods are very short, you may not be able to do much more than introduce yourself and your course and present rules and procedures. If so, you should begin the second day with a review of major class procedures and follow the first day's plan, beginning with a discussion of course requirements.

If your first day's class periods are of normal or nearly normal length, the following outline of activities may be followed on the second class day:

1. **Identify new students and get them seated.** Have them fill out class cards or any other forms from the first day. If these forms are time-consuming to complete or require extensive directions, you can wait until the rest of the students are engaged in a seatwork activity before having the new students complete them.
2. **Restate the beginning-of-class routine, and use it to start the period.** Perform your administrative chores, such as attendance check, at this time.
3. **Review your major rules and procedures.** Provide new students with a copy of the rules and procedures.
4. **If you did not discuss course requirements on the first day, do so now.** If students will keep a notebook or folder for your class, this is a good time to go over its organization and contents.

5. **Present a content activity.** Many teachers distribute textbooks, conduct a lesson, and then give a seatwork assignment from the text. If for some reason students cannot be assigned textbooks at this time, you can still distribute the textbooks and collect them at the end of the period. Alternatives are to provide lesson materials, such as worksheets, or to give students a pretest or some assessment of readiness for the first unit of the course. Readiness assessment is an especially good idea if you have not previously taught the subject, the grade level, or students with backgrounds similar to those of students in your classes.

6. **Close the period.** Use the procedure you introduced the first day.

After the Second Day

Continue using the procedures you introduced on the first two days, adding new procedures as needed. Monitor student behavior carefully. Review your procedures and give students feedback when their behavior does not meet your expectations. By the third or fourth class day, you should be giving regular assignments to be done in class and at home. Check work promptly and begin using your grading procedures at once so that students receive feedback about their work and are held accountable for it.

Further Reading

Emmer, E. T., Evertson, C. M., & Anderson, L. M. (1980). Effective management at the beginning of the school year. *The Elementary School Journal, 80,* 219–231.

Evertson, C. M., & Emmer, E. T. (1982). Effective management at the beginning of the school year in junior high classes. *Journal of Educational Psychology, 74,* 485–498.

The two articles cited above report the results of large-scale studies in which teachers were observed at the beginning of the school year and then subsequently throughout the rest of the year. The purpose of the studies was to identify the major teacher behaviors and strategies that contributed to successful classroom management. The large numbers of teachers and the diversity of school and classroom settings in these studies support the validity of their findings.

Freiberg, H. J. (Ed.) (1999). *Beyond behaviorism: Changing the classroom management paradigm.* Boston: Allyn and Bacon.

Chapters in this book describe several approaches to classroom management that have resulted in widely adopted programs. Also discussed are fundamental issues such as how much control is needed, how to involve students in decisions about discipline, and determining suitable goals for management and discipline.

Good, T., & Brophy, J. (2003). *Looking in classrooms* (8th ed.). Boston: Allyn and Bacon.

Research based and informative, this book offers many insights and ideas about classroom teaching. Several chapters provided a good foundation for beginning the school year by planning important classroom routines, activities, and instruction.

Mackenzie, R. J. (1997). Setting limits in the classroom. *American Educator, 21*(3), 32–43.

Reducing uncooperative attention-seeking, oppositional, and disruptive behavior requires that teachers use effective limit-setting strategies. Doing so helps students learn about the consequences of their actions.

Moskowitz, G., & Hayman, J. L. (1976). Success strategies of inner-city teachers: A year-long study. *The Journal of Educational Research, 69,* 283–288.

The authors observed junior high school teachers at the beginning and throughout the school year. Many differences were noted between teachers identified as "best" teachers and those who were in their first year of teaching. The article does a good job of identifying beginning-of-year behaviors that enhance or limit management effectiveness.

 ## Suggested Activities

1. Use Checklist 4 at the end of the chapter to be sure you have planned all aspects of the beginning of the year.

2. Read Case Studies 4.1, 4.2, and 4.3. They describe teachers beginning the year in quite diverse settings. These cases can be used for individual analysis or group discussion. Consider the following questions:

   a. To what extent are the principles described in this chapter in evidence in each case?

   b. Can you identify critical beginning-of-year planning and preparation activities for each case?

   c. What differences are apparent among the teachers in their beginning-of-year activities or approaches? Which one(s) would you be most likely to use? Why?

   d. In Case 4.3, a teacher uses a form of mastery learning; in Case 4.1, the teacher makes extensive use of groups for cooperative learning. How do these approaches affect the way each teacher begins the year?

3. Read Case Study 4.4, which depicts a teacher facing escalating disorderly behavior. What teacher actions or omissions contributed to the problem? Suggest some strategies for improving the situation.

4. What do you think your students' goals and concerns are or will be at the beginning of the year? How can a classroom management plan accommodate them?

5. The website http://712educators.about.com contains many useful items for secondary teachers. Open the site and browse around. To find materials that pertain to starting the year in secondary schools, enter "Beginning the school year" in the Search box.

CASE STUDY 4.1

**BEGINNING THE YEAR IN A FIRST-YEAR ALGEBRA CLASS
USING COOPERATIVE LEARNING GROUPS**

First-Day Activities

Activity	Description
Before the bell	Desks are clustered in seven groups of four or five each. The teacher collects a folder for each group of desks from the previous class, replacing it with another folder of a different color, marked with the period and group number. As students enter, Mrs. James tells them they may sit wherever they choose today but that seats will be assigned later in the week.
Initial greeting (4 minutes)	The teacher smiles and states her name. She introduces herself, telling students about her family and some out-of-school interests. She tells students that she is a hard worker and she also expects them to work hard. She says that she will be in her room an hour before classes begin and will stay in her room until 4:30 each day so that students can come in for help if they need more explanation or assistance. "The most important thing in this class is trying. We will all make mistakes and get stuck, but by working together, we will be able to solve the problems and learn a lot of new things."
Introduction (10 minutes)	Mrs. James notes that students have all had an introduction to algebra in the seventh and eighth grades but that she is curious about whether they know how important and useful it is. She leads a discussion in which she elicits their ideas about how algebra and other math might be useful. She asks students to raise their hands and wait to be called on before speaking during this activity. During the discussion, she also comments on the origins of the subject, the Arabic basis of its name, and some of its applications in science, business, and everyday math. She calls attention to a bulletin board that has several colorful posters highlighting math applications.
	During the discussion, Mrs. James thanks students on several occasions for raising their hands and for listening well. When a couple of students call out, she reminds them to raise hands before she calls on them.
	Mrs. James comments on the grouping of desks. She explains that in her classes students work in groups much of the time and that this activity can be very helpful in learning. She says that they won't always work in groups; students will keep an individual notebook and take tests by themselves. For many assignments, however, they will be expected to work together and to assist each other in understanding the content and solving problems. She comments that students often find this not only a good way to learn but also an enjoyable way. A student asks if she can choose her group. Mrs. James responds that she must reserve the right to arrange the groups. Because group membership will change at different times, however, students will have an opportunity to work with a variety of other students. Mrs. James also emphasizes that because this high school draws from many feeder middle schools many

(continued)

First-Day Activities *(Continued)*

Activity	Description
	students do not know each other, so working in groups with others is a good way to get to know other students.
Initial presentation of procedures (6 minutes)	Mrs. James thanks the students for raising hands before speaking. She says that she has a few other procedures for the class to run smoothly and that she will go over some of these now, saving the others for later, when they start group work. She tells her students that during class, when she is talking or when a student is presenting something to the whole class, they are to remain in their seats. If they wish to comment or ask a question, they should raise a hand and wait their turn. At other times, when they are working in groups or on individual assignments, they may talk if it is to someone in their group and it is about the work. If they need to sharpen a pencil or get some materials during work times, they may do so without permission, as long as they do not disturb other students.
Administrative activity and an initial group task (8 minutes)	The teacher tells students that she would like them to fill out a class card and make a name card to be used in class to help her and other students learn their names. She then designates students in each group as Chair 1, Chair 2, Chair 3, and Chair 4. She tells them that when they work in groups, different chairs will have different roles and that these will be rotated so that each student gets a chance to do different things. Then she says, "Chair 1, please open the group folder on the desk and look in the right-hand pocket. Take out a yellow card and a class card for each student."
	She has Chair 1 distribute these items in each group. Mrs. James then has students make name cards for their desks and fill out class cards. While students work on this task, she returns to her desk for a couple of minutes to attend to some administrative matters. She then asks Chair 1 to collect the cards.
Description of procedures folder (10 minutes)	Mrs. James asks Chair 2 to look in the left-hand pocket of the folder, take out the blue sheets listing classroom policies and procedures, and give one to each group member. She tells students that everyone will need a three-ring binder for this class and that this page should be the first one in it. She then reviews the classroom and school policies regarding absence and tardiness, leaving the room, make-up work, tests, and detention for violating rules. She explains that if she gives a warning to a student and it's ignored, she will assign a lunch detention and the student must bring lunch to the room at noon and eat it there. She says, "If I have to come find you, you will serve two lunch detentions."
End of period	Mrs. James notes that time is almost up. She says that she'll explain her grading policies and class activities the next day. Then she says, "Chair 3, if there is a new student in class assigned to your group tomorrow, would you please be responsible for helping them get a copy of the class policies, name card, and class card?"
	As the end-of-period bell rings, she asks the students to return their cards to the folder and to remain in their seats until she dismisses each group, which she does when materials have been returned to the folder and each group is seated and quiet.

Second-Day Activities

Activity	Description
Before the bell	Mrs. James collects folders from each group from the preceding period, replacing them with the next period's folders. She greets students as they enter, asking them to take seats with yesterday's group. She directs a few new students to join groups.
Beginning the period (3 minutes)	The teacher greets the students warmly as soon as the bell rings. She reminds students that they are in groups and that they have a designated number, which will be the same as yesterday's. She reminds those designated Chair 3 of their responsibility to help new members of the group.
Diagnostic test (15 minutes)	Mrs. James says, "Before we get started on today's lesson, I'd like you to answer some questions. This assignment is not group work, but must be done by you individually. This will not be for a grade, but I would like you to do your best. Your answers will help me understand what topics need review and also help me make group assignments. If you complete the work early, you should check it over, and then you may sit quietly and read."
	Mrs. James distributes the diagnostic test and tells students to show their work. She monitors as students do the work. When the time is up, she asks those designated Chair 4 to collect the papers in each group and bring them to her.
Description of procedures and grading policies (8 minutes)	The teacher reviews talk and movement procedures in groups. "Use procedures and group voices, please. Talk loudly enough to be heard by others in your group, but not so loudly that groups near you will hear. Like this." (She demonstrates.)
	She gives students a one-page handout describing grading policies. She explains these in detail and asks students to place this handout in their notebooks.
Preparation for group activity (4 minutes)	Mrs. James announces a first activity. She tells students that this activity will help them learn about working in groups and teach them some math concepts. She asks students to volunteer some ideas about what it takes to be a good group member. Stressing positive examples, Mrs. James supports especially the ideas of sharing, helping, listening, encouraging, and working hard.
Math lesson (20 minutes)	The teacher shows students a balance scale and relates it to the idea of an equation. She points out that if something is added to or subtracted from one side of the balance, it must also be added to or subtracted from the other side to preserve the balance. She asks for volunteers to come up and demonstrate how to put the equation in balance if an operation is performed on one side. Then she demonstrates how to add and subtract quantities to determine the value or weight of an unknown item.
	She gives the class similar problems to work in groups, stating that there are several ways to solve the problem and that they should use the materials in their group folder. She asks Chair 4 to open the folder and distribute the materials. She says she will ask someone in each group to report on the group's solution to one of the problems. After the groups have worked for a little while,

(continued)

Second-Day Activities *(Continued)*

Activity	Description
	Ms. James calls on one person from each group to report on a problem; she prompts students as needed while they demonstrate the process of arriving at a solution using the scale.
End of period (5 minutes)	Mrs. James asks students to comment on their roles in their groups. She also asks for suggestions about what works best for various roles. She praises the students for their creativity in developing solutions to the problems and for their efforts. About a minute before the end-of-period bell, she tells students they may put away their materials and get ready to leave. She asks those designated Chair 1 to return the materials to their group's folder. When the bell rings, Mrs. James dismisses the class by groups after materials are put away and the group's desks are properly arranged.

Third-Day Activities

Activity	Description
Before the bell	Mrs. James tells students to check the name list at each group of desks to find their group.
Group activity (5 minutes)	Mrs. James tells the students that they will stay in their groups for several weeks. She assigns chair numbers to the group members and asks students designated Chair 1 to open the folder and distribute a blank card so that each student can make a name tag. Then she has students play a quick name game for introductions within each group.
Textbook check-out (12 minutes)	Mrs. James has one student from each group distribute texts from several piles at the back of the room. While students cover their books, the teacher records book numbers.
Content activity and a new teaching strategy (15 minutes)	The teacher reviews concepts from yesterday's lesson with the balance scale. She has Chair 2 distribute materials from a box in each group. Students use the materials to work along with the teacher as she demonstrates various ways to solve several problems. Then she tells students that they will work in pairs in the next activity, and she writes "Think-Pair-Share" on the chalkboard. Students will first think about how to solve a problem, then work in pairs on it, and then take turns explaining the solution or demonstrating the steps to each other. "It's not enough just to work out a solution. Each of you must be able to explain to your partner how you did it." Afterward, Mrs. James has volunteers come forward to demonstrate and explain their solutions using the scale.
Group work (17 minutes)	Students are now given problems to solve as a group. These problems are somewhat more difficult, involving several steps. Mrs. James asks each group to work together to solve the problems. She asks Chairs 3 to be recorders of the solutions and Chairs 4 to be moderators. Based on yesterday's discussion, the teacher reviews briefly what these roles entail.

Activity	Description
	As the groups work on the problem, the teacher moves from group to group, checking on progress. She has several groups report back to the class. Afterward, students are given an assignment, due the next day, which they work on for the remainder of the class. They may work together on problems but are expected to show their own work on the assignment.
End of period (5 minutes)	With about five minutes remaining in the period, the teacher asks students to put away their work. She says that unfinished problems should be completed as homework. Then she initiates a short discussion about helping by asking students what it feels like not to understand something. She also asks about ways they might react when they're in that situation. "Everyone will experience those feelings and do some of those things, especially if they're made to feel dumb. In this class, though, we will learn from our mistakes, and no one should be embarrassed by not understanding something. Also, helping other students is a great way to gain in understanding. I certainly understand math much better now that I have taught it than I did when I was a student."
	Mrs. James explains that everyone will have opportunities to explain problems and answer questions in her class. If there is something they don't understand, they should ask for another explanation. She and the class then discuss how to explain in ways that are most helpful. The class is dismissed at the bell.

CASE STUDY 4.2

BEGINNING THE YEAR IN A HIGH SCHOOL BIOLOGY CLASS

First-Day Activities

Activity	Description
Before the bell	As students enter the room before the bell rings, Ms. Holly greets students at the front of the room near the doorway and tells them to take a seat near the front of the room.
Introduction (1 minute)	When the bell rings, the teacher moves to the front of the room and introduces herself. She tells students how to check their schedules to make sure they're in the right room. She gives her name and its spelling, announces the room number and course number, and tells students the abbreviations to look for on their schedule cards. Then she pleasantly welcomes them to her class.
Roll call (3 minutes)	Before the teacher begins to call roll, she explains to students the procedures she wants them to use. She expects them to raise their hands when she calls their names and also to tell her the name they would like to be called. After roll call, she records the names of two students not on her roll after checking their class schedule cards.

(continued)

First-Day Activities *(Continued)*

Activity	Description
Course overview (6 minutes)	Ms. Holly begins by giving an introduction to the course. She displays an overhead transparency that lists seven major topics to be covered during the semester. She describes each of the items on the list and mentions several of the activities and goals relating to each topic. Students listen quietly and ask a few questions when the teacher invites them to.
Presentation of classroom behavior policies and rules (12 minutes)	The teacher distributes copies of procedures and requirements for the class. She tells the students to put their name, the date, and the period at the top, and to keep these sheets at the front of their class folders at all times. The information sheet contains three sections. The first outlines eight areas of classroom procedures and rules. The second describes the notebook that is a major requirement for the course, and the third describes the grading system that will be used in the course. The teacher discusses each of the items in the procedures section in turn, and the students listen and follow on their sheets.
	Next the teacher covers policies for being on time to class and consequences for tardiness, the importance of daily attendance, procedures for making up work after absences, turning in classwork on time and consequences for late work, keeping all papers in the science notebook and replacing lost papers, safety rules for laboratory activities, and routines for ending the class period and dismissal. The teacher displays the school handbook for students and tells them that they will go over the handbook in greater detail in class later during the week.
Discussion of grading and notebook requirements (10 minutes)	Ms. Holly then describes in some detail the system that she will use for determining grades in the class. One of the major requirements will be a notebook for all student work. She explains the requirements for this notebook: the type of folder, the importance of keeping papers in the proper order, the heading for papers, the table of contents, and the requirement that all papers in the notebook be completed and/or corrected before the notebook is turned in. After answering student questions about the notebook, the teacher describes the grading system. (Tests in the class count 40 percent of the grade. Daily work is also 40 percent, and the notebook is 20 percent. There will be two or three unit exams during each six-week period.) The teacher also mentions extra-credit projects, which can be done later in the grading period.
Filling out information cards, checking out books, and covering books (12 minutes)	After this presentation of procedures and requirements for the course, Ms. Holly asks students to fill out information cards. She shows a model card on an overhead transparency and goes over the items with students. Then she explains to them the procedure they will use for checking out books and covering them. Because students have been assigned their lockers, the teacher passes out textbooks, directing students to check through them for damage and write their names inside the front cover. The teacher has the name of the text and the information that students are supposed to write in their book displayed on the overhead transparency, along with instructions for recording the number neatly on the class card, covering the book, and information about the cost of the book. The teacher passes out book covers, and students cover their books after completing their information cards.

Activity	Description
Discussions of textbook reading assignment (8 minutes)	Ms. Holly then asks students to look at a page in their text, and she introduces them to its format. She leads a discussion on how students can find the chapter objectives and use chapter titles and subtitles, along with the glossary and index, to guide them in their reading. The teacher briefly discusses their reading assignment (written on the chalkboard).
Seatwork (5 minutes)	Ms. Holly distributes assignment sheets and gives directions for answering questions on the sheets as part of the homework assignment. This assignment is a simple introduction to using various parts of the textbook to locate information. Students begin work on their reading or homework assignment while the teacher confers with one student about registration. When the bell rings signaling the end of class, the teacher reminds students of what to bring tomorrow and dismisses them.

Second-Day Activities

Activity	Description
Seatwork, roll call, and other administrative matters (6 minutes)	As soon as the tardy bell rings, Ms. Holly distributes a sheet for students to work on. This task is an extension of the students' classwork assignment from the previous day, an easy assignment in which students used the table of contents and book index to locate specific information. While students work on the assignment, the teacher calls roll and takes care of two new students.
Discussion of homework and seatwork assignments (12 minutes)	The teacher calls for the students' attention and begins asking questions from the previously assigned worksheets. Students volunteer answers, and the teacher leads a discussion. Students check their own papers during this discussion.
Presentation and discussion of textbook chapter (30 minutes)	Ms. Holly distributes an outline of the chapter that students were to have read for homework. The outline gives the main points and allows students room to fill in additional information from the presentation. The teacher also has a copy of the outline displayed on the overhead transparency. Students take notes as the teacher discusses the content.
End of period (2 minutes)	The teacher ends discussion of the first chapter and explains requirements for a short homework assignment. She then reminds students that each day they are to get ready to leave class by checking their work area for neatness and making sure they have all their belongings and materials ready. She shows them where the homework assignment will be written each day on the front chalkboard, along with the list of what they will need to bring to class the next day. Students are told to be sure to check this every day. The teacher answers several questions from students and leads an informal discussion until the bell rings. She then dismisses the class.

CASE STUDY 4.3

BEGINNING THE YEAR IN A HIGH SCHOOL ENGLISH CLASS
USING MASTERY LEARNING

First-Day Activities

Activity	Description
Before the bell	Student desks are arranged in rows. The teacher's desk is at one side of the front of the room, next to a lectern where the teacher stands. Ms. Lee makes eye contact with students and greets them as they enter, telling them that they may sit where they wish today. On the chalkboard in column format is written: First day of school: Bingo; Course Description; Begin Essay. The teacher's name and the name of the class are also written on the chalkboard.
Beginning the period (3 minutes)	The teacher welcomes students and asks them to check their schedules to be sure they are in the right room. She takes attendance by calling roll.
Introduction and get-acquainted activity (15 minutes)	Ms. Lee introduces herself, stating some of her outside interests, her reasons for teaching, and what aspects she especially enjoys. She introduces an activity called "Get-Acquainted Bingo," which requires students to fill a card with the names of classmates who match the descriptions in each of sixteen squares (e.g., has lived in another state; speaks another language; plays a musical instrument; has a hobby). Ms. Lee says that they'll need to go around the room to check with other students and that the same name may not appear in more than one square on each card.
	Because students will have to leave their seats and talk to other students to fill out the card, she asks what problems might occur during this activity. A student comments, "Everybody bumping into each other." The teacher agrees and asks what can be done to avoid the problem. Several students offer possible solutions, which the teacher accepts. She asks what other problems might occur. Another student comments that they might get too loud. The teacher thanks the student for his contribution and says that noise would be a problem if it were to disturb other classes or make it hard to hear. Ms. Lee asks whether anyone remembers other teachers' asking students to use "classroom voices" or "twelve-inch voices." She asks what that means and gets a couple of reasonable answers.
	Ms. Lee tells students to begin. While monitoring the activity, she talks briefly with several students who have entered late. After about eight minutes, most students have filled out their cards; Ms. Lee turns off the lights for a second and waits briefly until she has the students' attention. She then conducts a discussion based on information about students obtained in the preceding activity.
Initial course description, including an intro to mastery learning (10 minutes)	Ms. Lee displays a list of course topics on the overhead projector. This list is divided into three parts: literature, grammar, and writing, with three or four subtopics under each (e.g., writing: persuasive writing, research skills, creative writing). The teacher briefly describes the goal of each or states something about its importance or an interesting aspect of the topic. The teacher also says that because there are so many topics in the course, it will be important

Activity	Description
	to keep an organized notebook. She asks students to bring a three-ring binder with three dividers by Wednesday's class. She says that if anyone needs help in getting one, he or she should talk to her before or after class.

The teacher then mentions grading, stating that she uses an unusual procedure but that she thinks most students will be comfortable with it. She says that she bases her grading system on mastery learning. With this system, if students don't learn something the first time or if they do poorly on a test or assignment, they have another opportunity to master the concept or improve. She asks whether any of the students have experienced this system, and a few hands go up. The teacher says that they will talk about it more tomorrow and that she will give more information so that they understand what she expects. She tells her students, "The basic idea is straightforward. No one consistently learns new material the first time, so you will have the opportunity to succeed even if you run into problems initially. Often, I haven't understood something very well the first time I tried to learn it, but I improved a lot when I went back to it and tried again. Mastery learning gives you the opportunity to learn from your mistakes. If you do well the first time through, that's great, but if you don't, this system gives you a good chance to succeed." |
| Initial content activity and presentation of some behavior policies (20 minutes) | Ms. Lee introduces the activity by saying how much she appreciated their participation in the bingo activity and their staying on-task and not talking loudly. She says that she will have a variety of activities in which they will work in pairs or small groups—for example, checking each other's work, small-group discussions, and reviewing rough drafts. In those activities, student talk will be appropriate and desirable, and she is sure that they will handle this responsibly. At other times, however, they will be in more structured activities, such as class discussions and teacher presentations, in which to be fair to everyone, students will have to raise their hands and wait their turn to speak. "I'd like to have a lot of participation, but it's important to give everyone an opportunity to participate in the activity."

Ms. Lee then initiates a discussion of the first school day. She relates an experience she had when she was in high school, and she invites other students to share their own experiences. After a while, Ms. Lee asks for common themes or experiences, and a discussion ensues. Then she provides some directions for the first assignment, which is to write about the first day of school. Students may describe a particular incident, how the first day affects them generally, or the experience they are having this year.

Ms. Lee also uses this occasion to show students the form for heading their papers, the format of the papers, and related procedural matters. She says that they do not need to finish the assignment today, but she will pick up the papers and return them tomorrow for completion. She asks students not to talk during this activity because it might disturb others who are trying to concentrate on writing. She says that if they have questions, they should raise their hands and wait until she comes to them. |
| End of period (3 minutes) | With about three minutes remaining in the period, Ms. Lee collects the students' papers, stating that she'll return them the next day after she has looked them over. She says that she won't grade them at this time. During the last minute, she asks students to clean up around their desks, get their materials, and prepare to leave. She dismisses class when the bell rings. |

Second-Day Activities

Activity	Description
Before the bell	The teacher stands by the door and greets students as they enter. On the chalkboard is written in column format: Today's Activities: Spelling List; Class Procedures and Evaluation; Editing Practice; Finish First-Day Assignment. On another section of the chalkboard is written: On Wednesday: Bring Notebooks; Tardy Rule Begins.
Beginning the period (3 minutes)	Ms. Lee opens the period by calling roll. Four new students are in the class. Ms. Lee tells them that some information they missed yesterday will be covered on a handout she'll distribute later, but if they have questions, to be sure to ask. When two students enter late, they are reminded of the school's tardy rule and consequence. Ms. Lee tells students she will begin enforcing the rule the next day.
Spelling and the mastery criterion (10 minutes)	Ms. Lee tells students that spelling is a part of this class, and because the district has a curriculum for each grade level, the class will be spending some time each week working on the spelling of a set of words. She distributes a handout containing this week's words. She then leads the class in a short discussion of each word's meaning, and she points out potential problems in the spelling of each. Ms. Lee tells students that they will have a spelling test each Friday and that they must earn a score of at least eight of ten words on the test to achieve "mastery level." If they do not reach mastery, they will have the opportunity to study some more and take the test the following Friday, immediately after the teacher gives that week's test on the new words. If their score is below 80 the second time they take the test, they will receive a reduced number of points depending on the assignment.
Class procedures (10 minutes)	The teacher says that she wants to go over some important procedures. She distributes a page of policies to the students and says that they should place them in their notebooks. She asks students whether they have brought a notebook to class (about two-thirds have done so). She reminds the other students that they should have a notebook the next day because they will organize it in class.
	Ms. Lee tells students that now she will review her grading procedures. She distributes a one-page handout that summarizes the system and discusses it with the students. Each assignment during the grading period is worth a fixed number of points. Students who receive a grade of 80 or higher on the assignment will receive all the points. Some assignments, however, will require a grade of 90 to indicate mastery. If the grade on the assignment is below 80 (or 90), the student will be given an opportunity to improve his or her performance and receive the full number of points.
	The total of possible points for the grading period is 1,000, so the report card grade will be determined by dividing the total points earned by 10. If some students do not reach mastery on an assignment, they will receive a reduced number of points depending on their performance. Each grading period, students will be given an assignment sheet on which to record their grades and points. This will help them keep track of their work and also be available to show their parents if a question arises about their work. Ms. Lee shows students some stacked plastic trays marked with the period number, where they can turn in redone work and pick it up after it has been graded.

Activity	Description
	Ms. Lee then points out a table near the door and says that she will place copies of handouts on this table in case students are absent. She has an assignment calendar above the table. Students are asked to check the calendar for the numbers of handouts distributed on days they have been absent and then to pick up any handouts they need. Ms. Lee also explains absence procedures and out-of-room policies. She answers several questions.
Editing (10 minutes)	Ms. Lee tells students that one of the goals for the class is that they become skilled writers and that an important part of writing is correct usage and punctuation. She says that several times each week she will give them written matter that shows common errors. They will have an opportunity to rewrite it. Ms. Lee explains how she wants the corrections made, and she displays several sentences on the overhead projector. She works through two examples with the class and has them complete a third.
Completion of first-day essay (19 minutes)	Ms. Lee returns yesterday's first-day essays, commenting on how much she enjoyed reading their descriptions. She says that creative writing is an important part of the class and mentions a couple of titles that were especially creative. She says that many students had the same experiences, such as stuck lockers and scheduling problems, and also some common feelings about the first day, such as anxiety, confusion, and anticipation. She notes that new experiences are often accompanied by a variety of emotions and that they might use some emotion words in their descriptions to communicate their experiences.
	Ms. Lee distributes a list of adjectives describing feelings and asks students to circle those that describe feelings or emotions they have experienced on the first day of school. She gives some examples. Then, "just for fun," she has students select an adjective that does not describe their feelings about the first day of school and pass it on to other students in their row. For example, "anxious Al" passes his name to "disgruntled Darryl"; Darryl passes both names to "happy Hal" and so on down the row. Then the student at the end of the row begins the process and passes his or her opposite adjective up the row. Ms. Lee asks students to use "classroom voices" during the activity.
	The activity takes a couple of minutes, after which the teacher asks for a volunteer to repeat the adjective-name pairs for a row. She suggests that the adjectives on the list might be useful to the students as they finish their first-day descriptions, as a way to add clarity and interest to their writing. Ms. Lee then tells students that they have the remainder of the period to finish their first-day descriptions.
End of period (3 minutes)	About three minutes before the end of the period, Ms. Lee tells students that they have two minutes to finish. At the end of that time, she collects the assignment. She gets everyone's attention by standing at the front and saying, "Eyes to the front, please," while using eye contact to monitor students. When she has their attention, Ms. Lee reminds students to bring notebooks the next day because they will organize them in class. She also reminds students that tardy procedures will begin schoolwide the next day. This means that late students will be admitted only with a pass, and all other students must report to the office and later serve a lunch or after-school detention. Ms. Lee says that she'll issue literature books the next day and grammar books the day after that. When the bell rings, she dismisses the class.

Third-Day Activities

Activity	Description
Before the bell	Seating chart in hand, Ms. Lee rearranges the seating assignments of a half-dozen or so students as they enter the room. These arrangements are based on her observations during the first two periods, and students who appeared to distract each other are separated. When a student asks why, the teacher responds, "To be certain that everybody has a good opportunity to learn." Two students with schedule changes arrive; the teacher welcomes them to the class and points to the handouts from the first two days on the table. She asks them to read these and ask her if they have any questions. Ms. Lee asks two students to be "buddies" for the newcomers, and she tells the new students that they may also ask questions of their buddies. On the chalkboard is written in column form: Plan for the Day: Return First-Day Papers; Notebooks; Language Skills; Literature; Check-Out Books. In another area is written: Tardy Procedure Begins Today!
Beginning the period (3 minutes)	The teacher congratulates students on arriving promptly. When two students arrive after the bell, however, she sends them to the office per the school's procedure. She takes attendance using a seating chart. "We have a busy period ahead of us," she says, and she quickly summarizes the plan for the day.
Returning an assignment and more on the mastery system (6 minutes)	Ms. Lee returns the first-day writing assignment and also gives students a grade summary sheet listing the assignments and other student products for the grading period. She tells students to record the score and that if their first-day assignment received an 80 or higher, they should note "M" (for mastery) in the appropriate place and also give themselves the full number of points (50). If their score on the assignment is lower than 80, they have one week to redo it for a higher grade and receive the full number of points. A student asks what they get if they don't redo the assignment. The teacher says that if they didn't do it at all, or if their score is below 50, they don't get any points. If their score is between 50 and 79, they get half the points. She says, "If you don't quite reach 80 the first time, it's obviously to your advantage to rework the assignment because just a little effort will pay a big return in points. If you don't make any effort, you really do pay a price." Ms. Lee emphasizes that she grades the redone written assignments on improvement, so students should pay careful attention to any written comments. She also stresses that students may come to her room before or after school to receive assistance. "If you're working on a redo of an assignment, and you're not sure you're on the right track, bring it in and I'll take a look at it."
Organizing notebooks (8 minutes)	Ms. Lee asks students to get out their notebooks. Four or five students do not have one. The teacher thanks those who do and takes names of those who don't. She says that she expects them to have notebooks the next day. Anyone needing help getting one should check with her after class, and she will help them make arrangements. Ms. Lee then gives directions for notebook organization. During this time, the teacher circulates among the students, monitoring and assisting them as they arrange the handouts and assignments into the appropriate sections.

Activity	Description
Checking out textbooks (13 minutes)	Ms. Lee has the first student in each row get literature books and book covers from a pile at the front of the room and distribute them to students in his or her row. The teacher explains her procedure: Students should print their names in a space at the front of the book, next to where the teacher has already stamped her name. Then they are to inspect the book for damage. She will come around to verify and record their book numbers; if they have damage to report, she will record it so that they will not be charged when they return the book. While they are waiting, they should cover their books. She also provides some wide felt-tipped markers and suggests that students write "Literature" on the front and side of the book cover so that they bring the correct book to class. When they finish covering the book, they should begin reading a literature selection beginning on the page number she has written on the chalkboard. Ms. Lee tells students that in her classes she schedules literature activities on Tuesday, Wednesday, and Thursday of each week, so students will need to bring that book on those days. On Mondays and Fridays, they will need only their grammar books, which she will check out to them this Friday.
Introductory literature activity (12 minutes)	The teacher says that their first literature activity will be to read and discuss the descriptive essay, "My Mother, Rachel West," which students had begun to read earlier. She points out some words that may be unfamiliar and lists them on the overhead screen, asking students what the words mean, how they are used in the essay, and with what effect. After a few minutes Ms. Lee shifts the discussion to consider the importance of vocabulary, asking students to think of other words that might substitute for some of the identified words and what might be gained or lost. She has students copy eight words and definitions from the reading on a sheet to be placed in their notebooks. She provides students with some background information on the reading and asks them to finish it before the next session. She asks them to review some questions at the end of the selection and says that they'll discuss these the next day. She also says that students who need to do additional work on their first-day essays may use the time for that purpose.
Reading activity (12 minutes)	For the remainder of the period, students read the assigned selection. The teacher circulates, providing supplementary instruction to a few students who did not achieve mastery-level performance on the first essay assignment.
End of period (1 minute)	About a minute before the bell rings, the teacher tells students to begin putting away their materials. She reminds students about the materials they need for the next day's English class and dismisses them when the bell rings.

CASE STUDY 4.4

CONDUCT PROBLEMS IN A HISTORY CLASS

When the school year began, Mr. Davis told his American History classes that he had just one major rule for conduct—the Golden Rule. "If you'll treat others as you want to be treated, then we'll get along fine," he said. Then he added, "Just be sure to respect each other's rights, and that includes mine, and we'll all have a good year." Mr. Davis also told his students that he expected them to behave maturely because they were in high school and that if one of them got out of line, he would be quite willing to send that student to the school office to be dealt with by the assistant principal.

The classes did, indeed, function without major disruptions for several weeks. Gradually, however, almost imperceptibly, Mr. Davis began having difficulty getting students settled down to start the daily lesson. And once begun, presentations and class discussions seemed to be conducted with an undercurrent of noise as students whispered, joked, and socialized. Mr. Davis found himself interrupting the lessons more and more often to call for quiet or to remind students of what they were supposed to be doing. Problems were occurring in each class period but were worst in the sixth, the last period of the day. By the end of the fourth week of classes, Mr. Davis had sent two students to the office for persistent talking during class, including talking back to him when he asked them to be quiet. Sixth-period behavior was better for a day or so afterward, but students were soon back to being noisy and inattentive. The following description of the sixth-period class a few days later is typical.

At the beginning of the period, Mr. Davis wrote a discussion question on the chalkboard. While he checked roll and returned papers, students were supposed to write a paragraph answering the question in preparation for a class discussion. However, only about half the class actually did the work; other students talked, several sat doing nothing, and two students were out of their seats. Mr. Davis asked one student to sit down, but the student didn't. When he told a particularly noisy girl to "close your mouth," she responded, "I can't." During the discussion, students who were talking at the beginning of class complained that they did not understand the question. A few students raised their hands to volunteer responses during the discussion, and Mr. Davis called on them; other students called out responses, sometimes silly ones. Later, Mr. Davis assigned questions for the end of the chapter to be turned in the next day. Most students worked on this assignment in class, although some read magazines or talked. Three students passed magazines back and forth until Mr. Davis told them to put the magazines away. The noise level built up. Ten minutes before the end of the period, most students had stopped working and were conversing.

What are some things Mr. Davis might do to establish better behavior in his classes?

 ## Checklist 4

Preparation for the Beginning of School

Check When Complete	Item	Notes
☐	1. Are your room and materials preparations complete? (See Chapter 1.)	
☐	2. Have you decided on your class procedures, rules, and their associated consequences? (See Chapters 2, 7, and 9.)	

Check When Complete	Item	Notes
☐	3. Are you familiar with the parts of the building to which you may send students (e.g., library, bathrooms, etc.), and do you know what procedures should be followed?	_____
☐	4. Have you decided what school policies and rules you will need to present to students?	_____
☐	5. Have you prepared a handout for students or a bulletin board display of rules, major class procedures, and course requirements?	_____
☐	6. Do you know what bell schedule will be followed during the first week?	_____
☐	7. Is your lesson plan for the first few days of school ready for each class?	_____
☐	8. Do you have complete class rosters?	_____
☐	9. Do you have adequate numbers of textbooks, desks, and other class materials?	_____
☐	10. Have you decided on the procedures you will use for checking out textbooks to students?	_____
☐	11. Have you prepared time fillers to use if the period is extended?	_____
☐	12. Do you know whether any of your students have some disabling condition that should be accommodated in your room arrangement or instruction?	_____

5

Planning and Conducting Instruction

L et's assume that your classroom is organized, you've developed and taught your rules and procedures, and you have systems in place to manage student work. Now that your students are attentive and ready to participate, what do you do? It is at this point that management and instruction meet. Well-planned lessons with a variety of appropriate activities support the positive learning environment that your carefully considered management decisions have begun to create. Interesting, well-paced lessons are a key to holding students' attention; unimaginative or confusing lessons with limited opportunities for student participation are boring or frustrating to students, creating conditions for discipline problems to develop.

This chapter describes how to plan and conduct instruction in ways that support the kinds of learning you want for your students. Although this chapter is not intended to substitute for the study of specific methods of teaching particular subjects, some of the tasks of planning, organizing, and conducting instruction are basic to all content areas. Consequently, the ideas presented here should be helpful regardless of the secondary subject you teach.

Planning Classroom Activities

The term *activity* describes organized behavior that the teacher and students engage in for a common purpose. Typical activities in secondary classes include discussions, recitations, group work, presentations, seatwork, and checking, although this is by no means a complete list. Furthermore, activities are not always content based. For example, beginning-of-period activities may be mainly procedural.

Activities are an important aspect of instructional planning—they consume time, and time is a precious commodity. Unless your school uses block scheduling, class periods are usually less than an hour, so activities must be limited accordingly. Thus, given certain learning objectives, you will need to identify those activities that will most likely lead to meeting the objectives within the allotted period of time.

You will engage in several levels of planning—both long range (e.g., by the year or semester) and short range (e.g., weekly and daily). Each of these levels of planning should be coordinated. Thus, you can divide the semester plan into units of instruction, and within units, into weekly and daily plans. This type of organization allows you to coordinate the daily activities to produce a cohesive course focusing on the main objectives and goals. Without a master plan, daily activities can appear unrelated to each other and to long-range objectives.

Objectives for daily lessons will help you decide what activities should be used. Two important considerations should be kept in mind: First, what skills or concepts must be learned to reach the objectives, and second, what tasks and activities will help students the most. In other words, your plans provide road maps to transform curriculum and objectives into activities, assignments, and tasks for students.

In addition to their potential for helping students reach learning objectives, activities are selected in part for their potential for maintaining students' involvement throughout the period. For this reason, two or three activities—rather than a single long one—should be planned for most class periods. Activities that provide for student participation or that provide each student with an opportunity to practice or apply lesson content are also desirable; they help students learn the content, and they promote high levels of involvement in the lesson.

Even though much of your daily planning for classes will focus on organizing activities, you should keep in mind the broader perspective—your course as a whole. You need to know what knowledge and skills students are expected to develop and what units, topics, or textbook chapters are typically included in the course. Many of these outcomes are determined by state or local curriculum guidelines or by mandated testing, but you also need to keep in mind that you are teaching for understanding, appreciation, and application.

Examine the teacher's edition of your textbook and preview each major section, noting statements of overall objectives and the scope and sequence of content. Identifying reasonable expectations for your grade level will be helpful when you are deciding on course objectives and adequate coverage of topics. Other useful sources of information about appropriate content and reasonable expectations for students in particular age and grade levels may be found in school district or state education agency curriculum guides, courses and books on instructional methods in your subject, and yearbooks of national teachers' organizations in your academic field. Finally, your department chairperson, your instructional coordinator or supervisor, and other teachers in your subject area can provide helpful suggestions on course scope and topical sequence.

Some subjects, such as English/language arts and home economics, require extra effort when the teacher is developing an overall plan of content organization. Contents of these subjects include several discrete areas and frequently use more than one textbook. For example, middle school and high school English components include writing, usage and grammar, literature, and spelling. To cover diverse areas, it is common practice to use several textbooks. In such cases, the teacher must determine an appropriate sequence for all components and decide how they will be merged into one course. If you teach one of these subjects, it will be particularly important for you to consult one or more of the information sources on curriculum mentioned in the preceding paragraph.

Types of Activities

Some of the most frequently used types of classroom activities are described in the following sections. You can think of them as building blocks for constructing your lessons.

OPENING THE PERIOD

The chief concern in this activity is to help the students make an orderly transition into the classroom and be ready for the rest of the period, while the teacher handles administrative tasks such as the attendance check and helps previously absent students. We have described in Chapters 2 and 4 alternatives for structuring the opening, including the use of either academic warmups or an administrative routine with stated expectations for student behavior.

CHECKING CLASSWORK OR HOMEWORK

In this activity, students check their own work. The activity is appropriate only when a judgment as to the correctness of the work can be made easily. Checking provides quick feedback to students and allows the teacher to identify and discuss common errors on assignments. If performance on the assignment is given a grade, monitoring during checking may be needed to prevent cheating. Some teachers discourage cheating by requiring that checking be done with a different color ink than the assignment, with a pencil if the assignment was completed with ballpoint pen, or vice versa. When student checking is used frequently, you should collect and examine the students' papers, even when you record grades in class. This procedure will enable you to keep abreast of student progress and problems.

Remember that you must teach students the appropriate procedures for checking (e.g., make no mark if the answer is correct; neatly mark an X before the item if it is wrong). A uniform checking procedure helps students complete the activity efficiently; it also will be easier for you to review the students' work when you collect it if students have used the same set of marks and symbols.

RECITATION

This activity is a question-and-answer sequence in which the teacher asks questions, usually of a factual nature, and accepts or corrects student responses. This sequence of question/answer/evaluation is repeated frequently, with many students being asked to respond until a body of content has been covered. In effect, a recitation is a form of checking done orally. It can be used to provide practice, quickly review content, or check student understanding of a previous lesson or assigned reading. It can also be used to review spelling words, vocabulary definitions in any subject, or other recall of facts.

When using recitation to check student understanding, it is important to distribute questions to all students, not only to the eager beavers. Develop a way to check systematically who gets a turn to answer, perhaps by using a checklist or name cards. Sometimes teachers do not allow students enough time to respond, thus reducing opportunities for students who are slow to answer. Some experts recommend a "wait time" of several seconds (e.g., three seconds) before giving a prompt or calling on another student.

Dealing with incorrect answers during a recitation can be vexing. On the one hand, if the teacher gives extended explanations, the pace of the recitation may become unacceptably slow; on the other hand, if the teacher pushes on by giving the correct answer or obtaining it from another student, a lack of clarity may result. Other problems include maintaining student self-esteem in the face of incorrect (and public) answers and implying low attributions for ability by asking some students only "easy" questions. Ways to address these problems include paraphrasing partially correct responses in order to "credit" the student but also to add a brief elaborating teacher explanation. The student who gives a wrong answer can be asked a follow-up question (unless the student appears lost). Most recitation questions should be easy, by definition, because they review content and are factual. Frequent wrong answers are a sign that reteaching is needed or that more student practice should be provided.

CONTENT DEVELOPMENT

In this activity, the teacher presents new information, elaborates or extends a concept or principle, conducts a demonstration, shows how to perform a skill, or describes how to solve a problem. During content development activities, the teacher's questions are used to check student understanding and to maintain involvement. They also encourage students to contribute to the steps in problem solving, to apply concepts or principles, or to analyze the ideas being presented. In addition to questioning for comprehension, it is often a good idea to obtain work samples or other student demonstrations of the skills being taught during content development activities. Important skills for effective content development are described later in this chapter in the section, Instructional Management.

DISCUSSION

In most secondary school classes, discussions are conducted as teacher-led, whole-class activities. The purpose of using discussion is to encourage students to evaluate events, topics, or results; to clarify the basis for their judgments; and to become aware of other points of view. Sometimes discussions are begun with a recitation activity in which the facts of the content to be discussed are reviewed. Compared to a recitation, however, discussion questions are more likely to elicit student judgments and opinions, and teachers are less likely to evaluate the students' responses directly. Instead, students are encouraged to examine their opinions and beliefs and to understand other perspectives. Students may respond to each other rather than only to the teacher. The teacher's role then becomes one of clarifying and using student ideas rather than evaluating their correctness.

Management of a discussion activity calls for a number of skills, including warmth or friendliness (to promote security), listening skills, conflict resolution, and encouraging expression of divergent points of view (to foster acceptance and openness). Although it is common for some students to contribute more to a discussion than others, the teacher should not allow a few students to monopolize the discourse. Asking reticent members for their opinions or views of what has previously been discussed is a good way to do so. Giving students opportunities to paraphrase, clarify, and elaborate on their own or other students' remarks is a useful way to keep a discussion moving along and on-target, perhaps allowing the teacher to transfer some of the responsibility for discussion maintenance to students. Getting students to listen to each other, rather than treating the discussion as a dialogue with the teacher, is sometimes difficult. It's important, therefore, to emphasize that students should respond to each other, not only to the teacher's comments and questions.

When using a discussion format, careful planning of questions is needed. Students should also be made aware of your ground rules for participation (e.g., raise hands, listen carefully, respect each person's right to self-expression). Some secondary classes, especially at the middle school level, have difficulty sustaining a discussion for very long, so plan short ones (e.g., ten to fifteen minutes) until you have an idea of what you and your classes can handle. After students have acquired good discussion skills, the length of this activity can be increased when appropriate.

SEATWORK

In this activity, students engage in assignments that build on previously presented material. Often, the portion of the seatwork assignment not completed in class becomes a homework assignment, unless the material or resources needed to finish it are available only in the classroom.

Good management of seatwork activities has several components. First, adequate content development must precede the independent student activity so that students can work productively on their own. Next, the teacher must communicate clearly the requirements and objectives of the students' work and arrange for access to needed materials or resources. A good strategy is to begin the seatwork assignment as a whole-class activity (e.g., by working several of the exercises, problems, or questions together) before the independent work phase. This gets students started, gives them an opportunity to ask questions, and enables the teacher to observe and correct common problems in a whole-class format rather than having to deal with the same problem with multiple individuals. Subsequently, the teacher should actively monitor the students' work so that problems are detected early and corrective feedback is provided.

Seatwork activities are best used for consolidating or extending prior learning rather than for acquiring new content. Therefore, we urge you not to overuse it. A rule of thumb is to devote at least as much time to content development as to seatwork. Moreover, student engagement is harder to maintain in lengthy seatwork activities. Try breaking the activity into smaller segments and having a discussion or review between them. The change in lesson format will help refocus student attention, and it will give you an opportunity to check student comprehension and clear up problem areas before students continue.

SMALL-GROUP WORK

This activity format can be used for many objectives. For example, to promote greater comprehension and facilitate retention of important content, pairs of students can explain concepts to each other or describe how they solved a problem. Group work can also be used for completing laboratory observations or other assignments, drilling on spelling words or new vocabulary, reviewing for a test, or generating different ways to solve a problem. Small groups can be used for gathering the information needed to prepare a project, planning a group report, or discussing an issue or topic.

Small groups work best when objectives are clear and when steps or procedures for achieving them are understood by the students. Careful monitoring of the groups is helpful in keeping them focused and on-track, although the teacher's role depends in part on the nature of the group task (Cohen 1994). When students are working on a closed-ended objective in which the outcome is clear and a course of action to achieve it is apparent, specific teacher direction along with close monitoring, prompting, and redirection, when necessary, is an efficient management approach. If the task outcome is not well defined, however, and the approach to the task is divergent, a hovering teacher can reduce the likelihood that a group will take responsibility for developing its own approach or achieve optimum results. To maximize student involvement in such group tasks, it's best to give groups more latitude in determining how to develop their ideas, while still providing direction about acceptable behavior. The management of small groups is treated extensively in Chapter 6, so we postpone further discussion of this topic for the present.

CLOSING

The goal of this procedural activity is to bring the period to an end in an orderly manner, with students ready to pass to the next class, leaving your room in good condition for your next period. Teachers usually give students a warning before the end of the period so that they have enough time to put materials away and get their own things ready. Other procedures for the closing activity were discussed in Chapter 2.

In the preceding discussion, each activity was treated as a discrete event; in practice, activities are sometimes combined. Thus, a teacher may combine recitation and content development or discussion and recitation. If you find that using some combination of activities is more suitable for your lesson goals than planning separate activities, by all means pursue the lesson structure that helps accomplish your objectives more effectively.

Organizing Activities

The center stage of instruction is occupied by content development because it is a major vehicle for new learning. However, all class periods include other activities, so one must plan an appropriate sequence. A commonly observed sequence of activities in secondary school classrooms is as follows:

1. Opening routine
2. Checking
3. Content development
4. Seatwork, group work, or discussion
5. Closing

Advantages of this sequence are that it has a minimum number of transition points, allows checking and feedback of previous work, provides for the presentation of new material, and has a practice or an application activity.

A disadvantage of the preceding sequence is that it does not easily allow for the presentation of different topics within the same period, and it also requires that the content be amenable to presentation and practice in two lengthy segments. A variation of the sequence that accommodates more than one type of content or more complex content is as follows:

1. Opening
2. Checking
3. First content development activity
4. First seatwork or group-work activity
5. Discussion or checking
6. Second content development activity
7. Second seatwork or group-work activity
8. Closing

This sequence can be used when two different types of content must be taught within the same period and the teacher wants to provide a period of practice using classwork exercises following each content development activity. Teachers whose schools use block scheduling, in which classes meet for "double" periods, can use the activity sequence to organize their instruction. The sequence can also be used when a complex lesson is separated into two phases of content development, each followed by short periods of student work either alone or in groups. Subdividing new content into two different parts, with an intervening practice activity, helps students consolidate learning from the first part before they are asked to contend with the new learning required in the second part. It also allows the teacher to check student understanding and provide prompt feedback. Another advantage of this sequence is that student attention is usually easier to maintain when individual activities are divided into shorter segments. A disadvantage of this sequence is that it requires more transition points. However, as long as the teacher is sensitive to the need to manage these transitions, the lesson format can be a useful one.

Kounin's Concepts for Managing Group Instruction

A central theme in managing activities well is the idea of activity flow. This means the degree to which a lesson proceeds smoothly without digressions, diversions, and interruptions. Lessons with a good flow keep student attention and are less likely to offer opportunities for deviance because most of the cues for students are directed toward behaviors appropriate for the lesson. When lesson flow is jerky, with frequent interruptions and side trips, there is more competition for student attention from cues external to the focus of the lesson. Therefore, there is a greater tendency for students to go off-task.

A series of classroom research studies by Kounin and his colleagues (Kounin 1970; Kounin & Gump 1974; Kounin & Obradovic 1968; see also Perron & Downey 1997) identified several concepts that contribute to the effective management of interactive group activities such as content development, discussion, and recitations. In Kounin's studies, classroom lessons were videotaped and teacher behaviors were analyzed to determine which ones predicted classrooms with high amounts of student involvement and low levels of deviant behavior. The concepts that emerged from this research provide a rich source of ideas about conducting instruction, so we will take some time to present and discuss them.

Activity flow is maintained through three types of teacher behaviors: preventing misbehavior, managing lesson movement, and maintaining group focus. Within each type of behavior are two or three related concepts. Let us look at how each is defined and consider some examples. These concepts are defined and examples are given in Table 5.1.

Preventing Misbehavior

Classrooms are complex settings. Many events can take place at the same time, and one cannot always anticipate what will occur or when. New teachers especially are at risk of focusing too closely on single events or on selected areas of the classroom, thus overlooking developing problems until they have spread or become disruptive. Understanding two of Kounin's concepts, withitness and overlapping, helps to prevent this mistake.

Withitness is the degree to which the teacher corrects misbehavior before it intensifies or spreads and also targets the correct student. A teacher who is not very "with it" fails to stop a problem until it has escalated and then may require a major intervention to bring it to a halt, or else the teacher fails to catch the perpetrator and instead targets either the wrong student or a Johnny-come-lately to the scene of the crime. It is apparent that underlying aspects of withitness include good monitoring and prompt handling of inappropriate behavior.

Table 5.1 How Effective Managers Maintain Activity Flow

Issue	Skill	Definition	Example
Preventing misbehavior	Withitness	General awareness of the classroom, which is communicated to students; prompt and correct identification and correction of misbehavior	The teacher makes eye contact with a student who is about to "shoot a basket" with a wad of paper. The student puts the paper away. A student behind him, who has seen the interaction, decides he's not likely to get away with shooting a basket either.
	Overlapping	Attending to two or more simultaneous events	The teacher is leading a class discussion when a student comes in late. The teacher nods to him, continuing the discussion. Later, when students have begun a seatwork assignment, she attends to him and signs his tardy slip.
Managing movement	Momentum	Keeping lessons moving briskly; planning carefully to avoid slowdowns	The teacher notices that the explanation of a relatively minor concept is taking too long and distracting attention from the primary focus of the lesson. The teacher makes a mental note to go more deeply into this concept in a separate lesson the next day and moves on.
	Smoothness	Staying on track with the lesson; avoiding digressions and diversions that can lead to confusion	While being responsive to student interests, the teacher avoids comments that tend to draw attention away from the key points of the lesson.
Maintaining group focus	Group alerting	Taking action to engage the attention of the whole class while individuals are responding	Each student has a number that was drawn from a hat on the way into class. The teacher draws numbers and uses them to call on students during a fast-paced review.
	Encouraging accountability	Communicating to students that their participation will be observed and evaluated	At the end of discussion and practice of a new skill, students are told to turn to a neighbor and explain the process to him or her.
	Higher participation formats	Using lessons that define behavior of students when they are not directly answering a teacher's question	While some students work problems at the board, students at their desks are instructed to check them by working the problems on paper.

Overlapping refers to the way the teacher handles two or more simultaneous events: For example, a visitor comes to the door in the middle of a lesson; a student leaves his seat without permission while the teacher is leading a discussion; several students get into a squabble while the teacher is busy helping other students across the room. A teacher who has good overlapping skills handles both events in some way instead of dropping one to handle the other or ignoring the second event. To handle a long interruption, for example, a teacher might tell students to get out some work; after they have done so, the teacher might then deal with the interrupter. The squabble away from the teacher might be handled by eye contact or a brief verbal desist while the teacher stays in contact with the original group.

Notice that a teacher who is "withit" and exhibits good overlapping skills is able to insulate lessons from the intrusions that student misbehavior or external interruptions might cause. Furthermore, by reacting promptly to problems (but not overreacting), the teacher can often use simple measures (eye contact, redirection, a quiet desist) that do not interfere with ongoing activities or distract students. If a teacher is not very withit or does not overlap when needed, lessons may be interrupted by student misbehavior and subsequently by the teacher's more visible and tardy reactions.

Managing Movement

Whereas withitness and overlapping are accomplished by handling external interruptions and student intrusions into the flow of the lesson, movement management is accomplished by avoiding teacher-caused intrusions or delays. Good movement management is achieved through momentum and smoothness.

MOMENTUM

Momentum refers to pacing and is indicated by lessons that move along briskly. Teachers can cause slowdowns in momentum by dwelling too long on individual parts of a lesson, direction, or skill and by breaking an activity into too many parts. For example, students should be taught a standard heading for assignments so it can be used routinely rather than having its form altered so that it must be explained repeatedly.

SMOOTHNESS

A lesson that exhibits continuity, rather than jerkiness, epitomizes the concept of smoothness. A smoothly flowing lesson keeps student attention; one that is jerky can be distracting. Kounin used graphic labels to depict ways that a teacher might diverge from a smooth lesson. He described these divergences as "dangles," "flip-flops," "thrusts," and "stimulus-boundedness." These problems are described and compared in Table 5.2.

Table 5.2 Common Problems in Maintaining Momentum and Smoothness

Problem	Definition	Example
Dangle	Teacher leaves a topic or activity "dangling" to do something else or to insert some new material	"All right, please take out your math books. Turn to page . . . Oops, I forgot to send this form to the office. Raise your hand if you ride the bus. All right, where were we?"
Flip-flop	Like a dangle, except that the topic inserted is left over from an earlier activity	"OK, let's leave vocabulary now. We'll pick up the discussion tomorrow. Please move your chairs into your writing groups. Take your pencils and a blank piece of paper, and that's all." (Students move into their groups and the teacher begins to give instructions for today's writing activity.) "All right now, does everyone understand what I want you to do? Oh, and did everyone remember to write down their vocabulary workbook assignment? I put it on the board, pages 235–242. OK, go ahead and start."
Thrust	Teacher intrudes with some information when students are involved in another activity, and it seems irrelevant to them	Students are working quietly on a test. The teacher has been circulating and monitoring. The teacher interrupts and comments, "When you're finished, bring your test booklets to the front table and put your answer sheets in this box." Students continue to work quietly. When they begin completing their tests, the teacher must explain again where to put the test booklet and answer sheet.
Stimulus-bound	Teacher is distracted by some outside stimulus and draws the class's attention to it and away from the lesson	Students are taking turns reading their writing aloud. Each student's reading is followed by comments from the rest of the class. During one such discussion, the teacher notices a student reading a paperback. "What are you reading, Alice?" she asks. "Have you read anything else by that writer?"

Maintaining Group Focus

Classroom instruction involves teaching students in groups, usually a whole class at a time. The teacher must be conscious of the group influence on instruction. Like a conductor leading an orchestra, the teacher must elicit the performance of individuals and still provide signals and directions that keep the whole class together. Group focus can be maintained through several techniques.

GROUP ALERTING

This term means taking some action to engage the attention of the whole class while individuals are responding. It can take the form of creating suspense, telling students they might be called on next, calling on them randomly, asking students not reciting to listen carefully because they might be called on to add to the answer, or using some visual aid, display, or attention-capturing strategy. In contrast, examples of poor group alerting are engaging in a dialogue with one student or calling on a student before asking a question so that the rest of the class does not feel the need to pay attention to the question.

ACCOUNTABILITY

Accountability occurs when the teacher lets students know that their performance will be observed and evaluated in some manner. It does not require a letter grade or a score (although it might), but only communicating some degree of awareness of how individual students are performing. For example, the teacher might ask everyone who knows an answer to raise a hand and then call on one or more of those students; or the teacher could have all students write down answers, perform, or display work and then circulate to check it.

HIGHER PARTICIPATION FORMATS

Lessons that cue or program the behavior of students when they are not directly involved in answering a teacher's question have a higher built-in rate of participation than do lessons that merely assume that students will sit and watch when other students respond. Higher participation formats occur when students are expected to write answers, solve problems, read along, manipulate materials, or perform some other task during instruction.

Some activities lend themselves more to one type of group focus than to another. When teachers are planning instruction, it is helpful for them to consider which of the three aspects to use. For example, it might be difficult to use a high participation format during a demonstration that involves expensive materials, but group alerting might be easy to incorporate in the lesson.

Kounin's concepts are a stimulating addition to our repertoire for understanding how to engage students during instruction. Not only do they help identify key aspects of effective teaching, but they can also be used to diagnose instructional problems and identify possible solutions. For example, if lessons seem to drag and student response is unenthusiastic, there may be a problem with group focus; a solution may be to work on alerting or accountability or to increase the degree of participation. Activities that take too long and that seem to get off-track constantly might have a problem in the area of movement management; perhaps the teacher should check for the incidence of slowdowns and jerkiness.

໑໑ Transition Management

The interval between any two activities is a transition. In addition, the beginning and ending of periods are transitions. The goal of a transition is to bring the preceding activity to a successful conclusion and begin the next one without undue delay. Several management problems can occur at these times, such as long delays before starting the next activity or high levels of inappropriate or disruptive student behavior that can spill over into the next activity. Arlin (1979) found that the amount of off-task behavior increased during transitions, but when teachers structured transitions, off-task behavior was substantially reduced. Also, classrooms populated by students with learning and attention disorders are more susceptible to transition problems (Marks et al. 2003). Some of the causes of transition problems include a lack of readiness by the teacher or the students for the next activity, unclear student expectations about appropriate behavior during transitions, and faulty procedures. Examples of transition problems are listed next, along with some suggestions for correcting them.

Transition Problem	Suggested Solution
Students talk loudly at the beginning of the period. The teacher is interrupted while checking attendance, and the start of content activities is delayed.	Establish a beginning-of-period routine with clear expectations for student behavior. Have a content activity ready for students to begin at once.
Students talk too much during transitions, especially after a seatwork assignment has been given but before they've begun working on it. Many students do not start their seatwork activity for several minutes.	Be sure students know what the assignment is; post it where they can see it easily. Work as a whole class on the first several seatwork exercises so that all students begin the lesson successfully and at the same time. Then walk around the room, check students' work, and give corrective and/or encouraging feedback.
Students stop working long before the end-of-period bell; they then engage in excessive talking and leave the room a mess.	An end-of-period routine should be established: Students work until the teacher gives a signal, and then they clean up around their desks or work areas before being dismissed.
Whenever the teacher attempts to move students from one activity into another, a number of students don't make the transition but continue working on the preceding activity. This delays the start of the next activity or results in confusion.	The teacher should give the class notice a few minutes before an activity is scheduled to end. When it ends, students should put up material from the first activity before getting out new materials for the second. The teacher should monitor the transition to make sure that all students complete it.

Transition Problem	Suggested Solution
A few students always seem to be slowpokes during transition, delaying the rest of the class.	Don't wait for one or two students and hold up the rest of the class. Go ahead and start, but be sure to monitor to find out why they are having trouble. It may help to move closer to these students during the transition.
Students frequently leave their seats to socialize, come up to the teacher to ask questions, attempt to get a bathroom permit, go to the wastebasket, or wander around the room during transitions.	Define appropriate behavior during transitions and explain the rationale for limiting student behavior during these times. Monitor students and be sure procedures are established to handle out-of-seat behavior.
The teacher delays the beginning of activities to look for materials, finish attendance reporting, return or collect papers, or chat with individual students while the rest of the students wait.	The teacher needs to have all materials ready, and once transitions begin, the teacher should avoid doing anything that interferes with his or her ability to monitor and direct students.

 ## Instructional Management

Planning

Organize the parts of your lesson into a coherent sequence. If the lesson is complex, write down the main components. Review the unit and lesson in the teacher's edition of your textbook(s). Pay careful attention to suggestions for lesson development and activities. Study the exercises, questions, or problems provided in the textbook and decide which items would provide appropriate review of lesson objectives. Note examples, demonstrations, and key questions and activities to use in developing the main concepts. If some items in the seatwork assignment go well beyond your lesson's scope, don't assign them as classwork or homework until you can teach the necessary content. If the content is not essential and you do not plan to teach it later, assign such items for enrichment or for extra credit.

Try to anticipate problems students may encounter in the lesson or assignments. Check for new terms and be ready to define them and present examples. Do some of the classwork or homework assignment yourself to uncover hurdles students will face. You can then build into your lesson some helpful hints or extra emphasis in these areas.

Consider the interest the lesson is likely to have for students. Will you be enthusiastic about teaching this material to your classes in this way? Your enthusiasm about the lesson is contagious and signals to students how you feel about its importance. If you find it interesting and exciting and you communicate this excitement to your class, students will probably respond with interest. If, however, you are unenthusiastic about a lesson, chances are that your students will share your feelings. Consider changing your approach in some way to put a little more spark in the activities.

Presenting New Content Clearly

Tell students what the lesson objectives are either at the beginning of or during the activity. If the lesson is at all complex, provide an outline. Displaying the topical sequence helps organize the content for students and provides a road map to keep them on course.

If students are expected to understand content from silent reading, viewing a film or tape, or completing an Internet search, provide a content outline with a few items filled in and spaces for students to supply the rest. This task focuses attention and provides motivation for careful reading or viewing.

As you present a lesson, stay with the planned sequence unless an obvious change is needed. Avoid needless digressions, interruptions, or tangential information. Inserting irrelevant information into a lesson only confuses students about what they are expected to learn. Displaying key concepts, new terms, major points, and other critical information on the overhead transparency screen or writing them on the chalkboard will underscore their importance. If students are required to take notes, the display will guide the information students record.

Presentation should be as focused and concrete as possible. Use examples, illustrations, demonstrations, physical props, charts, and other means of providing substance and dimension to abstractions in the lesson. Avoid vague expressions and verbal time fillers that communicate little information and make presentations difficult to follow.

Checking for Understanding

Student understanding should be checked during instruction, not only as a part of formal evaluations, such as tests and assignments. Doing so allows the teacher

to reteach essential content as needed. It also helps the teacher gauge when to adjust instruction.

Comprehension and skills can be checked at the beginning, during, and at the end of instruction. The amount of informal assessment that is feasible depends on the available time and the importance of the information. Informal assessments are carried out by obtaining samples of oral, written, or other performance and using these to judge the degree to which students possess desired knowledge or skills. Examples of checking for understanding include the following:

- At the beginning of a presentation, the teacher asks several students to define basic concepts that were covered previously and that will be needed to comprehend the presentation.
- During a presentation, the teacher asks students to write their answers to a pertinent question. She then moves among the class to read the answers.
- Students, who are seated in groups, are given a problem to discuss and solve. Then the teacher asks one student in each group to summarize its solution.
- Halfway through a presentation, the teacher conducts a recitation on the lesson's main ideas up to that point.
- At several times during a lesson, the teacher displays on the overhead screen a multiple-choice question on a critical point. After students record an answer, she asks for "hands" to indicate response choices.
- During a content development activity, the teacher looks around the room frequently, observing student behavior; he also moves among the students as they work on a short classwork exercise, looking for evidence that students can perform the task.

In these examples, pertinent information was obtained from several students. In addition to providing potentially useful information about student comprehension, the strategies also provide for a more active student role than simple listening and thus may encourage student involvement in the flow of the lesson.

Further Reading

Alvermann, D. E., O'Brien, D. G., & Dillon, D. R. (1990). What teachers do when they say they're having discussions of content area reading assignments: A qualitative analysis. *Reading Research Quarterly, 25,* 296–322.

Although teachers often say that they utilize discussion activities, this study found that the nature of discussion varies greatly from class to class. Maintaining control was very important to many of the teachers, and the more this dominated their perspective, the more their discussions resembled a recitation rather than an open forum for expressing views.

Bransford, J. B., Brown, A. L., & Cocking, R. R. (Eds.) (1999). *How people learn.* Washington, DC: National Academy Press.

This is a research-based examination of learning with an emphasis on applications for schools and teachers. It's very readable and is packed with good ideas for instruction.

Brophy, J., & Alleman, J. (1991). Activities as instructional tools: A framework for analysis and evaluation. *Educational Researcher, 20*(4), 9–23.

The authors provide a detailed analysis of the design, selection, and evaluation of activities, with a central concern being how activities contribute to student learning. Several major principles underlying activity design are proposed in this comprehensive analysis.

Marzanno, R. J., Pickering, D. J., & Pollock, J. E. (2001). *Classroom instruction that works: Research based strategies for increasing student achievement.* Alexandria, VA: Association for Supervision and Curriculum Development.

The authors present chapters on instructional practices that have substantial research support for improving student learning. Topics included are note taking, homework and practice, cooperative learning, objectives and feedback, generating and testing hypotheses, and questioning strategies. The book is an excellent source of ideas to use when planning instruction.

Stigler, J. W., & Stevenson, H. W. (1991). How Asian teachers polish each lesson to perfection. *American Educator, 15*(1), 12–20, 43–47.

If you have a stereotype of Chinese or Japanese classrooms led by an authoritarian lecturer endlessly drilling students in rote tasks, your view will change after reading this article. Teachers in these two Asian cultures emphasize well-constructed, coherent lessons that focus on meaningful learning and active participation by students.

 ## Suggested Activities

1. Case Studies 5.1 and 5.2 describe difficulties two teachers are experiencing with organizing and presenting instruction. After reading each paragraph, review the relevant sections in this chapter and in earlier parts of this book and decide what strategies would be helpful in overcoming the problems. You might also use each case as a basis for a group discussion and generate a list of many possible solutions or strategies. Case Studies 5.3, 5.4, and 5.5 provide further opportunities for review of and practice in applying concepts from this chapter.

2. See how many examples of Kounin's concepts you can find in Case Study 5.4. Compare your list with the key in the Appendix.

3. Analyze the lesson in Case Study 5.5 by first identifying the sequence of activities used by the teacher and then discussing what occurred within each activity. Where problems are evident, describe alternative approaches or strategies that might be used. Compare your answers with the keys in the Appendix.

4. If you have access to a secondary classroom for observation, watch a class period and note how transitions are managed. Observe which students seem to lose their way during transitions and how the teacher brings them back to the next activity. Note any structure supplied by the teacher, such as signals or routines. Also note how the teacher uses proximity, movement, monitoring, and eye contact during the transition.

5. Prepare an outline of a lesson plan for a class period at a grade level and in a subject you might teach. Alternatively, download a lesson plan from a website; www.eduref.org has a compilation of educational resources for many subjects and grade levels. Other websites with large numbers of plans are www.712educators.about.com, www.lessonplanspage.com, and www.teachervision.fen.com, which have tips for teachers and a lesson plan center. Analyze the plan with one or more colleagues, paying attention to the goals, types of activities, their sequencing and length, and transitions.

CASE STUDY 5.1

OVER AND OVER

In Ms. Liu's class, there almost always seem to be some students who don't understand presentations or assignments and who need a lot of reexplanation. While she is lecturing, students continually ask questions about what they should write in their notes. When an in-class assignment is made, Ms. Liu finds herself answering many questions about information just covered in the lecture. Sometimes she has to reexplain parts of the lesson to the whole class. As a result, there is often not enough time to complete activities before the end of the period. In an attempt to avoid the problems associated with note taking, she decides to write important information on the chalkboard during the lecture. What else can Ms. Liu do?

CASE STUDY 5.2

TRANSITION PROBLEMS

Mr. Miller feels that too much time is wasted in his ninth-grade class while students get settled after class changes, get supplies ready, or move from one activity to another. While the teacher deals with students' problems, make-up work, or questions at the beginning of class, students talk and begin to play around or wander. It then takes some time to get their attention and get class started. Also, when activities change during the class period, students sometimes delay activities while they sharpen pencils or borrow supplies. Trading papers to check work in class usually results in some confusion.

Mr. Miller has already spoken with his class about the problem and has reminded them of the rules for sharpening pencils immediately upon arriving and taking seats before the bell. He tries to enforce these two rules, but he is also required to monitor the hall. What else can he do to cut down on wasted time?

CASE STUDY 5.3

A CHANGE IN PLANS

During the second week of school, Ms. Kendall is informed that too few students have signed up for her fifth-period elective humanities class. There is, however, an overflow in fifth-period general science. Because she is certified in both English and science, the administration's solution to the enrollment problem is for her to begin Monday with the fifth-period science class. Although certified in the subject, Ms. Kendall has never taught it before. What steps should she take as she begins to construct her general science curriculum for the year? What will she need to know before she can prepare her lesson plans? What should her daily plans include?

CASE STUDY 5.4

KOUNIN CONCEPTS

As his fourth-period class begins, Mr. Case makes eye contact with two students who are exchanging notes; the students quickly get out their class materials. "Let's begin by working some of the exercises at the end of the chapter; you'll need your notebooks." As students begin to get out their materials, Mr. Case calls out, "Oops, I forgot to tell you to bring money tomorrow for the field trip. How many of you will be going?" After a brief discussion, students finish getting out their materials. Mr. Case says, "We'll go through these exercises orally, but I also want you to write the answers in your notebooks as part of today's classwork. I'll come around and check on your notebook work later in the period. Now, who can answer the first question? Hands please. Tyrone?" Mr. Case conducts the lesson by calling on various students, some with hands up, others seemingly at random from the nonvolunteers. About halfway through the exercises, a student enters the room and says that he is new to the school and has been assigned to the class. Mr. Case goes to his desk, sits down, and says, "Okay, come here. I'll check out a text to you. I wish the school office wouldn't send people in the middle of a period. Where are you from, anyway?" After giving the student a syllabus and a text, Mr. Case leaves his desk and says to the class, "Now where were we? Oh yes, question seven. Say, where did Kim and Lee go? I didn't give them permission to leave." After several more minutes, Mr. Case calls a halt to the activity and says, "Now I'd like us to discuss the test coming up this Thursday. Let's make sure that you are all clear on what will be on the exam and what you will need to study to get ready for it." After a pause, he adds: "I almost forgot. Get out your questions from before and look at the next to the last one. We need to add an important point that was left out." After finishing the item, Mr. Case turns the topic back to the upcoming test: "Now, where were we? Oh, yes. I need to show you some items that will be similar to those on the test. Here's one." He writes it on the chalkboard, then pauses: "Well, I don't want to give away the test, do I?" Without discussing the test further, he turns to another topic: "Just wait until you hear about the videotape we will be viewing tomorrow. I borrowed it from another teacher, and she said that her students thought it was one of the most thought-provoking, exciting stories they had ever seen!"

CASE STUDY 5.5

A SCIENCE LESSON

After checking roll, Ms. Grant tells students that the day's activity will be their first lab assignment and that they will work in groups. "The purpose of the lab work is to get practice with the scientific method," she says, and she lists the stages: observation, formulation of a hypothesis, gathering evidence, analysis, and conclusions. Ms. Grant tells students that they must work together in an assigned lab group, and she calls out the group assignments, forming six groups of four or five students each. Students are then told to arrange their desks according to groups. Students are very noisy as they do so, with much playing and talking occurring. Ms. Grant has to speak very loudly to regain the students' attention and give directions for a lab sheet that she distributes to each student. Standing at the front of the room, the teacher reads the directions on the lab sheet while several students continue to converse. Two groups at the back of the room do not pay attention to the teacher's presentation of directions. Ms. Grant tells students that each group will get a box with something inside and that they should try to determine what it is. They must work together as a group. Having said that, Ms. Grant distributes to each group a small box wrapped in construction paper. Students immediately treat the boxes as noisemakers, causing more commotion. Ms. Grant yells above the din, "Be sure to fill in three guesses at the bottom of the page."

During the ensuing activity, only one group discusses what possibilities exist and how they might determine what the box contains. The other groups mainly record the first three guesses that are offered by group members. The teacher observes the groups from a stool at the front of the room. After four minutes, she says, "List the tests that you performed. Then put down your three best guesses." After six minutes, four of the groups are finished, and students put the boxes back on the teacher's desk. Two groups continue to work on the problem, while the remaining students sit idly or talk. One boy calls out, "When are we going to start?" The teacher responds, "Soon, when everyone is ready." After two more minutes, the teacher says, "Listen up, we are ready for the group reports." Some students are still talking while Ms. Grant gives directions for each group's oral report. One student from each group will give the group report, which is a statement of each guess and the reasons for it. The teacher also reminds students to follow class rules for listening when other students talk and for not leaving their seats during discussions. "If you can't keep your mouths shut, we won't be able to do activities like this," she notes. While giving reports, students speak softly; it is difficult to hear each report because of talking and fooling around by a number of students. The students' reports are short, and the teacher's comments are limited to brief evaluations and indications of acceptance, such as "Okay," "Good," or "Good observation." Ms. Grant does not record or compare group observations or guesses, but she occasionally asks for clarification, such as, "What makes you guess that?"

After about ten minutes, each group report has been given, although many students have not paid attention to any report except the one from their own group. Ms. Grant tells students, "You used a lot of good observations, like the last group that distinguished between round objects and objects with flat sides. Most of the groups were close, and tomorrow I'll tell you what was in each box. Please pass your papers in." After papers have been collected, Ms. Grant asks two students to distribute a classroom set of books. She tells the class to begin reading a chapter on molecules for the next day. After several minutes of commotion, students settle down and read silently for the remaining thirteen minutes of class.

What problems are evident and what changes would be appropriate?

Checklist 5

Planning for Instruction

Check When Complete	Before the Lesson, Ask Yourself	Notes
☐	1. What are the most important concepts or skills to be learned?	
☐	2. Are there difficult words or concepts that need extra explanation?	
☐	3. How will you help students make connections to previous learning?	
☐	4. What activities will you plan to create interest in the lesson?	
☐	5. What materials will be needed? Will students need to learn how to use them?	
☐	6. What procedures will students need to follow to complete the activities?	
☐	7. How much time will you allocate for different parts of the lesson?	
☐	8. If activities require students to work together, how will groups be formed? How will you encourage productive work in groups?	
☐	9. What examples and questioning strategies will you use?	
☐	10. How will you tell during and after the lesson what students understand?	
☐	11. What are the presentation alternatives if students have trouble with concepts or skills? Peer explanation, media, textbook, etc.?	
☐	12. Will any students need extra help or more explanation?	

Check When Complete	Before the Lesson, Ask Yourself	Notes
☐	13. How will you make sure that all students participate?	_____
☐	14. How will you adjust the lesson if time is too short or long?	_____
☐	15. What kind of product, if any, will you expect from students at the end of the lesson?	_____
☐	16. What will students do if they finish early?	_____
☐	17. How will you evaluate students' performance and give them feedback?	_____
☐	18. How will the concepts or skills be used by students in future lessons?	_____

6

Managing Cooperative Learning Groups

Cooperative learning is a form of instruction in which students are organized into groups to complete assignments and projects collaboratively, to assist each other, to solve problems, to share materials, and to participate in discussions. Teachers who use cooperative learning groups do so because they believe that the method increases student learning and involvement. Many teachers also value the increased student independence from the teacher's direction that results from an emphasis on group planning, assistance, and decision making. Such teachers often describe their role as that of facilitator rather than director of group activities. Finally, teachers value the social skills and problem-solving abilities that are enhanced through frequent group work. These important life skills will serve the students well in many work and social settings that they encounter in or out of school. The following are some examples of cooperative learning activities in different subjects and grade levels:

Students in a blocked English and history class complete a "diary project" in groups of three or four. Each group selects a historical person and prepares a diary written from their subject's perspective. Diaries consist of a description of the era, a persuasive essay, an advertisement for a product the person might sell or endorse, and several daily "diary" entries detailing reactions to events of the era. Students complete the project over a two-week period, which includes library research, computer searches, and in-class writing sessions. Group presentations as well as written products are utilized.

In an English class, students work in pairs to rewrite fairy tales using the style of a selected author. Although each student is responsible for his or her own version, students assist each other when identifying the features of the author's style they wish to incorporate into the rewritten tale and when outlining their versions. Students also edit each other's work and provide suggestions for revision.

Students in a middle school social studies class work in groups of four on an "explorers" assignment. In each group, students read text materials, discuss them, and write answers to questions about an explorer's life, actions, and impact. At a designated time, students change seats to go to new groups, where they share their information with other students who incorporate it into their reports.

In a math class, students explore different ways to solve a problem in order to discover a preferred approach. Each group is responsible for generating at least two approaches to the solution and then deciding which approach it prefers and why. After about ten minutes, the teacher extends the problem by changing one of the conditions. Groups discuss the effect of the changed condition on their choice of a solution.

In a world geography class, students work in groups of four or five, using Hyperstudio to prepare a computer-based report on a South American country. Different students assume responsibility for assembling information about their group's country, such as physical geography, economics, government, climate, culture, and customs. Individual student roles in the group include producer, technical director, and researchers.

In a science lesson on observation, groups of four students generate a list of ten to twenty characteristics of an unshelled peanut. Students weigh, measure, shake, examine, and discuss their group's peanut. After a while, the teacher mixes up the peanuts and then each group tries to find its original peanut. Next the teacher has groups exchange descriptions and use them to find the associated peanut. The lesson concludes with a whole-class discussion of different types of observational data and validity criteria.

These examples illustrate that cooperative learning can be used in a wide array of subjects at all secondary grade levels from middle through high school. Furthermore, groups may be used in single, self-contained lessons, or they may be used in long-term projects. Whatever the use, some changes in traditional managerial routines will be needed. Although a number of the procedures from earlier chapters for managing student work and behavior in whole-class and individual formats will continue to apply to cooperative groups, some of the *talk* and *movement* procedures may need to be modified. In addition, the teacher's managerial tasks of *pacing* activities, *monitoring,* and *giving feedback* to students become especially important. The process of introducing cooperative groups is also crucial and deserves careful consideration. In particular, your focus will be on *teaching students the skills* necessary for working effectively in groups.

The defining features of cooperative groups vary somewhat depending on the particular application (Slavin 1995, Johnson & Johnson 1999; Cohen 1994; Putnam 1998), but common elements among these variations include group goals or task interdependence, some degree of individual accountability, and good group interaction processes. The management strategies presented in this chapter apply to group activities that utilize these generic features rather than to only one model of group work. It should also be noted that cooperative learning is only one type of instructional format available to you as a secondary teacher. Teachers should not depend on cooperative groups for all of their content development work. Whole-class presentations, demonstrations, and discussions will continue to be essential formats for delivering and applying content, and seatwork and classwork exercises will continue to be important formats for consolidating individual student learning through practice. Cooperative learning activities can, however, add a very useful methodology to more traditional instructional approaches.

Research on Cooperative Learning

Substantial research on cooperative learning has focused on its effects on student achievement and other outcomes of interest such as interpersonal relations and student attitudes toward learning (Slavin 1995; Johnson & Johnson 1999; Nastasi & Clements 1991). Several studies have found that cooperative learning typically results in achievement levels that are equal to or greater than those for individualistic or competitive classroom teaching methods. Results for other outcomes such as motivation, attitudes, and behaviors often favor cooperative group methods (see also Wade, Abrami, Poulsen, & Chambers 1995, and Educational Research Service 1989, for extensive summaries and reviews of this research literature).

Explanations of the positive benefits of cooperative groups usually point to students' increased engagement with the content as an important factor. Compared to large-class or individual seatwork formats, small groups have greater potential for participation, feedback, and mutual construction of meaning among students. The group format encourages students to become active participants rather than passive recipients of information. Lower achieving students profit from explanations provided by their peers, while students who are higher achievers benefit from constructing explanations for other students. All students develop interpersonal skills by engaging in tasks with a common goal in groups that contain students with diverse backgrounds. Furthermore, all students can benefit from the affective support they receive in a cohesive group. Such support can help create positive norms for achievement and learning.

Although cooperative groups can improve learning and other outcomes for students, such results are by no means assured simply by the use of groups. For example, although research has shown that student achievement is promoted by helping behaviors such as giving and receiving explanations (Nattiv 1994; Webb & Farivar 1994; Whicker, Bol, & Nunnery 1997), such assistance does not occur automatically. Students who need help do not always ask for it, nor do they necessarily receive assistance when they do. Helpers may, moreover, simply give a correct answer or share a solution rather than engage in constructive dialogue. Without feedback and instruction on how to collaborate, higher achieving students may retreat to a less advanced level of cognition (Tudge 1992). More frequent use of group activities promotes positive outcomes when the quality of group interaction is high, but when group interactions are of low quality, outcomes may be negatively affected (Battistich, Solomon, & Delucchi 1993). Students with disabilities especially need supportive, positive partners, and teachers must be proactive about arranging group membership, teaching group behaviors, and monitoring to promote their successful participation in group activities (O'Connor & Jenkins 1996).

Research has identified a number of strategies that you can use to promote the effectiveness of cooperative groups (Emmer & Gerwels 2002; Cohen 1994; Slavin 1995). Such actions include teaching students how to work in groups, practicing the role of facilitator, carefully choosing and pacing academic activities, and promoting interdependence along with individual responsibility within a group context. Characteristics of more effective cooperative group lessons also include some form of daily accountability (versus later or no evaluation of individual or group performance), teacher monitoring of and feedback to groups, and the use of manipulative materials (Emmer & Gerwels 2002).

The importance of these and other skills will depend in part on your goals and the nature of group-based academic tasks. Some teachers use groups as the primary means of instruction and develop projects and an integrated curriculum to deliver much of their academic content. Other teachers use groups primarily as a supplement to whole-class and individual instruction, relying on groups during the classwork portion of lessons to provide short practice activities. Whichever approach you decide to adopt, you will find the skills described in the remainder of this chapter helpful. You will, however, need to tailor them to your own application.

 ## Strategies and Routines That Support Cooperative Learning

Room Arrangement

If you plan to make extensive use of groups, it will be advantageous to arrange student seating in groups rather than have students move to group seating each time the format is used. Some classrooms are equipped with tables; to facilitate monitoring, these should be arranged to permit your unrestricted movement among them. In the absence of group tables, desks can be pushed together to form groups.

In some classrooms, it will be necessary to move from whole-class seating arrangements to small groups. Plan ahead to speed these transitions. Mark on the floor with masking or colored plastic tape the location of tables or desks in each arrangement. Then, when it is time to make the transition, teach students how to move to groups just as you would teach them any other classroom procedure.

Teachers often begin group activities with pairs of students rather than larger groups, but seating arrangements can still accommodate larger numbers; for example, when using table groups of four, divide the larger groups into pairs.

Some teachers place a small box or bin in the middle of each table or group of desks for materials used by everyone in the group. A common materials center in each group eliminates the need for borrowing these supplies from other students, and it reduces the need for trips to out-of-group storage areas.

Talk and Movement Procedures

Teachers often report that when they begin using groups, the increased noise level bothers them. After a while, they get used to it and are less anxious when they realize that the noise is coming from engaged, involved students. Nevertheless, to prevent excessive noise, teachers should discuss this issue with the class and develop some guidelines. A common guideline is to use "six-inch" or "twelve-inch" voices. Another guideline is to speak quietly enough so students in nearby groups can't hear or aren't distracted. "Whisper voices" do not work well as a guideline because groups usually can't work efficiently and conduct discussions while whispering. If noise becomes excessive, you can use a group attention signal (see below) to restore it to an acceptable level.

Movement will not be a major problem if students are already seated in their groups, although it may be useful to provide a guideline such as "Stay with your group" or "Take care of out-of-group business promptly" to limit unnecessary wandering and visiting. Some movement will be necessary, of course, when students obtain materials. Assigning a "materials manager" role in each group will help take care of such business efficiently.

Some teachers change group composition for different activities, resulting in student movement during the transitions. Such transitions can be real time-wasters and make it difficult to start the next activity. An efficient routine is to announce the beginning of the transition, state the expectation, and tell students how much time they have to get ready ("All of you need to bring materials and be in your group in one minute."). Continue to monitor throughout the transition to cut down on stragglers ("thirty seconds left, . . . fifteen seconds, . . . Everyone should be in their group now."). You can also state your expectation about what they are to do when they arrive at their group's location ("Sit in your seat and put your supplies—book, paper, pencil, etc.—on the table/desk." Or "Start work on your project right away.").

Group Attention Signals

When your students work in groups, you may need to stop their work to provide some additional directions or to make a transition to another activity or task. You may also need to provide some feedback to the whole class, modify some aspect of the assignment, or provide additional instruction. In addition, noise may rise to unacceptable levels, requiring you to intervene. In all of these cases, you will be faced with the task of interrupting students who are already engaged in a task or interacting with each other, making it difficult to gain their attention. The solution to this problem is to use a signal.

Efficient signals for group attention require students to make some overt response, which interrupts whatever else they may be doing. When teaching middle school students, you can give a verbal signal such as, "Raise a hand if you can hear me," "Fold your hands if you can hear me," or "Clap if you can hear me." These signals gain students' attention by requiring that they substitute a behavior, thus effectively stopping the prior activity. They are especially useful when students are working with manipulatives that might distract them from attending. Another common signal, appropriate for any grade level, is to turn on the overhead projector and at the same time request, "Eyes to the front, please." Because you are interrupting the students, capturing their attention will not be instantaneous; you may find it useful to pace the transition by counting down: "Five, four, three, two, one . . ." and then begin the next activity promptly.

When students are not as interactively engaged, a less dramatic or intrusive stimulus can be used to get their attention. Ringing a bell and giving a simple verbal direction such as, "Stop, look, listen," "Eyes to the front," or "Eyes on the teacher" will often suffice. It's a good idea to teach several signals to students to avoid overworking one of them and to give you some options. Finally, avoid interrupting students unnecessarily. Try to present information or directions ahead of time, or post them on the chalkboard or the overhead to minimize the need to break into ongoing student activities.

Promoting Interdependence within the Group

When either the group's product or the performance of individual group members is enhanced by the actions of other group members, positive interdependence has occurred. In addition to improving group and individual performance, interdependence builds group cohesion and helps create group norms that support learning. Interdependence can be fostered in a number of ways.

■ Assignments or projects can require varied skills and abilities, such as drawing, organizing data into charts, the use of computers, oral presentations, and construction, in addition to the more traditional skills of reading, writing, and computing. Such variation in tasks gives more students the opportunity to contribute to the final group product.
■ Each student can be responsible for contributing a unique component to the group's product. For example, students might do research on different aspects of a topic for a group report.
■ Each student chooses a specific part of a topic to teach to the rest of the students in the group. Or, in groups of four students, pairs work together to prepare information for the other two students in the group.
■ In groups of two, students work as drill partners to help each other learn.
■ The teacher assigns different roles to students (e.g., reader, checker, recorder, and materials manager) to ensure that each student makes a contribution to the group's activity.
■ Group assignments (e.g., projects, reports, performances, constructions, or oral group presentations) can be given a group grade, recognition, or points.

Individual Accountability

Although interdependence is important, students must also feel individually responsible for their learning. This is not as much of a problem when students are expected to complete the assignments as individuals with group support. When group assignments are the outcome, however, establishing group accountability—for example, by giving the group's product a grade or by asking the group to report orally—may not be sufficient for some students, who may be content to loaf or ride other students' coattails. It may be necessary to give individual grades in addition to the group grade, for example. Individual accountability in the context of a group-based assignment may be increased in several ways, as noted in the following examples.

■ Require that individual students perform an identifiable portion of the group assignment.
■ Ask groups to turn in a list of each student's contribution to the final product.
■ Use peer evaluation of group members' participation and contributions.

- Ask students to record observations in individual notebooks that you will collect and grade at various times.
- Have students turn in individual work—even if it is just individual class notes—along with the group's product.
- Require students to keep a daily record of their individual work in spiral notebooks.
- Let students know that when their group reports to the class, each student should be ready to explain its work. Better yet, require that each student be responsible for some part of the group presentation.
- Have selected students report individually on their group work.
- Give students a quiz based on the group assignment.

You can also foster individual responsibility when you set expectations: Stress to students that even though they are working on a group assignment, each of them is responsible for learning the material. Tell students that it is important for the members of a group to help each other understand what they are learning and for each person to contribute. Finally, when you monitor student work in groups, note participation by individual students. If particular students are not contributing, try to determine why and take corrective measures, such as redirecting them. When simple interventions don't work, teachers often ask the group to help solve the problem, or they may have a conference with the student to try to assess the situation and work out a solution.

Maintaining individual responsibility in a group setting is not always easy. Adding individual assessments on top of group assessments may increase the amount of time the teacher needs to spend on planning and preparation as well as evaluation. Focusing on individual accountability, moreover, may deflect attention from group outcomes. Procedures for accountability, therefore, should be planned carefully and amended as necessary, until you develop a balance between accountability needs and available time and energy.

Monitoring Student Work and Behavior

Good monitoring of group work is essential and typically requires you to walk among the groups, scanning the rest of the class from time to time. Try not to spend too much time with a single group at the expense of keeping abreast of the activities of the rest. When teachers do this, they lose awareness of the class. Goals for monitoring include keeping track of individual performance and growth in academic areas, group skills, and individual behaviors. A complicating factor is the extent to which individual versus group performance needs to be distinguished.

How you keep track of student work in groups will depend on the nature of the group activity. When individual assignments are used and the group's function is to support individual learning, monitoring academic performance is not much different than in classrooms in which whole-class and individual seatwork are the primary formats. You can circulate among the groups and note individual student performance, and you can also collect the individual assignments and check them. Critical to the effective utilization of groups to support individual learning is the quality of interaction among students. It is important to note the degree to which students provide explanations and demonstrations for each other instead of only giving answers or ignoring peer questions. A good way to encourage quality interaction is to ask students to be sure that *everyone* in the group—not just one or two students—can explain the ideas or concepts.

An effective monitoring technique is the use of a clipboard with the students' names and enough space to record ratings or notes about performance and behavior during group activities. This technique encourages teachers to record information about all students, not only the active, visible ones. The information can later be used to give feedback to groups and individuals or to add to performance evaluations. Use of this strategy as seldom as once or twice a week can add important information about individuals and supplement other types of monitoring. If you let students know what you are looking for when you use the clipboard, a side benefit of this strategy is that it will improve the identified behaviors.

When group assignments are used, the focus of monitoring shifts to the group's collective progress, along with individual performance. If you provide checkpoints, reminders, and time limits, you will not only give yourself some monitoring milestones, but you will also help students self-monitor. Asking groups to report to you on their progress, plans, or difficulties will also provide additional information about comprehension that you might not obtain through observation alone. As noted in the preceding section on individual accountability, it may be beneficial to include an individual component to a collective assignment. Not only will such data increase your information about each student's achievement, but the procedure itself will also improve individual accountability.

Teachers use various indicators to determine satisfactory group functioning. Because students usually have a specific task to perform in the group, it is not difficult to determine whether students are engaged in a suitable activity. When students are talking with each other about the task and performing behaviors needed to complete an assignment such as writing, assembling materials, practicing, or constructing, then teachers can easily identify appropriate on-task behavior. Teachers also watch for signs that individual students may be uninvolved or disengaged. Momentary off-task behavior usually can be ignored, but if it is prolonged, some form of intervention may be needed. Another indicator is the level and nature of emotion exhibited by students. Teachers should take note of students in a group when they exhibit tense, angry, or hostile behaviors. Such emotional reactions suggest frustration or potential conflicts that could escalate and therefore call for an early intervention to prevent the development of more serious problems. Occasionally, a student will exhibit very oppositional behaviors in a group, refusing to compromise or share in the work. Intervention by the teacher will be required to help divert the group's focus from the negative behavior and toward constructive action.

Interventions for Groups

These are closely tied to the monitoring features just described. The most common interventions are simple ones—easy to use and brief. Individual students and groups who are off-task may be verbally or nonverbally redirected to the task. Students who persist in inappropriate behaviors can be given a short time out (e.g., one or two minutes initially) or sent to work alone for a longer time if they don't respond to milder interventions. Other interventions for individuals are described in detail in Chapter 9.

Conferences with students can be used more readily during group time than during whole-class activities because other students will be occupied with their group tasks. Conferences typically are brief—less than a minute or so—and consist of listening to concerns and providing feedback to the student or group, along with redirection and a plan for changing the behavior. Such an approach is more effective than simple reprimands because it offers an alternative behavior. A brief conference also allows the teacher to provide feedback on the spot rather than delaying it so long that it would prove ineffective.

Teachers also engage groups in a conference when a group process has broken down. Examples include groups in which students don't ask or give assistance constructively, make poor progress toward the group's goal, or encounter a problem they aren't able to overcome. Teachers often describe their role as that of *facilitator* or *mediator* in this type of conference. While the teacher may provide feedback about the problem and a reality check for the group's perceptions, students are encouraged to solve the problem themselves. Strategies teachers use to facilitate a solution include asking students to identify the problem and suggest alternatives, asking for reactions and comments, and calling for the group to select a different approach to try. As a last resort, teachers may offer a solution or change group membership if the problem proves intractable.

Effective Group-Work Skills

To work effectively in a group, students need to practice a number of group-work skills. These include *social skills,* such as active listening, sharing, and supporting; *explaining skills,* which convey understanding and meaning in academic tasks; and *leadership skills,* such as planning and demonstrating initiative and enthusiasm.

Social Skills

Active listening includes listening to others without interrupting, being able to summarize others' ideas, incorporating them into the ongoing discussion, and using them constructively in completing the group's assignment. Sharing materials and taking turns are also necessary for effective cooperation. Another social skill is giving support, which includes accepting differences, being friendly, and encouraging others. Students who lack social skills may insist on doing things their way, argue frequently, ignore or put down another student's contributions, or not participate in the group's work.

The ability to work in a group depends on social skills, so teachers usually emphasize their development. One way to do so is to teach students what skills are needed for group work when group activities are first introduced and later as the need arises. Teachers may even teach certain phrases for students to use when summarizing, asking questions, expressing disagreement, and so on. Another way to promote social skills is to assign roles that require their use. For example, some teachers assign the role of encourager (who makes certain that each group member has an opportunity to contribute to the group's work and interaction and who gives positive feedback to others when appropriate) or summarizer (who helps keep track of ideas and progress).

Explaining Skills

These skills are an important aspect of group work, and they are critical to the development of academic outcomes. Indicators of explaining skills are student comments that describe a problem, assignment, or goal. Student comments might also identify steps to be accomplished or followed to complete a task as well as reasons for the steps. Students might summarize the work they have done or plan to do. If a group assignment includes answering questions, students could give their answers and describe how they obtained them.

Another important component of the explaining process is seeking explanations from others. This may involve students' describing what they do and do not understand and asking for help from other group members. Seeking such help is unlikely to occur unless other students in the group practice good social skills. To encourage seeking help, the teacher might say, "No one knows everything. If there's something you don't understand, it's smart to ask for help from the group. And if someone asks for help, the friendly thing to do is to give a good explanation."

Student interactions about content are essential to the process of constructing meaning. Interactions enhance comprehension and are the basis for learning. Most students will need encouragement to engage in these behaviors because conversations about content are not a natural part of their interactions. Some ways to do so include the following:

- Assign the role of summarizer to a student and rotate the role.
- Have students turn to a partner and explain something; then have the partner "explain back."
- Have each student in the group write one question; members of the group then answer it.
- Lead a discussion about how to give a good explanation and how to ask for help.
- Conduct role-plays of asking for help and explaining.

- Have students write their group's ideas on a chart and present them to the class.
- Give the groups one question to answer and have each member record other members' contributions or restate them.

Leadership Skills

When a group has someone who steps up and says, "Let's figure out what we need to get this job done," it has someone who is practicing a leadership skill. Desired attributes include demonstrating initiative, planning, and enthusiasm. Good social skills also complement this repertoire, as does basic competence in the content relevant to the group's task. Many teachers value these skills highly and try to form groups with at least one student who exhibits them "naturally."

Although leadership skills are developed over time and students possess them in varying degrees, all students can make some progress toward acquiring or improving them. You can help develop leadership skills by assigning roles such as presenter or discussion leader, which give students the opportunity to demonstrate initiative and gain confidence. You can also identify various student leadership actions, such as planning steps for the group to reach a goal, encouraging and supporting other group members, finding alternative ways to complete the group's assignment, or volunteering for a difficult job. Discuss these behaviors with the class, perhaps making a list to which students could refer. Give positive feedback to students who engage in these and other leadership activities. Opportunities to practice leadership skills are especially important for the quiet though competent students, who might not otherwise be noticed and who need encouragement to develop these skills.

FOR REFLECTION

Supporters of the use of cooperative learning emphasize the interdependent nature of social life, including work and family settings. They also emphasize the social nature of learning and the importance of interaction in constructing meaning. Some educators and commentators, however, have expressed concerns about overreliance on groups, arguing that group learning wastes time, especially of gifted students who must help their less able peers. These critics also dislike the focus on group rather than individual performance. What is your position on these issues? Should groups be used more or less frequently in your teaching field? To accomplish what goals?

Beginning the Use of Cooperative Learning Groups

Whether you begin to use groups at the start of the year or wait until later, there are several matters you should address. It will be important that the physical arrangement of the classroom supports the use of groups, especially if you plan to use them extensively. You should also choose carefully the initial tasks for the groups because you will want to set the stage for subsequent group activities. Group composition will be important to determine; students need to be able to work constructively with each other and aid each other's learning. Finally, you will plan how to teach the group skills needed for effective group functioning.

In some schools and school districts, cooperative group activities are very prevalent. If you teach in such a district, your students may have developed some group skills, and they may need less coaching from you. It's best not to assume too much, though, at the start. You can modify your use of groups to accommodate the students' capabilities when you begin to observe them in this format.

Room Arrangement

Try to arrange places for groups to meet so that you can monitor them easily. Establish a central materials storage area with easy access so that your "materials managers" can obtain needed supplies quickly. Other important aspects of room arrangement were discussed earlier in this chapter, as well as in Chapter 1.

Procedures and Routines

Don't assume that because students follow the rules during whole-class and seatwork activities, they will automatically do so during group work. Instead, be prepared to articulate to students your specific expectations for talk and movement during group work (e.g., "Keep talk within your group only"). Also teach a group attention signal so that you can refocus class attention as needed (see the earlier section on group attention signals). These procedures should be explained to students and reviewed when necessary.

Forming Groups

Initially, you may have students work in pairs, with students simply reviewing each other's work or discussing a question or problem. You also might use pairs to work on a classwork exercise or to practice spelling words or number facts. When pairs are used in such straightforward ways, most students generally will not need to move to new locations, and the activity will be brief, placing fewer demands on the students and you.

When assigning students to larger groups, a main consideration of most teachers is to represent in each group a *range of achievement* in the subject. A second concern is often to place a leader (see the earlier section on leadership skills) in each group. Teachers also try to avoid grouping students together who don't get along or who are argumentative. Such a student often works best in a group with someone who has good leadership abilities, including social skills.

Some teachers avoid placing in the same group students who are at opposite *extremes* in achievement levels in the content area; for example, they would not place a very high achiever and a very low achiever in the same group. Instead, they seek less variation, though their groups are still more heterogeneous than separate groups of high- and low-achieving students. These teachers' concern is that the pace of work and the discourse patterns in the groups with very high students may be inappropriate for and intimidating to the lower performing students, resulting in their withdrawal and task avoidance. In groups having midrange achievers, the pace of work is more likely to encourage the lower achiever's participation. This principle is obviously dependent on the degree of social and explaining skills possessed by the various students.

No hard-and-fast rules can be stated about how long groups should stay together. Some teachers change group membership frequently—as often as every few weeks. Most leave students in the same group for longer periods but reshuffle the deck at least a few times each semester. Some teachers allow students to form their own groups for special activities or projects or for a change of pace but rarely allow self-selected groups for an extended time, except in a special project.

At the beginning of the year, before you know your students very well, it may be instructive to allow students to choose partners for a few initial activities. Doing so will provide valuable information about who works well with whom, which you can use when forming more permanent groups. After groups are formed, they should be monitored for signs of conflict. Don't be too quick to step in with a solution, but do ask groups to address such problems. Giving students responsibility to deal with group problems can create an opportunity for learning. As students acquire group skills and experience success working together, conflict usually diminishes. When conflicts cannot be resolved in a reasonable time within the group, however, most teachers choose to move antagonistic students to new groups. Later in the year, when such students have become more cooperative, they might be given an opportunity to work together again.

Initial Group Tasks

Students who don't have much experience working in groups will need to develop their skills in uncomplicated tasks rather than in complex projects. Holubec (1992), a pioneer in the development of cooperative learning groups, describes a number of simple, easy-to-implement activities for beginning group work. Her suggestions include the following:

> *Turn to your partner.* Ask students to explain something or compare answers to a problem or exercise. Students might also choose the next step or add to an answer. As the students gain experience, this format can be used for problem solving.
> *Drill partners.* Use this for practicing material that must be memorized.
> *Reading buddies.* Students read to each other. This activity can be built on after a while by asking students to summarize or make up a question for the partner.

Checking. Students compare answers and resolve discrepancies. Each student must be able to explain the answer.

Reviewers. Students review for a quiz or test or prepare for an oral report by working together to develop questions or by asking and answering each other's questions.

It is important not to rush into complex group work until you build a foundation of practice and skills. Teaching group-work skills is easier in simpler formats with uncomplicated procedures. After your students have had success in some of these initial group tasks, they will be ready for more complex group formats and assignments.

Teaching Group Skills

Decide on a set of basic skills that your students should acquire. One such set might include *listening, explaining, asking for help, encouraging,* and *sharing.* A good way to begin the teaching process is to have a whole-class discussion about what is needed to work cooperatively with others. To build a rationale for working together, some teachers like to broaden the scope of the discussion to include home and neighborhood or extracurricular groups as well as classroom groups and to discuss the character and life skills that are needed. Eventually, of course, the discussion needs to address concrete behaviors that constitute good listening, explaining, and so forth. Signs can be posted listing desired group behaviors (a local school supply store may have some that pertain specifically to group activities).

Descriptions of desirable group skills can be included in a handout, or they can be listed on an overhead for students to copy into their notebooks. This activity naturally permits discussion of group processes and goals, along with opportunities to give examples and model desired behaviors, perhaps through role-plays.

Providing students with examples and models of desired group skills should be accompanied by opportunities for practice and feedback. Remember that it will take many weeks for some students to feel comfortable with the new demands of group participation. Be patient. Rather than reviewing all desirable group skills, pick one and spend time discussing it. Let students practice it, and give them feedback as they work in groups. Introduce other skills in subsequent days or weeks.

Mrs. Walker focused on one group skill a week until her social studies class developed an effective repertoire by the end of the first six weeks of the school year. During the first week, she emphasized participating during group work; during the second week, she focused on remaining on-task. Subsequent weeks were devoted to cooperating, encouraging, explaining, and active listening. Mrs. Walker introduced each skill in a whole-class discussion, soliciting examples, suggestions, and a rationale from her students. During the first week, she displayed on the overhead a five-point rating scale for "participating" and indicated what she would be looking for as students worked in groups. At the end of several group-work activities that week, she engaged students in a discussion about the skill, asked them to review their performance, and then shared her assessments with the groups. In each subsequent week, Mrs. Walker added a new scale so that groups received feedback about their progress in acquiring the skills.

Students need feedback about how they are performing group skills. Mrs. Walker's use of scales is one way to focus students on specific components of group work. Another way is to conduct whole-class discussions about group-work activities. Such a discussion can begin with a request that students evaluate an aspect of their group work, indicating what went well and what could be improved, or they might be asked to describe how someone in their group performed one of the group skills effectively. Students might also be asked to describe what makes it difficult to perform a particular skill and how that problem might be overcome. Getting students to talk about their group experience is one of the best ways to help them develop good monitoring and self-regulation skills.

Teachers can also provide feedback to a particular group or to an individual, as needed. Usually, such feedback occurs as the teacher moves around the room, monitoring the activity. During the initial stages of group work, when students are acquiring group skills, it is especially important that appropriate behaviors be identified and supported. Interventions with students who aren't practicing good group behaviors can sometimes be addressed as a group problem. Assigning the role of encourager (one who monitors participation and makes sure each student has a turn) may help stimulate reluctant students. At other times, discussing the situation with the individual student may be the best way to encourage the student to practice group behaviors.

Some group skills can also be taught by assigning roles to individual students in a group. Roles such as materials manager, recorder, discussion leader, encourager, discussant, or reporter entail the use of specific skills. By assigning some of these roles to students, teachers encourage them to practice new behaviors. Rotating the roles among group members permits all students to gain experience. Using roles also helps promote interdependence among the group members because each student has a unique job to perform for the group. Frequently used roles can be written on cards, along with key behaviors, and laminated. Posters with role descriptions can also be displayed at easy-to-see locations until students have mastered the basics.

Using Group and Individual Rewards

Most students consider working in groups a desirable activity, so it is not usually necessary to establish an extrinsic group or individual reward structure to accompany the use of cooperative learning groups. Teachers do sometimes find using rewards helpful as an extra motivational tool to encourage students to practice appropriate group skills or to improve participation of undermotivated students.

Mr. Galvan used a weekly raffle system with his middle school students, rewarding them with "tickets" for desirable group behavior. A group also received bonus tickets when all of its members did well on an assignment. Students initialed their tickets, and at the end of the week, Mr. Galvan drew four or five from a box; winners received small toys or privileges as prizes.

Ms. Frank gave points to groups for desirable behaviors, such as getting ready or cleaning up promptly, helping and sharing, or listening and explaining. She would award points during group work, accompanied by feedback when it wasn't obvious what the points were for: "I really like how you have been explaining the ideas to each other rather than just giving the answers." She also awarded points during wrap-up discussions with the whole class, noting when she observed good examples of some desirable behavior during group work. She kept a tally of points, and when a group reached a set number of points, it got to choose a reward from a menu of desirable activities, such as extra time on the class computers.

Judicious use of rewards can direct student attention to important behaviors and make it more likely that students will employ them. Group rewards, moreover, can strengthen cohesiveness through a common goal and the shared positive affect that results when the group succeeds. As we note in Chapter 7, in the discussion on intrinsic motivation, extrinsic rewards should be a *supplement* to other more natural consequences of student accomplishment, such as recognition, positive feedback, other forms of praise, and the satisfaction that accompanies learning and goal attainment. As long as these consequences are abundant, the use of some additional group and individual reinforcers should not interfere with intrinsic motivation.

Further Reading

Cohen, E. G. (1998). Making cooperative learning equitable. *Educational Leadership, 56,* 18–21.

Status differences among students reduce the participation and learning of lower status students. Cohen provides some practical strategies teachers can use to improve lower status students' opportunities, including teacher emphasis on the multiple abilities needed to accomplish many group tasks and altering student expectations about the competence of the lower status students.

Edwards, C., & Stout, J. (1990). Cooperative learning: The first year. *Educational Leadership, 47*(4), 38–43.

In this article, two teachers offer suggestions about critical elements in the process of implementing cooperative learning activities. These ideas will be helpful to anyone trying it out, whether at the beginning of the year or later.

Johnson, D. W., & Johnson, R. T. (1999). *Learning together and alone: Cooperative, competitive, and individualistic learning* (5th ed.). Boston: Allyn and Bacon.

The authors are well known for their extensive research program on group processes and have been leaders in the development of cooperative group teaching methods. This book surveys research comparing cooperative learning to other traditional classroom methods and also presents the authors' suggestions for implementing effective group learning.

Pederson, J. E., & Digby, A. D., (Eds.) (1995). *Secondary schools and cooperative learning: Theories, models, and strategies.* New York: Garland.

Various models of cooperative learning are reviewed. Different chapters describe applications in secondary mathematics, science, social studies, English, and other subject areas.

Slavin, R. E. (1995). *Cooperative learning: Theory, research, and practice* (2nd ed.). Boston: Allyn and Bacon.

This authoritative book provides a good overview of cooperative learning approaches, along with a careful description of research. The author has done extensive research and development in this field, and this book provides a thorough review of his and his colleagues' work.

 ## Suggested Activities

1. Observe a class using cooperative learning. As you do so, note room arrangement features and routines that support group learning. Use Checklist 6 as an observation guide.

2. Choose a lesson or unit that you have observed being taught in an individual or whole-class instructional format, or find one in a teacher's edition or curriculum guide. Identify how you might use cooperative learning groups to teach some component of the lesson or unit. Discuss the modifications you would make to incorporate concepts presented in this chapter.

3. In a group, discuss (a) problems associated with fostering individual responsibility in a group-based task and (b) how to give feedback to individuals about academic performance and individual behaviors in the group setting. What are some workable, efficient strategies for enhancing responsibility and providing feedback?

4. Reread Case Study 4.1, which illustrates one teacher's approach to introducing cooperative groups at the beginning of the year.

    a. Note concepts described in this chapter that are evident in Ms. James's procedures and strategies. What functions do the associated procedures and strategies serve?

    b. Are any areas discussed in this chapter not present in Ms. James's classroom during the first three days? Would you suggest introducing them? Why or why not?

5. Review some lesson plans at the website www.eduref.org (click on the "Lesson Plans" button). You can search this site's large collection by grade level and subject. You can find examples of cooperative group lessons if you type "cooperative groups" in the search descriptor. Share a favorite lesson plan with colleagues. Try to anticipate possible management issues that could arise if you were to teach this lesson, and get feedback from others in your group.

6. Browse some other informative websites for cooperative learning. These include www.co-operation.org, the website for the Cooperative Learning Cen-

ter at The University of Minnesota, and www.psychologymatters.org/ jigsaw.html, sponsored by the American Psychological Association. The latter site has updated research on using jigsaw grouping in classrooms.

 Checklist 6

Planning for Cooperative Group Instruction

Check When Complete	Item	Notes
	Room Arrangement	
☐	A. How will student seating be arranged?	_____
☐	B. How will group materials/supplies be stored?	_____
	Routines and Expectations	
☐	A. What are your expectations for student movement to/from and during group work?	_____
☐	B. What expectations about talking will you communicate to students?	_____
☐	C. What group attention signals will you use?	_____
☐	D. Will students have specific roles?	_____
☐	E. What group skills need to be discussed, modeled, or practiced?	_____
	Monitoring, Accountability, and Feedback Procedures	
☐	A. When will group work have individual products, group products, or both?	_____
☐	B. How will individual or group work be assessed?	_____
☐	C. How will you monitor student behavior and work during group activities?	_____

(continued)

Check When Complete	Item	Notes
☐	D. How will students receive feedback about individual and group performance?	
☐	E. How will students receive feedback about their behavior in groups?	
	Group Skills That Need to Be Discussed/Modeled/Practiced	
☐	A. Social skills	
☐	B. Explaining skills	
☐	C. Leadership skills	

7

Maintaining Appropriate Student Behavior

As you have seen in the first six chapters, good classroom management depends on very careful planning of classroom organization, rules, procedures, and instruction. All the preparation will pay large dividends when the students arrive. Readiness alone, however, is not sufficient to sustain good behavior throughout the year. You will have to be actively involved in maintaining student cooperation and compliance with necessary classroom rules and procedures. You cannot assume that students will behave appropriately just because you once discussed what was expected of them.

In particular, do not be lulled into complacency by the good behavior of your students during the first few days of school. Most classes are cooperative initially even if the teacher does not pay careful attention to maintaining good behavior, but a class that seems to begin very well may ultimately become disruptive and difficult to control. Behavior problems can have a gradual onset, developing over several weeks or even months. It is usually possible to avoid these problems, but doing so depends on understanding why they occur and what to do to prevent them. Because problems develop gradually, the causes are not always apparent to the teacher or even to an observer unfamiliar with the history of the classroom.

Teachers who are able to maintain a high level of cooperative, appropriate student behavior often share a number of characteristics and skills. One of these is observant monitoring of students. Such teachers have greater awareness of classroom events and behaviors, which improves their ability to detect and treat problems and help students who are having difficulty. Another characteristic of good managers is consistency in the use of rules and procedures and in their dealings with students who do not follow them. A third attribute is prompt management of inappropriate behavior, before it escalates or spreads. Finally, good behavior is maintained by creating a positive classroom climate, with an emphasis on encouraging appropriate behavior. This chapter discusses ways in which these concepts can be implemented.

Monitoring Student Behavior

To be an effective monitor of classroom behavior, you must know what to look for. Two categories of behavior are especially important.

1. Student involvement in learning activities
2. Student compliance with classroom rules and procedures

Student involvement is indicated by many behaviors, including attention during presentations and discussions, and progress on seatwork and other assignments. Students' compliance with classroom rules and procedures will be easy to monitor if you have a clear set of expectations for student behavior and have communicated them to the class.

Monitoring student behavior during presentations requires that you stand or sit so that you can see the faces of all of the students and that you scan the room frequently. Actively monitoring a class by walking among students tends to increase student attention (Fifer 1986). Some teachers are not very good monitors of student behavior during whole-class activities because they focus their attention on a limited number of students, especially those seated in the middle rows and at the front desks. Other teachers "talk to the chalkboard." In either case, the teacher does not have a very clear perception of overall student response to the presentation or of what may be occurring at the periphery of the class. During your presentations, therefore, try to move around and develop "active eyes." If you notice commotion involving several students and you have no idea what is going on, this is a sign that you have not been monitoring closely enough.

When students are working on individual assignments, monitoring should be done by circulating around the classroom to check each student's progress periodically and to provide individual feedback. You will, of course, help students who request assistance; however, you should not just "chase hands." If you do, you will not be aware of the progress of all students. It is very difficult to monitor student progress on assignments from your desk or from any other fixed location, so spend as little time as possible at one place. If you must work at your desk for a time, get up periodically and circulate around the room to check on students' progress and to make sure that directions are being followed correctly. If you must spend a long time (e.g., more than a minute or two) helping an individual student, avoid doing it at the student's desk unless you can monitor the rest of the class from that position. For instance, if the student's seat is in the middle of the room, half of the class will be behind you. In such a case, call the student to your desk, to the front of the room, or to some other location from which you can easily see all students. Finally, if for some reason you must work at your desk or at any other location, don't let students congregate around the area. They will obstruct your view of the class, and they may distract students seated nearby. Instead, call students to you one at a time.

A technique for monitoring at the beginning of seatwork that is effective in getting everyone started is to begin the work as a whole-group activity. Have students get out the necessary materials (be sure to look for these on the students' desks), head their papers, and then do the first exercise or answer the first question or two under your direction. Check and discuss this work with the class. This makes it easy for you to scan the room to be sure that everyone has begun and to determine whether students understand what to do.

A critical monitoring task is checking assignments. Collect them regularly and look them over even when students do the checking in class. Keep your grade book current so that you will be able to detect students who are doing poor work or who skip assignments. If you give a long-term assignment, be sure to check progress regularly. You may even wish to give a grade or assign points toward a grade at these progress checkpoints. To encourage self-monitoring, you may also have students keep their own checklists of assignments.

Consistency

The dictum "be consistent" has been repeated more frequently than the Pledge of Allegiance. It is still worth some discussion, however, because its meaning is not always clear. In the classroom, consistency means retaining the same expectations for behaviors that are appropriate or inappropriate in particular activities; it also means that these expectations apply to every student on all occasions. For example, if students are expected to work silently during seatwork activities on Monday, the same procedure is in effect for all students on Tuesday, Wednesday, and so on. Consistency also applies to the use of penalties. For example, if the penalty for tardy arrival to class is detention, the teacher makes sure that all tardy students receive the penalty and that this procedure is followed even on the days when it is inconvenient to administer it or in spite of the pleading of individual students that an exception be made. Obvious inconsistency in the use of procedures or in the application of penalties usually causes students to "test the limits" by not following the procedure or by repeating whatever behavior was to have evoked the penalty. These events can rapidly escalate and force the teacher either to abandon the procedure or to tolerate high levels of inappropriate behavior. Because neither outcome is desirable, it is best to avoid the problem by resolving to be consistent in the first place.

Of course, it is not possible to be totally consistent, as there will be occasions when the most reasonable course of action is to make an exception to a rule or procedure. For example, if a student's individualized education program stipulates a particular way to handle rule violations for a special student, the plan must be followed even if you might respond differently to other students who committed the same infraction. Or a deadline for an assignment may be extended when a student has a valid reason, or some procedures might be changed to accommodate a special event. Note that procedures used routinely for some activities but not for others are not inconsistent. For example, you may stipulate that students should remain in their seats during discussions or presentations but that during seatwork they may get materials, sharpen pencils, or turn in papers as needed without permission. As long as you have differentiated between the activities when you explain the procedures to the students, no problems should occur.

Undesirable inconsistency usually arises from three sources. First, the procedures or rules are not reasonable, workable, or appropriate. Second, the teacher fails to monitor students closely and does not detect inappropriate behavior. This gives the appearance of inconsistency when the teacher does detect misbehavior and tries to stop it. Finally, the teacher may not feel strongly enough about the procedure or rule to enforce it or to use the associated penalty. If you find yourself caught in an inconsistency that is becoming a problem, you have the following alternatives:

- Reteach the procedure. Take a few minutes to discuss the problem with the class and reiterate your desire that the rule or procedure be followed. Then enforce it.
- Modify the procedure and then reintroduce it.
- Abandon the procedure or consequence and possibly substitute another in its place.

The alternative you choose depends on the circumstances and on the importance of the component to your classroom management system.

Prompt Management of Inappropriate Behavior

Prompt handling of inappropriate behavior helps to prevent its escalation. Behaviors of concern include lack of involvement in learning activities, prolonged inattention or work avoidance, and obvious violations of classroom rules and procedures. Effective managers have a high degree of "withitness"; that is, they are so attuned to the class that they are able to detect off-task behavior and stop it before it escalates (see Chapter 5 for more discussion of withitness). It is not a good idea to ignore persistent off-task behavior because prolonged inattention makes it difficult for the students both to learn and to complete assignments. Violations of rules and failure to follow procedures create many problems we have already discussed. These behaviors should be dealt with directly but without overreaction. A calm, reasoned tone or approach is more productive and less likely to lead to confrontation. The following alternatives are recommended.

Four Simple Ways to Manage Inappropriate Behavior

We will assume that the classroom tasks are within the capabilities of the students. If not, then the first priority in addressing problem behaviors is to provide suitable instruction or to modify the tasks. If the suitability of the task is not at issue, the following simple strategies are often effective.

1. Make eye contact with or move closer to the student. Use a signal, such as a finger to the lips or a head shake, to prompt the appropriate behavior. Monitor until the student complies.

2. If the student is not following a procedure correctly, a simple reminder of the correct procedure may be effective. You can either state the correct procedure or note other students who are doing what is expected.
3. When the student is off-task—that is, not working on an assignment—redirect his or her attention to the task: "Robert, you should be writing now." Or "Becky, the assignment is to complete all of the problems on the page." Check the student's progress shortly thereafter to make sure that work is continuing.
4. Ask or tell the student to stop the inappropriate behavior. Then monitor until it stops and the student begins constructive activity.

Sometimes it is inconvenient or would interrupt an activity to use these procedures immediately. In such a case, make a mental note of the problem and continue the activity until a more appropriate time occurs. Then tell the student you saw what was occurring, and discuss what the appropriate behavior should have been. When possible, discussions with individual students about their inappropriate behaviors should be conducted as privately as feasible. Of course, privacy in a classroom is not likely to be complete unless you remove the student from the room, a strategy that you will usually not employ because of your responsibility for the entire class. Ways to achieve partial privacy include conferring with a student at your desk, whispering or speaking in a low tone, and using nonverbal signals to convey a message to a student. When you use such strategies, you also communicate to other students your intention that the conversation be considered private. This will reduce the amount of peer attention the student receives and is less likely to intrude into the ongoing activity.

The four procedures just listed are easy to use, cause little interruption of class activities, and enable students to correct their behavior. If a student persists in the behavior, however, some other alternatives must be used. If the rest of the class is working and does not need your immediate attention, a brief talk with the student and/or assessing an appropriate penalty may be sufficient. If that doesn't settle the matter or if an immediate conference isn't desirable or feasible, tell the student to wait after class to speak to you. If the student is being disruptive, send him or her either to a "time-out" desk in another part of the room or to the hall. Then talk with the student when you have time. Your goal in discussing the problem behavior with the student is to determine the reason for the problem, to make clear what the unacceptable behavior is and what the student should be doing, and then to obtain a commitment from the student for acceptable behavior. Some teachers like to have the student put the commitment in writing in a brief "contract" or "plan," specifying what he or she agrees to do, before being allowed to return to class. Additional strategies for dealing with problem behaviors are discussed in detail in Chapters 8 and 9, so we do not pursue this topic here.

Building a Positive Climate

This chapter has emphasized maintaining appropriate behavior by applying procedures and rules consistently, handling problems promptly, and using nonintrusive interventions when possible to maintain activity flow and student involvement in lessons. We now want to emphasize the importance of keeping a positive perspective and avoiding overdwelling on student misbehavior or inadequacies. Sometimes teachers get caught in the trap of seeing only faults and problems and overlooking the better features of students' behavior. Instead of rejoicing when twenty-nine students are involved in learning, we complain about the one student who is off-task.

> Mr. Acerbic's ninth-grade physical education class could do no right. Although most of the students initially participated willingly in the class activities, students never seemed to perform quickly or well enough for their teacher. "Come on, you horseflies, quit buzzing and listen up," he would yell when he heard talking. "Laps" around the gym were given for even slight infractions such as inattention; there always seemed to be three or four students making the rounds at any given time. Instead of feedback about good performance, criticism was usually given for inadequacies. Although students took the constant carping in stride, they displayed little zest for the class.

Although poor performance should not be ignored—students need specific, corrective feedback to know what to improve—it is important that the climate for learning be positive. This means that students should look forward to the class. They should expect to learn and to receive assistance when they encounter difficulty and should feel supported in their efforts. Such a climate can be fostered by communicating positive expectations to students, praising good performance, and at times, using additional rewards.

Teacher expectations can be communicated in a variety of ways, some obvious and others subtle. (For a thorough description of this aspect of teacher behavior, see Good & Brophy 2003, chap. 3.) Teachers can:

- Identify appropriate instructional goals and discuss them with students so that they are clear about what is expected.
- Insist that students complete work satisfactorily.
- Refuse to accept excuses for poor work.
- Communicate acceptance of imperfect initial performance when students struggle to achieve new learning.
- Convey confidence in the students' ability to do well.
- Display an encouraging, "can do" attitude that generates student excitement and self-confidence.
- Avoid comparative evaluations, especially of lower ability students, that might cause them to conclude that they cannot accomplish the objectives.

By communicating positive expectations, teachers lay the foundation for students to attempt new tasks and reach new goals. When students know that their teacher believes them to be capable, they are more likely to work harder.

A positive climate for learning is also created by appropriate teacher praise. When used well, teacher praise can be uplifting and provide great encouragement to a student. The most powerful type of teacher praise provides the student with information about what aspect of student performance is praiseworthy and also demonstrates that the teacher is impressed with the quality of the student's work. In other words, effective praise provides both informative feedback and genuine teacher approval. It can also accompany suggestions for improvement (constructive criticism) without loss of effect.

Public praise that focuses on student *accomplishment* works better than praise for student effort. When the teacher praises only for "working hard," students may assume that the teacher thinks they aren't very able. When you know that a student put forth considerable effort and you want to acknowledge it, be sure the praise also includes an emphasis on the student's achievement. "Gloria, all your hard work paid off because your project was beautifully done. The organization of ideas and the extra details in the descriptions were outstanding!" Likewise, praise should be deserved and it should not be too easily obtained. Public praise of a student for success on an easy task can suggest to the rest of the class (and the student who was praised) that the teacher believes he or she has little ability.

It is a good idea to look for private ways to provide praise. Written comments on papers, tests, and other assignments offer excellent opportunities for quality praise. Private conversations, conferences with parents, notes home, and informal contacts also offer opportunities for praising students. Private praise avoids some of the complications of public praise and permits the teacher to include a greater variety of performances and behaviors as its focus. Further discussion of the uses of teacher praise can be found in Emmer (1988) and Brophy (1998).

 ## Improving Class Climate through Incentives or Rewards

Extra incentives or rewards can help build a positive climate. The improvement in class climate occurs because the incentives add interest or excitement to the class routine, while also directing attention toward appropriate behavior and away from inappropriate behavior. Moreover, when students are rewarded rather than punished, they are more likely to respond positively to the teacher, contributing to a mutually supportive pattern of interaction.

Before introducing an external incentive, you should consider several factors that might affect its appropriateness and effects. Check your school or district policies because sometimes the use of incentives is restricted. You would not want to promise a field trip or party only to find out that it was prohibited by school board policy.

Your rewards should target the behaviors you would like to encourage. Rewards too easily earned or too difficult to achieve lose their motivational effect. Also, you should be concerned about whether the use of a reward takes too much class time for recordkeeping or other administrative tasks. Avoid using complex systems that distract you and your students from a focus on learning. Start with simple procedures and add to them when reasonable.

Be careful not to set up incentives that only the most able students can achieve. Systems that encourage excessive competition for scarce rewards will discourage students who don't have much chance. The examples in this section and in the case at the end of the chapter include a variety of types. Combine these ideas with those of other teachers and your own experience to develop some alternatives for use at various times of the year. Many different types of rewards, including symbols, recognition, activities, and materials, can be used with secondary students. Each of these types is described in the following sections with examples.

Grades and Other Symbols

The most prevalent form of incentive is the letter or numerical grade, although other symbols such as checks or stars are sometimes used with students in middle school classes. Good grades are a powerful incentive for most students when they are perceived to be a direct reflection of their achievement and competence. Therefore, it is important to tie as many facets of student work to grades as possible. In addition, you should make clear to students the basis for determining grades to help them know what they have to do to achieve good grades. Procedures for managing student work have already been discussed at length in earlier chapters, so we do not dwell on them here.

One caveat is worth noting. Occasionally, teachers react negatively to the grading system because they feel that too much emphasis is placed on grades and not enough on learning. This feeling may cause the teacher to project a casual attitude about grades and be vague about the grading criteria. This is a mistake; the teacher is still required to assign grades, and the students are left with less control over their fate. A more constructive reaction would be for the teacher to work hard to make the grading criteria reflect the course's learning objectives.

Recognition

These rewards involve some means of giving attention to the student. Examples are the display of student work; awarding a certificate for achievement, improvement, or good behavior; and verbally citing student accomplishments. Some adolescents are embarrassed by being singled out for attention, so giving public recognition to several students at the same time is a better strategy. At a school or grade level, recognition awards are often given at the end of the year or semester, with teachers nominating the recipients. If this is the case in your school, be sure to find out what awards are commonly given. Then tell your students what they are (e.g., awards for attendance, achievement, improvement, honor students, hard work, conduct, good citizens, etc.) early in the year. Early discussion of these awards may motivate your students to work toward them. A similar procedure is to establish and display an honor roll (e.g., an all-star list, honor society, gold record club) to reward students at the end of each grading term. Certificates, stickers with designs appealing to teenagers, or treats can be used in conjunction with the awards, especially for younger secondary students. It is a good idea to spread the honors

around to include a good portion of your students. Thus, don't give awards only for outstanding achievement; have awards for improvement, excellent effort, good conduct, and so on.

FOR REFLECTION

Think back to your middle school and high school years and recall a class that had a very positive climate. List some of the characteristics of that class and what the teacher did to promote it. Compare notes with a friend. To what extent do you recognize concepts from this chapter in these recollections? How can you put these into practice in your own teaching?

Activities as Rewards

Granting privileges, such as working with a friend, free reading time, visits to the school library, or helping to decorate a bulletin board, are examples of activity rewards. A more elaborate activity reward would be a field trip or party. Because school policy may affect your use of the latter activities, check these out before announcing them to your classes. You should, of course, be certain to describe clearly what students need to do to receive such privileges.

Teachers who use activity rewards as incentives for the whole class can permit students to participate in their identification and selection. Thus, a list of possibly desirable (and acceptable) activities can be presented to a class or solicited from students during a discussion; either way, the class can vote on whichever one it wishes to seek. Some whole-class activities that might be used include watching a videotape, fifteen minutes of free time, playing games, listening to music, having a popcorn party, or no homework. A group activity reward should be made contingent on specific desirable behaviors; if the group cooperates, students will receive the incentive. If not, they will lose some or all of the time in the activity. Because the purpose of an activity reward is, at least in part, to promote positive climate building, it is important not to let one or two students spoil the fun for the rest of the class. A chronically uncooperative student or two can be invited to participate, but if they persist in noncompliance, the teacher may exclude them from the activity. Of course, they should be encouraged to participate and given the opportunity to make that choice.

Finding a supervised place for the excluded student during the activity is a drawback to using this incentive. Sometimes teachers solve the problem by arranging ahead of time for the student to go to another teacher's classroom. The student then works on assigned seatwork during that time.

Material Incentives

These rewards include awarding objects of value to students. Examples include food, discarded classroom materials, games, toys, or books. In addition to ascertaining school policy, you must consider your own financial circumstances before deciding to use such rewards. Because you will have a large number of students and limited resources, your use of material rewards will be restricted at best.

When you consider what types of rewards to use in your classes, several factors should be kept in mind. Your rewards should be related to the student behaviors that are most important to you. Obviously, one such set of student behaviors is satisfactory completion of assignments, participation in academic activities, and attainment of learning objectives. For these student behaviors, grades are effective and relevant rewards. Another set of important student behaviors are those related to following rules and major procedures. For these behaviors, recognition and activity rewards can be used effectively. Some teachers hold competitions among their class sections, rewarding the class that has the best behavior record, punctuality, or homework completion rate for a grading period. With the cooperation of other teachers and administrators, good student behavior can be rewarded by a party or dance at the end of the semester for all students who have stayed off the detention list and maintained good attendance records. An incentive on such a grand scale requires much planning and effort as well as the cooperation of large numbers of people.

Caution in the Use of Rewards

Some researchers (e.g., Deci & Ryan 1985; Lepper & Greene 1978) have urged caution in the use of extrinsic rewards, pointing out that under some circumstances their use may reduce students' intrinsic motivation to engage in the rewarded activity. In studies conducted by motivational researchers, subjects are given a reward for engaging in an activity or for reaching some predetermined level of performance. Later, the reward is withdrawn and the subjects are observed when they are free to choose the activity and how long to engage in it. Compared to subjects who do not receive an external incentive, the previously rewarded subjects tend to choose other

activities more or to engage in the rewarded activity for a shorter time. From such results, it is inferred that receiving a reward reduces motivation for an activity if subsequently the extrinsic reward is no longer available.

Explanations of this dampening effect on motivation usually focus on the thinking processes that occur when individuals are given rewards. "This is an unpleasant or boring task, so a reward is needed to maintain engagement" is the implicit message communicated by the use of external rewards. Consequently, the recipient tends to devalue the rewarded activity.

Before concluding that teachers should never use incentives, however, it should be noted that research in this area has a number of limitations with respect to its generalization to classroom practice. For one thing, much of the research has been conducted in laboratory settings in which the activity or task and its accompanying reward occur on only one occasion; in addition, the rewarded activity or task has usually been a highly interesting one, such as a game or puzzle. Thus, the research setting and the tasks are often not very representative of the nature of classroom work for which rewards might usually be used. Furthermore, some research has found that incentives can enhance interest rather than reduce it. After reviewing numerous studies, Cameron and Pierce (1994) concluded, "The present findings suggest that verbal praise and positive feedback enhance people's intrinsic interest. . . . Rewards can have a negative impact on intrinsic motivation when they are offered to people for engaging in a task without consideration of any standard of performance" (p. 397). Bandura (1986) argues that the conflicting findings mean that the effect of extrinsic rewards on intrinsic motivation is weak and that many other factors operate to mediate the effects of the use of incentives.

We believe that the most reasonable application of the research results for classroom use of rewards is to be thoughtful about their use. No purpose will be served by adding a reward to an activity that is already highly interesting to students, and the evidence suggests that to do so may cause reduced motivation. However, many classroom tasks are not highly interesting, especially during the extensive repetition that is needed to produce skilled performance and learning. When student motivation flags, external incentives help to maintain engagement. In fact, the use of incentives is much more desirable than lowering expectations and accepting poor performance or using punishment and threats to attempt to keep students working. Finally, when rewards are used, the teacher can counteract the potential for negative effects on intrinsic motivation by making the reward contingent on some desired level of performance (not only completion of the task), by pointing out the usefulness of the skill, by choosing materials and activities that have more potential for sustaining student interest, by describing long-term outcomes of value to the students, and by demonstrating personal interest in and enthusiasm for the task.

Further Reading

Freiberg, H. J. (1996). From tourists to citizens in the classroom. *Educational Leadership, 54,* 32–36.

An emphasis on creating a positive classroom climate characterizes this article. Based on research he has conducted, Freiberg recommends including increasing student participation in rule setting, allowing students to volunteer for classroom jobs, and making the school a more caring and personal place.

Hidi, S., & Harackiewicz, J. M. (2000). Motivating the academically unmotivated: A critical issue for the 21st century. *Review of Educational Research, 70,* 151–179.

The authors review research on how goals and interests influence motivation for school tasks. While acknowledging the benefits of intrinsic motivation, external reinforcement, situational interest, and performance goals are reviewed and suggested as helpful when working with unmotivated students.

Mueller, C. M., & Dweck, C. S. (1998). Praise for intelligence can undermine children's motivation for performance. *Journal of Personality and Social Psychology, 75,* 33–52.

In a series of six studies, the authors demonstrate that students who receive positive feedback based on their effort continue to exert effort in learning. These students associate struggles with a lack of effort. Students who receive positive feedback based on their intelligence seek to continue looking smart and may choose activities with less challenge. These students associate struggles with lack of ability and therefore may not make further attempts.

Positive school climate. (1998). *Educational Leadership, 56*(1), 1–85.

This issue of the journal has articles that describe a variety of approaches to positive climate setting. Included are such ideas as what makes a high school an inviting place for students, preventing violence, modifying in-school suspension to make it more effective, helping students avoid risky behavior, and building a sense of community.

Raffini, J. P. (1996). *150 ways to increase intrinsic motivation in the classroom.* Boston: Allyn and Bacon.

Many useful strategies are presented in this compendium of classroom activities designed to enhance student motivation. Teachers looking for alternative ways to build classroom climate will find Chapters 4 and 6 especially appealing.

Suggested Activities

1. Find out about school policies that affect your use of rewards and penalties. Also, note any schoolwide policy that you will need to incorporate into your own classroom's procedures.

2. Read the descriptions of the various incentive systems and rewards in Case Study 7.1. What are some of the hoped-for consequences and what are some potential drawbacks of their use? Consider, for example, effects on student attitudes, motivation, and behavior in the short and long run, as well as teacher time and effort. Are there any incentives that especially appeal to you? Any that you would not use with middle school or high school students? Discuss the rationale for your preferences and dislikes. Are there circumstances that would make you more or less inclined to use any of these incentives?

3. Review Checklists 2 and 3 in Chapters 2 and 3 and identify any individual or group rewards you intend to use with major conduct and work procedures. By planning ahead, you will be better able to explain these incentives and be consistent in their use.

CASE STUDY 7.1

EXAMPLES OF INCENTIVES AND REWARDS

Some examples of incentives and rewards that we have observed in secondary school classrooms are described in the following pages. These examples are grouped according to type, although it should be noted that some incentives combine features of several types.

AWARDS AND OTHER RECOGNITION

An attractive award certificate was designed by a teacher and used for individual students at different times during the year. The certificates were especially impressive because each was signed by the principal as well as the teacher. Students were recognized for outstanding effort, along with improvement or accomplishment. To save time, the teacher made many copies of the blank certificates before school began and asked the principal to sign them all at once. She filled them in as needed with students' names and accomplishments. The certificates were awarded both publicly and privately, according to the student and the accomplishment. (Note: Blank achievement/appreciation certificates can also be purchased from school supply stores.)

Honor roll systems are common. Generally, these schoolwide systems have incentive value for better students and don't provide much motivation for the less academically successful. One teacher who taught several classes of low achievers in a school that used ability grouping developed an in-class honor roll that was more accessible to his students. At the end of each grading period, students who had improved their performance or who had participated well in class activities were named to a "Best in the West" honor roll. Their names were placed on a bulletin board honor roll, and they received attractive stickers to display on their notebooks or textbook covers.

COMPETITIONS

For some subjects, long-range incentives are available in the form of city, regional, or statewide competitions (e.g., spelling or composition contests, science and math fairs). Other competitions can be conducted within a school, with classes competing against one another, or they may even be limited to the classes taught by one teacher. The teacher can establish a reward for the first class completing a project or for the class in which all students complete the project first. Within-class rewards can also be offered. One teacher posted spelling grades by class on a bulletin board display. The class with the highest overall score at the end of each month received a special prize or treat.

Teachers who use some form of cooperative groups frequently use group competitions. Students in winning groups may receive a reward, such as extra time in desirable activities (e.g., free reading, computer use, library passes), recognition, certificates, appreciation notes sent home, or bonus points. Competitions can be based on average test scores of students in the group, performance criteria for projects or assignments, desirable group behavior, or improvement on some criterion. When using group competitions, it's best to have a fairly short time frame (e.g., group-of-the-week rather than group-of-the-semester awards).

ENCOURAGING IMPROVEMENT

One of the defining characteristics of the mastery learning approach is the opportunity to re-take tests and redo assignments until a predetermined criterion, such as 80 or 90, is reached. Even if mastery learning is not adopted *in toto,* some teachers allow students to redo incorrectly done assignments to improve their grade. Students might be allowed to earn enough points to bring their grade up to a B level, for example.

EXTRA-CREDIT ASSIGNMENTS

Extra-credit activities are frequently popular with students, and the extra credit earned toward improving a grade is an important incentive for most students. One teacher kept an extra-credit logic problem on the side board, changing it every week or two depending on its difficulty. She also had extra-credit puzzles and worksheets on a front table. These puzzles covered material currently being studied by the class, and students were encouraged to work on them after they had finished their required work. They could also copy them and work on them at home. This teacher had students keep their completed extra-credit problems in a special section of their notebooks, where they were checked when the teacher graded the notebooks. Each correct problem was worth one point and was added to the notebook grade at the end of the grading period.

A science teacher kept a list of extra-credit projects for students to work on individually or in groups. Along with the list of projects was a description of the requirements for each project, its complexity, a deadline for completion, and the number of points earned toward a report card grade. English and social studies teachers frequently have book lists from which students may choose extra-credit reading. A form for students to use when reporting on the book should also be available.

Sometimes bulletin boards are used to display extra-credit work. One math teacher had a picture of a mountain, with math problems relevant to current lessons at each of several elevations. Beneath the mountain were lines for ten student names. The first ten students (from all classes) correctly completing the problems had their names posted under the mountain. When the tenth name was posted, the teacher taped a piece of gum or candy beside each name for the student to remove.

SPECIAL ACTIVITIES AND PRIVILEGES

Allowing students special privileges or permitting them to participate in desired activities is a commonly used reward, and it is often combined with another kind of reward such as recognition. For example, one teacher chose outstanding students each week, based on their attitude, grades, and attendance. The teacher would put students' names on a bulletin board display, and students would receive a special treat on Friday. The teacher also included in the special activity or treat all students who had not received demerits for misbehavior during that week. Another teacher recognized consistent performance by naming all students who had turned in all their work during the previous week as a "Student of the Week" and by placing their names on a special bulletin board display. After being named "Student of the Week" five times during a six-week grading period, the student was entitled to claim an A for one of the four major components of the report card grade. One teacher allowed fifteen or twenty minutes of free reading or game time on Friday when a class had been well behaved throughout the week. Another teacher made an "activity chain" from construction paper, adding a link when class behavior was good each day. When the chain reached a certain length, the class was permitted to have part of a period for a special activity such as free reading or a class competition.

WEEKLY POINT SYSTEM

Point systems are useful because in addition to giving students clearly specified incentives, they encourage them to take responsibility for keeping track of their own work. One teacher gave a handout to students at the beginning of each week with the week's assignments on it. The students recorded points they earned for each assignment, with up to 100 points awarded weekly. Some bonus points were also available for extra-credit assignments, and the teacher could add extra points for good behavior and class participation. These weekly records of points were then used along with test scores to determine report card grades. A common modification of this system is to allow the summary sheet to cover a longer period of time, such as two or three weeks, instead of one week. With older and more mature students, such as those in the upper grades in high school, teachers who apply this system often use a summary sheet for the grading period rather than for each week.

8

Communication Skills for Teaching

Throughout this book, we have emphasized classroom management's preventive and instructional aspects. Not all problems can be prevented, however, and sometimes unobtrusive handling of inappropriate behavior during instruction is not sufficient. The approaches described in this chapter provide some additional means for dealing with problems that persist. The following example illustrates such a situation.

> During the past several days, Debra and Diane have been increasingly inattentive in Ms. Harris's fifth-period class. Their off-task behavior has included whispering with other students and each other, teasing boys seated nearby, and displaying exaggerated boredom with class discussions. Ms. Harris first asked the girls to stop bothering the class, and when that had no effect, she moved the girls to different seats. However, Debra and Diane continued to disrupt by passing notes and calling out loudly to one another.

We will not second-guess Ms. Harris by wondering whether she had communicated expectations clearly or had taken action promptly enough; let us suppose that she had in fact practiced good preventive management skills but that the students misbehaved anyway. No strategy works all the time. What options are now available to Ms. Harris to deal with the situation? Some possible approaches include the following:

- Ignore the problem and hope it goes away.
- Refer the students to an assistant principal.
- Call the students' parents and ask for their help.
- Apply a consequence, such as detention or some other punishment.

Each of these approaches has advantages and limitations. For example, ignoring the problem requires little effort and might work if the students are mainly seeking teacher attention. The description does not, however, suggest that this is a likely reason for the behavior, and ignoring the problem may only allow it to intensify and spread to other students. Referral has the advantage of demanding little of the teacher's time, at least in the short run; it also temporarily removes the disruptive students, and it can have deterrent value. However, it may do nothing in the long run to deal with the problem the students are causing in the class, and although referral may sometimes be a reasonable approach to serious misbehavior, it can easily be overused.

A telephone call to parents sometimes works wonders and is usually worth a try. Unfortunately, parents cannot always stop misbehavior. They do not, after all, accompany their child to your class, nor do they control the cues that are eliciting the misbehavior. Punishing the students by assigning detention or withholding some desirable activity or privilege is another possible reaction. Punishment can stop misbehavior, at least temporarily, and it can deter other students. But punishment can have the disadvantages of creating hostility or resentment and of trapping the teacher and students in a cycle of misbehavior-reaction that leads to power struggles. By itself, punishment does little to teach the student self-control and responsibility.

Because each of these approaches has limitations, you need additional means of coping with problems. This does not mean that other approaches such as ignoring, referral, applying consequences, or involving parents will be supplanted. It does mean that communication strategies should be added to your repertoire to deal with problems that cannot be corrected with minor interventions and to help students learn to take responsibility for their own behavior.

In addition to being helpful when dealing with students whose behavior is creating a problem for the teacher or for other students, communication skills can be used to assist students who are themselves experiencing problems. Teachers frequently become aware of students' problems caused by factors both inside and outside the classroom. Teachers can help these students by being good listeners and by encouraging them to consider alternative ways to solve problems or to adapt to difficult situations.

We use the label *communication skills* for the set of strategies described in this chapter to emphasize that the approach focuses on communicating clearly and effectively with students to help bring about a change in their behavior, in their thinking, or in the situation that has caused the problem. In addition, communication also means being open to information, so teachers also need to be good listeners and try to understand the student's (or parents') concerns and feelings. To become an effective communicator, you need three related skills:

1. **Constructive assertiveness.** This includes communicating your concerns clearly, insisting that misbehavior be corrected, and resisting being coerced or manipulated.
2. **Empathic responding.** This refers to listening to the student's perspective and reacting in ways that maintain a positive relationship and encourage further discussion.
3. **Problem solving.** This component includes several steps for reaching mutually satisfactory resolutions to problems; it requires working with the student to develop a plan for change.

The three elements are derived from a variety of publications, including Egan's *The Skilled Helper,* Gordon's *Teacher Effectiveness Training,* Carkhuff's *The Art of Helping in the 21st Century,* Kottler and Kottler's *Teacher as Counselor,* Glasser's *Reality Therapy,* Alberti's *Assertiveness,* Zuker's *Mastering Assertiveness Skills,* and other standard sources. These books are listed in the References. The treatment of communication skills in this chapter is intended to be an introduction; if you are interested in further reading, we suggest that you refer to one or more of the cited books.

Although this chapter's treatment of assertiveness, empathic responding, and problem solving focuses on their use with students, the skills are very helpful when dealing with parents—especially during parent conferences—and other adults. Thus, the skills described in this chapter have a variety of applications and will improve your effectiveness in handling many classroom and school-related situations.

⟨⟨⟩⟩ Constructive Assertiveness

Assertiveness is the ability to stand up for one's legitimate rights in ways that make it less likely that others will ignore or circumvent them. The adjective *constructive* implies that the assertive teacher does not tear down or attack the student. Constructive assertiveness can be thought of as a general characteristic or attribute that is used in a wide variety of settings or as a set of skills that are more situation specific. Some individuals are assertive in an array of situations (e.g., interacting with strangers, on the job, at parties, in school, etc.), while others lack assertiveness in many of these settings.

Even if you are not generally assertive, you can learn to use assertive behaviors while you are teaching. In fact, doing so may help generalize the behaviors to other situations as you become more confident of your skills. People who are very unassertive (e.g., they feel very nervous whenever they are expected to lead a group; they are unable to begin conversations or to make eye contact with others; they accede to inappropriate demands readily; they are unable to ask others to respect their rights) will find teaching uncomfortable and will have particular difficulty with discipline. Such persons can help themselves in several ways, especially by reading about assertiveness and practicing some of the skills, preferably in situations that are not too uncomfortable, until they begin to develop confidence. It is also possible to obtain professional help, such as from a counseling center, or to enroll in a course or workshop on assertiveness training. A good assertiveness training program usually includes anxiety-reduction exercises, skills training and practice in developing more effective behaviors, and cognitive restructuring to reshape negative thought patterns that interfere with appropriate social interaction.

The elements of constructive assertiveness include

- A clear statement of the problem or issue
- Unambiguous body language
- Insistence on appropriate behavior and resolution of the problem

Assertiveness is not

- Hostile or aggressive
- Argumentative
- Inflexible
- Wimpy, wishy-washy, doormat behavior

Assertiveness lies on a continuum between aggressive, overbearing pushiness and timid, submissive, or weak responses that allow students to trample on the teacher's and other students' rights. By using assertiveness skills, you communicate to students that you are serious about teaching and about maintaining a classroom in which everyone's rights are respected.

Assertiveness has three basic elements:

1. *A clear statement of the problem or concern.* Student misbehavior usually causes problems for teachers by making it difficult to conduct lessons, by slowing down activities, and by subverting routines that help a class run smoothly. When misbehavior persists, it is time for the teacher to let the student know what the problem is from the teacher's point of view. Sometimes a simple description of the problem is enough to produce behavior change because the student becomes more aware of the behavior and begins to monitor it better. Stating the problem has two parts: (a) identifying the student behavior and (b) describing its effects if they are not obvious:

> "Talking and passing notes during discussion distracts other students from the lesson."
>
> "Calling out answers without raising your hand prevents others from participating."
>
> "Wandering around the room disturbs the class."
>
> "Calling other students names causes hard feelings."

By focusing on the behavior and its effects, you can reduce the potential for student defensiveness and keep open the opportunity for achieving a satisfactory resolution.

Notice that the problem descriptions above avoid labeling either students or their behavior (e.g., accusing them of being bad, rude, annoying, inconsiderate, or infantile). Labeling should be avoided because it interferes with behavior change by communicating a negative expectation that the student might accept as valid. Notice also that statements rather than questions are used. Quizzing students (e.g., "Why are you talking?" "Do you think you should be calling someone that name?") invites defensive, sarcastic, or oppositional responses.

2. *Body language.* Constructive assertiveness with students needs to be reinforced by appropriate body language in three areas. The first is making eye contact when addressing the student, especially when describing the problem and when calling for behavior change. Note that there is a difference between eye contact that communicates seriousness and resolve versus an angry glare that emits hostility. In the former case, breaking eye contact from time to time relieves tension. A second area of assertive body language is maintaining an erect posture, facing the student (but not so close as to appear to threaten) to communicate your attention and involvement in the conversation. A third area is matching your facial expressions with the content and tone of your statements (e.g., not grinning when making serious statements).

3. *Obtaining appropriate behavior.* Assertiveness requires that the teacher not be diverted from insisting on appropriate behavior. Students may deny involvement, argue, or blame others (including the teacher). When dealing with such diversionary tactics, remember, "There are many reasons for misbehavior, but no excuses." Although it is possible that others contributed to the problem, the student

needs to accept responsibility for his or her behavior. It is important to listen carefully to and understand the student's situation, but in the end, if the student's behavior is interfering with your ability to teach, the behavior must change. Thus, if a student begins to argue or to deny responsibility for the behavior, you should avoid being sidetracked.

When working with students who are evasive or who are not taking matters very seriously, a little dramatic emphasis may help move them to reconsider the situation. Consider Ms. Harris during a conference with Debra and Diane:

> "I've asked you to stay after class because I'm very concerned with the behavior in the fifth period. Please sit down." (Pauses, looks at the girls.) "I had to stop class three times today because of your loud talking." (Rises from behind desk, voice slightly louder.) "I cannot teach when noise interferes with our discussions." (Sits down, looks at the girls.) "This cannot go on anymore." (Calmer.) "I would like us to work out a solution to this problem. Do you think we can?"

Being an assertive teacher means that you let students know your concerns and needs in a manner that gets their attention and communicates your intent to carry through with consequences and to deal with the situation until it is resolved. It is not necessary that you lose your sense of humor or treat students impolitely. A little humor can reduce tension, and treating students with courtesy models the kind of behavior that you expect of them. Developing a level of assertiveness that is comfortable for you and understanding how your behavior is perceived by others are important. Working through activities at the end of this chapter will help develop your skills and self-awareness.

Empathic Responding

Another important communication skill is the ability to respond with empathy to students. This skill allows you to show you are aware and accepting of the student's perspective as well as to seek clarification of it when necessary. Empathic responding helps keep the lines of communication open between you and students so that problems can be understood and resolved in mutually acceptable ways. Such skills are especially appropriate when students express their concerns, show stress, or display other strong emotions. As a teacher, you should respond in a manner that helps the student deal constructively with those feelings or at least avoids adding to the student's discomfort or distress. Empathic responding can also be used as a part of the problem-solving process when dealing with students who must change their behavior. In such situations, students can be resistant and express negative feelings; the teacher's empathic responses can help defuse these reactions and increase the acceptance of a plan for change.

Empathic responding complements constructive assertiveness. Whereas assertiveness allows teachers to express their concerns, empathic responding solicits and affirms the student's viewpoint. The use of empathic responding skills does not imply that misbehaving students are entitled to "do their thing" without regard for others; rather, the implication is that the student's views should be taken into account to reach a satisfactory solution. If the teacher shows some openness to the student's perspective, there is a better chance that the student will make a commitment to change. Conversely, a teacher who shows no interest in the student's feelings is more likely to encounter defiant behavior and an unwillingness to cooperate or to accept responsibility.

Compare the following two episodes.

Episode A

STUDENT: I'm not staying. You can't make me.
TEACHER: You'll have to stay after school. You've been tardy three times.
STUDENT: Oh man, I can't stay.
TEACHER: That's life. If you don't serve your time now, it's doubled. That's the rule.
STUDENT: (*Angry*) I'm leaving.
TEACHER: You'd better not.
STUDENT: Buzz off! (*Student leaves.*)

In this episode, the teacher's response does nothing to resolve the situation. It's likely that the student is aware of the consequences of skipping detention, so the argument only provokes a confrontation which the student wins, at least temporarily, by leaving.

Another way to handle the situation is illustrated below.

Episode B

STUDENT: I'm not staying. You can't make me.
TEACHER: I agree. It's up to you.
STUDENT: I can't stay.
TEACHER: Staying after school is a problem for you?
STUDENT: I can't be late to practice.
TEACHER: Oh, I see. The detention would make you late for practice.
STUDENT: Right, and if I'm late one more time, I'll have to sit out the next game.
TEACHER: That's a difficult situation. What are your options?

In Episode B, the teacher avoids arguing with the student and instead acknowledges the student's concern and invites further discussion. The student responds to the teacher's approach by stating his or her concern more explicitly. Notice that the teacher's role in this conference is that of listener or helper rather than opponent. Notice, too, that the teacher does not offer to solve the student's problem by dropping the detention penalty. Instead, the student is led to consider what options are available. Of course, there is no guarantee that the situation will be resolved to everyone's satisfaction. Yet, the approach at least offers the possibility of resolution, and it avoids the confrontation that occurred in Episode A. Further, it maintains the student's responsibility for dealing with the situation rather than giving the student yet another excuse for avoiding responsibility.

Empathic responding has several advantages. It allows the teacher a way to deal with strong emotions without taking over responsibility for solving the student's problems. At the same time, the strategy helps defuse emotionally charged situations: Often, intense feelings are transient and persist only when fed by an intense response. By not responding with similar emotional intensity, the teacher avoids fueling the fire. Also, the calm, empathic teacher serves as a good model for constructive problem solving.

Empathic responding has two components: listening skills and processing skills. Listening skills acknowledge or accept the student's expression of feeling or ideas and are intended to encourage the student to continue discussing the situation. At a minimal level, the listener merely indicates attention. Sometimes, just an interested look will encourage the student to continue speaking. Other examples of nonverbal listening behaviors are nodding, making eye contact with the speaker, and other body language that communicates openness to discussion. Verbal encouragement is indicated by utterances such as, "Um-hm," "I see," "Go on," "That's interesting," and the like. At other times, a little more encouragement may be needed. In such a case, the teacher can invite more discussion with phrases such as, "Tell me more," "I'm interested in hearing your ideas about this," "Would you care to comment?" "What do you think?" and "You've listened to my opinion. I'd like to listen to yours."

Processing skills allow you to confirm or clarify your perception of the student's message. At the simplest level, you can repeat back or summarize what the student says. When the student has provided multiple messages or a confusing array of statements, you can select what seems most important and paraphrase it. You can then "reflect" or "bounce back" this paraphrase as a question. Often, the student will acknowledge the correctness of your perception or offer clarification. For example, consider this interchange from a short after-school conference.

STUDENT: I hate this place. School is stupid!
TEACHER: Would you like to talk about it?
STUDENT: I just don't like it here.
TEACHER: School really turns you off.
STUDENT: No. Not school, I mean here, this place.
TEACHER: You like some schools, but not this high school?
STUDENT: Right, there's too many rules, no one listens to you, you can't talk to your friends. You know, it's just do this, do that, shut up.
TEACHER: You feel too restricted here, like you can't do what you want and no one cares?
STUDENT: It's always teachers telling you to be quiet, do your work. There's never time to be with friends and to have fun.
TEACHER: It sounds like you'd like more opportunities to socialize and hang out.
STUDENT: Right. If I could only have some things to look forward to, that I'd feel like coming here for, it'd be more bearable.
TEACHER: I wonder if you're aware of the activities we have after school . . .

In the example, the teacher uses a variety of responses with a turned-off student and progresses to a point where the student can express, at least partially, some of the basis for the feelings. Note that as the discussion unfolds the student becomes more communicative and reasonable. Although one cannot expect that major problems will usually be resolved via a single empathic interchange, it is not unusual for the sharp edge of negative emotions to be blunted and for the conversation to end on a positive note. At the least, the student knows that an adult cares enough to listen, and the teacher is in a better position to guide the student in the future.

The skills of empathic responding—both listening and processing—have been presented in the context of interactions with individual students, but they are also helpful when problems arise in group settings. In particular, using these skills helps prevent teachers from responding defensively when students react emotionally or express a problem during class. They also "buy time" for the teacher to consider alternatives for dealing with a problem. In addition, listening and processing skills are useful for leading group discussions.

Although empathic responding skills are very helpful in some situations, they are not intended as the primary means of dealing with students who are acting out, breaking class rules, or interfering with other students. Such misbehavior needs to be dealt with using approaches discussed in Chapters 7 and 9 and in the other sections of this chapter. However, listening and processing can be used to support these other measures.

A limitation of these skills is finding the right time and place to use them. It would be awkward, to say the least, to respond empathically to every expression of emotion or opinion during class activities. Such reactivity would cause slowdowns and might undermine your students' attention to lessons. The frequency and circumstances in which you choose to use these skills will depend on a variety of factors, including opportunities, your goals and values, and how competent you feel.

FOR REFLECTION

Many of us are sensitive to or self-conscious about some aspect of our image or background. Height, weight, appearance, content knowledge, inexperience, ethnicity, marital status, and acceptance or respect are among the areas that may be a source of insecurity or concern. Because teaching is such a public event, and because adolescents are astute observers of teachers' reactions, teachers often reveal much of themselves as they react when their students find the right "button" to push. Think about an area that represents a source of insecurity for you. Then consider how your communication with students may be affected if a student pushes that button. What can you do to minimize the negative effect or, better still, turn it into a plus?

🌀 Problem Solving

Problem solving is a process used to deal with and resolve conflicts. Conflicts arise between teachers and students because different roles give rise to different needs and because individuals have different goals and interests. If conflict arises, teachers need a way to manage it constructively so that teaching and learning can continue in a supportive classroom climate. An effective means of accomplishing this is the problem-solving process, in which the teacher works with the student to develop a plan to reduce or eliminate the problem. Steps in the process include (1) identification of the problem, (2) discussion of alternative solutions, and (3) obtaining a commitment to try one of them. Depending on circumstances, a problem-solving session may also include attempts to identify the basis for the problem and may specify the consequences of following or not following the plan. Because it generally requires more than a brief intervention, a problem-solving session is usually conducted during a conference with the student. Often, the skills of constructive assertiveness and empathic responding are helpful in reaching a workable agreement.

Problem-solving conferences are usually reserved for chronic situations that have not yielded to simpler remedies. Some action needs to be taken to stop the behavior because allowing it to continue would interfere with your ability to teach, other students' opportunities to learn, or the student's long-term functioning in your class or school. Consider the following examples.

1. Brad likes to be the center of attention. Whenever you ask a question, he calls out the answer without raising his hand and with no regard for the fact that you have already called on another student. Although you have reminded him of correct behavior and have tried to ignore his call-outs, the behavior continues to interfere with your class discussions.
2. Alice and Alicia always seem to be in a hurry to leave your room at the end of the fourth period. Unfortunately, they do not clean up their art supplies and they fuss and argue when you have them return to finish their jobs. Then they complain that they will be late to their next class. Their foot dragging seemed trivial at first, but it has become a daily source of irritation that disrupts the last several minutes of the class each day.
3. Terrence has not turned in his last three assignments, even though you allowed ample time in class to work on them. He seems to have a lackadaisical attitude about academic work, and he uses his time in class for goofing off whenever he can get away with it. During the previous grading period, he was within one point of failing your course, and not turning in his work is sure to drop him below the failing point.

Each of these examples illustrates a situation that has reached a stage at which a problem-solving conference might be useful. In each case, routine intervention has not altered the student's behavior, and more of the same teacher response will result only in a continuing power struggle or in a deterioration in the student's ability to behave constructively.

What is evident in each example is that the students are not accepting responsibility for their behavior. Perhaps what is needed is a stronger consequence (e.g., a penalty) that is clearly contingent on a repetition of the misbehavior. In fact, this strategy can be an alternative discussed with students during a problem-solving conference. Until the students make a commitment to change the offending behavior, however, the use of punishment may be perceived as coercive and controlling, rather than as a logical consequence, and thus may do little or no good. It also appears that the basis of the problems in each of the three examples is not clear. Why won't Brad wait his turn? Why can't Alicia and Alice follow a simple cleanup procedure? Doesn't Terrence understand or care about what will happen to his grade? Giving the students a chance to discuss their situations might produce insights that would lead to better solutions. It would also permit the teacher and students to become more aware of each other's perceptions and possibly prevent the development of additional problems. Steps in a problem-solving conference are described next.

STEP 1: Identifying the problem. You can begin the discussion by stating the purpose of the meeting and asking the student to express his or her viewpoint. Obtaining the student's view provides useful information for later steps, and it also enables you to gauge the student's understanding of the situation and willingness to cooperate. An alternative opening is to describe the problem yourself and ask the student for a reaction; this alternative is especially needed when you are dealing with young children, with students having limited verbal skills, and with evasive and dissembling students. Unless the student's attitude is very cooperative, you must be assertive about expressing your concerns. As explained earlier, this can be done by describing, without labeling, the behavior of concern and the problem it is causing. You may also need to stress that the problem will not be allowed to continue and that something must be done to solve it.

Glasser, in his Reality Therapy model (cf. Bassin, Bratter, & Rachin 1976), recommends asking students to evaluate whether the behavior is helping or hurting them or has good or bad effects. The logic is that a student who understands and admits that a behavior has negative consequences will be more likely to participate in the search for and commitment to a solution. A student who denies responsibility or who sees no harmful effects seldom makes a meaningful commitment to change. It may be helpful to ask such a student what the consequences might be if the behavior continues.

During this initial phase of the conference, a student may react defensively or emotionally and may try to avoid responsibility by blaming others, arguing, citing extenuating circumstances, and so forth. When such behaviors occur, you must decide whether the student's reaction is primarily for the purpose of evading responsibility or if it has some validity. If the latter is the case, you can use listening and processing skills to respond; this communicates a willingness to hear the student's point of view and may increase subsequent cooperation. There is considerable reciprocity in interaction, and if you model desirable behavior, you encourage its use by the student. A disadvantage of using empathic responding during this phase of problem solving is that the student's excuses, arguments, and extenuating circumstances may simply be a means of avoiding responsibility. Because you do not want to get sidetracked from the issue that brought the student to the conference in the first place, be sure to return the focus to the main problem after student concerns have been expressed. When the problem has been identified and agreed on, the conference can move to the next step.

STEP 2: **Identifying and selecting a solution.** One way to begin this phase is to invite the student to suggest a solution to the problem. If the student is unable to do so, you can offer one. Whenever possible, it is best to have two or more alternatives so that options can be compared and the most desirable one chosen. Frequently, the student's solution is stated negatively, focusing on simply ending an undesirable behavior. Although this is a step in the right direction, it is best to include a positive focus as well by including a plan for increasing desirable behavior. Thus, you should be ready to work with the student's idea and also suggest modifications.

If you are the one who suggests a solution, seek the student's reaction to check on whether the plan is understood and accepted. Also, evaluate the plan's appropriateness: Is it realistic? Will it significantly reduce the problem? Does it call for changes in other students or in the classroom environment, and are such changes feasible? Can it be evaluated readily? Occasionally, a student may try to avoid responsibility by proposing a solution that places the burden for change on the teacher or other students—for example, to design more interesting lessons or to get other students to "leave me alone." Consider such changes to the extent that they are appropriate and reasonable, but don't allow a student to shift responsibility to others unless that is where the responsibility for the problem lies. A reasonable response is, "Yes, such changes might help, but what will you contribute?" When a mutually agreeable solution is reached, you are ready for the third stage.

STEP 3: **Obtaining a commitment.** In this step, the teacher asks the student to accept the solution and to try it for a specified period of time, usually with the understanding that it will be evaluated afterward. The student's commitment can be given orally or in written form, as in a "contract." Sometimes such contracts are printed with an official-looking border, seal, and script, with space for student and teacher signatures and for listing contract terms and consequences if the plan is or is not followed.

Whether or not consequences are specified depends on the severity of the problem and whether it is a first conference or a follow-up for a broken contract. Some teachers like to give students a chance to correct their behavior without resorting to penalties; the rationale is that long-range cooperation is better when the teacher uses the least controlling or coercive approach. However, if the student is not making a reasonable effort to comply with the plan, or if the misbehavior is dangerous or too disruptive to be allowed to continue, spelling out the consequences may well be needed to get the student's attention and to communicate the seriousness of the situation: "You must either follow our agreement or discuss your behavior with the assistant principal—Mr. Dreadnaught—and your parents."

If the plan fails to solve the problem, you'll have to follow through with whatever consequence was stipulated or work with the student to alter the plan and produce a more workable solution. A major consideration is how much time and energy you can or should devote to pursuing the plan versus using a referral, detention, or some other consequence available in your school. You might also consult with a counselor, assistant principal, or another teacher before taking further action to get another perspective on the problem.

When problem-solving conferences fail to make progress (e.g., the student does not make a sincere commitment to a plan or simply does not cooperate), the teacher should evaluate his or her assertiveness and empathic responding skills before concluding that a problem-solving approach does not work with that student. Poor assertiveness skills—hostile, critical, or attacking behaviors—and their opposite—timid, tentative responding—interfere with the problem-solving process. An overly assertive, hostile style reflects a reliance on the teacher's power and cuts off communication. An unassertive style is easily ignored; the teacher is not seen as credible, and students simply won't believe that the teacher will insist on correct behavior or will follow through with consequences if they push past the limits. A constructively assertive teacher, however, captures the students' attention and communicates serious intent to change the situation. Empathic responding communicates a willingness to listen to the student's point of view and permits the teacher to clarify and react to a student's statements without closing off further discussion. Such skills are especially needed during problem-solving discussions because they allow the teacher to deal constructively with defensive student behavior. They also help to clarify solutions as they are discussed and improve the chances of obtaining a sincere commitment to change.

When you use these skills, be patient and give them a chance to work. Often, teachers use a problem-solving approach only after a situation has reached a flashpoint or for behavior that has been established over a long period of time. In such cases, you cannot expect miracles; change may occur gradually and imperfectly. However, problem-solving conferences can be helpful in many cases and should be a component of your set of management and discipline skills.

A Note on Parent Conferences

As we have already mentioned, constructive assertiveness, empathic responding, and problem solving can be useful in your interactions with parents as well as students. In your interactions with parents, it is helpful to remember the following:

- Approach parents as team members. Both you and the parents want what's best for the child; the point of the meeting is to find ways to work together.
- Parents who had difficulty in school themselves may be intimidated by schools and teachers. This may come across as avoidance, anger, or defensiveness. Be respectful and nonthreatening.
- Respect parents' knowledge of their children.
- Show your appreciation for parents' efforts to rearrange work schedules to meet with you. Use the time wisely by being prepared and organized.

- Stick to descriptions of behavior rather than characterizations of students (e.g., "Abigail calls other children names" rather than "Abigail is mean").
- Whenever possible, document your concerns. For example, if you believe that a student's work is sloppy, have samples available to show parents.

Further Reading

Berger, E. H. (2000). *Parents as partners in education: Families and schools working together* (5th ed.). Upper Saddle River, NJ: Merrill.

This handbook provides a comprehensive look at parent-school relationships and offers practical suggestions to aid collaboration between teachers and parents. Topics include diverse families, the exceptional child, programs to enrich parent-school environment, and communication necessary for partnerships.

Carkhuff, R. R. (1999). *The art of helping in the 21st century* (8th ed.). Amherst, MA: Human Resource Development Press.

The helping process is presented as a thoughtful, compassionate application of a series of skills. Critical concepts in the helping model are clearly explained and illustrated.

Egan, G. (1998). *The skilled helper: A problem management approach to helping* (6th ed.). Pacific Grove, CA: Brooks/Cole.

In addition to providing a very thorough description of skills needed for effective counseling, Egan presents an in-depth analysis of critical issues and common problems that occur in helping relationships.

Hill, C. E., & O'Brien, K. M. (1999). *Helping skills: Facilitating exploration, insight, and action.* Washington, DC: American Psychological Association.

This textbook outlines a three-stage model of helping and presents basic skills used at each stage, emphasizing the role of affect, cognition, and behavior in the change process.

Kottler, J. A. (2002). *Students who drive you crazy: Succeeding with resistant, unmotivated, and otherwise difficult young people.* Thousand Oaks, CA: Sage Publications/Corwin Press.

The book blends theory and research with examples from practicing teachers, counselors, school administrators, and students. It offers tools for dealing with frustrating, hostile interactions.

Suggested Activities

ACTIVITY 8.1: DEVELOPING ASSERTIVENESS SKILLS

The purpose of this activity is to provide some situations for practicing assertiveness skills. For each situation described, prepare an assertive response. Use the following sequence of steps with each situation until you are comfortable with the approach. Then combine the steps so that you have the experience of responding to situations "on your feet."

STEP 1: Write out a statement that describes the problem clearly or that insists that your rights be respected. Compare and discuss your statements with other participants. Revise your statement if you wish.

STEP 2: Use role-playing to portray the situation, with you as the teacher and someone else as the student. During the role-play, try to use appropriate body language (eye contact, facial expression) to support your intervention.

STEP 3: Get feedback from observers regarding your use of assertiveness skills. Use the Assertiveness Assessment Scales (see below) to assess your own behavior, and check out your perceptions by comparing your self-ratings to those of observers. Be sure to discuss any discrepancies and any problems you experienced enacting an assertive role. Repeat Step 2 until you feel comfortable with your handling of the situation.

It is not necessary to continue the role-play to a complete resolution of the situation. The purpose is only to provide experience in enacting assertive behaviors. The person playing the student role should respond as naturally as possible.

- *Situation A.* Bubba has been sliding by lately, doing the minimum and barely passing. At the end of class today, he asks you if it would be all right to turn in his project a few days late. He knows that you have already given similar permission to two other students who had difficulty obtaining needed materials.
- *Situation B.* Martha and Marie are supposed to put the equipment away, but they have left much of it strewn about the gym. Now they are heading for the door in anticipation of the end-of-period bell.
- *Situation C.* Victor has not been working on his assignment. You caught his eye, but he looked away and has continued to talk to nearby students. As you move around the room checking other students' progress, he begins to make a paper airplane.
- *Situation D.* As you walk down the hallway, you hear two students trading insults: "Your mama . . ." and so forth. The students are not angry yet, just "fooling around," but several other students are gathering and you think they may encourage the two students to fight.
- *Situation E.* As you begin class, you observe Donalda eating a cookie in violation of the rule prohibiting food in the room. When she sees that you notice her, Donalda stuffs the cookie into her mouth and gets another one out of the package.
- *Situation F.* During your current events discussion, Jack and Jill trade notes and laugh inappropriately. You sense that other students' attention is being captured by the duo's antics, and you begin to be annoyed at having to compete for class attention.
- *Situation G.* When you were absent yesterday, your fourth-period class gave the substitute teacher a hard time; according to the note he left for you (with a copy sent to the principal), many students refused to work at all, four or five left for the bathroom and never returned, and a paper-and-spitwad fight

raged all period. As the tardy bell rings, you enter the room to greet the fourth-period class.

᯿ Assertiveness Assessment Scales

When using the following scales, note that a midrange rating represents an appropriate degree of assertiveness. When rating your own or another teacher's behavior as either nonassertive or hostile, circle the descriptive term that best reflects the basis for your judgment, or write a note on the scale if the descriptors don't adequately capture your perception.

	Unassertive	Assertive	Hostile
	1 ——— 2 ———	3 ——— 4 ——— 5	
Eye contact	Teacher avoids looking at student.	Teacher maintains eye contact with student.	Teacher glares at student; stares student down.
	1 ——— 2 ———	3 ——— 4 ——— 5	
Body language	Teacher turns away, gestures nervously, trembles, fiddles with papers or pen.	Teacher faces student; alert posture but not threatening. Gestures support statements.	Teacher crowds student, points, shakes fist threateningly.
	1 ——— 2 ———	3 ——— 4 ——— 5	
Message	Obsequious, self-denigrating; excuses student behavior; pleads with student; apologizes.	Clearly states the problem or insists that the behavior stop. Makes own feelings known, may use humor to relieve tension.	Name calling, labeling, blaming, threatening, sarcastic, long lecturing.
	1 ——— 2 ———	3 ——— 4 ——— 5	
Voice features	Tremulous, whiny, hesitant, broken, or too soft.	Appropriate volume, natural sounding, varied for emphasis.	Too loud; shouts, screams.
	1 ——— 2 ———	3 ——— 4 ——— 5	
Facial features	Smiles inappropriately; nervous twitches and tics.	Expression suits message.	Excessive affect; contorted, disgusted, enraged expression.

ACTIVITY 8.2: RECOGNIZING LISTENING RESPONSES

Each of the following dialogues depicts a statement and a variety of teacher responses. In each case, decide which one is closest to a listening response—that is, invites further discussion or best reflects the idea or feeling.

1. STUDENT: School sucks.

   a. Don't use that type of language.
   b. You seem upset about school.
   c. Come on, things aren't that bad.
   d. That attitude will get you nowhere.

2. STUDENT: I can't understand algebra. Why do we have to learn this stuff?

   a. You'll need it to get into college.
   b. Just keep at it. It'll make sense after a while.
   c. Something isn't making sense to you?
   d. Would you like to come in for extra help after school?

3. STUDENT: I don't want to sit near those boys anymore.

   a. Sorry, but seats have been assigned for the semester.
   b. If they're bothering you, I can move you.
   c. Can you handle this on your own?
   d. What's the situation?

4. PARENT: My child is very upset and needs more help or she won't be able to pass. She says she doesn't understand anything.

   a. Please go on. I'd like to hear more about this.
   b. She needs to pay closer attention in class.
   c. She's very anxious but actually she'll do just fine. She only needs to review more before tests.
   d. Most students find my explanations to be quite clear. Perhaps she isn't listening.

5. TEACHER NEXT DOOR: That fifth period is going to drive me up a wall. They have been impossible lately!

   a. Have you considered being more assertive with them?
   b. I know, everyone in this wing can hear them.
   c. They are really a handful!
   d. You think they're bad, you should have my sixth period.

ACTIVITY 8.3: PRODUCING EMPATHIC RESPONSES

You will need to work with a colleague during this activity. Take turns role-playing the student and the teacher. The person role-playing the teacher should practice empathic responding skills, and the student should try to behave as naturally as possible. Note that it is assumed that the dialogue is occurring at a time and place that permits this type of interchange and that the teacher is interested in allowing the student to describe the problem. In this exercise, you should avoid giving solutions to the student's problem; instead, concentrate on using listening and processing skills to encourage the student to talk about the situation and think through the problem.

- *Situation A.* Teresa is an ESL student who is doing well in math and science; however, she has difficulty with writing. With tears in her eyes, she approaches you after class with an essay you have given a failing grade. "I thought that I did okay on this assignment."
- *Situation B.* David, a bright student, offers you some advice: "This class would be a lot more interesting if we didn't have to do all these worksheets. Couldn't we choose our own work sometime?"
- *Situation C.* While the rest of the class is at work on an assignment, Barry closes his book, throws away his assignment sheet, and slinks down in his seat disgustedly.
- *Situation D.* For the second time this week, Sue Ann has not turned in an assignment. Last week she "forgot" to bring her homework twice. After class, you remind Sue Ann that assignments count for half the grade. "I don't care," she responds.
- *Situation E.* Armand, a new student, has been having trouble making friends. Lately, he has been getting into arguments with some of the more popular boys and has been teasing a few girls, apparently to gain some attention. He has not, however, succeeded in breaking into the social scene. After class one day, he says to you, "I wish I could transfer back to my old school."

ACTIVITY 8.4: PROBLEM-SOLVING EXERCISES

Use role-playing to practice the problem-solving steps (identify the problem and its consequences, identify and select a solution, obtain a commitment to try it out) with the following situations. In situations in which the student is mainly experiencing the problem, assume that the teacher's initial listening response is received positively by the student so that there is a basis for continuing the discussion and for the teacher to assist the student in thinking through a solution. If the student's behavior is affecting the teacher's ability to teach or interfering with other students' rights, the student may initially be reluctant to participate in a discussion, and the teacher will have to use assertive skills to overcome this resistance. In addition to the situations listed here, you can use some of the situations presented in Activities 8.1 and 8.3 for more practice.

- *Situation A.* Bob and Ray are noisy and distracting when they clown around and vie for other students' attention. Reminders and penalties have only fleeting effects on their behavior. You decide to have them come in for a conference.
- *Situation B.* Darnell is good natured as long as no demands are placed on him. However, when reminded that class time is for learning and for working on assignments, he becomes defiant and insists that it is his right to do whatever he wishes, as long as "I don't hurt no one."

- *Situation C.* Lucy is a bright student but often turns in work late; frequently, it is incomplete. She is able to pass your tests, however, and she could easily be a top student if she were prompt and better organized. Recently, you sent her parents a progress report because of missing assignments, and Lucy and her mother have come in for a conference to discuss the situation. As things now stand, Lucy will fail your course this grading period. Her mother wonders whether you will allow Lucy to make up the missing work to avoid the failing grade.
- *Situation D.* Tina has been off-task during class, not turning in her assignments, and showing disrespect to you when you try to discuss her work with her. You've scheduled a conference with her mother, and now the two of you are sitting together to decide how you can work together to help Tina.

CASE STUDY 8.1

THREE DIALOGUES

Discuss the following three vignettes. To what extent did the teachers use the problem-solving steps as well as constructive assertiveness and empathic responding? Were they appropriately used? What other approaches might the teachers have tried for dealing with these problems? What are their advantages and disadvantages?

Dialogue 8.1: Brad

TEACHER: Brad, I asked you to stay to talk with me because of a problem we've been having during discussions. Often, when I ask a question, you call out the answer without waiting to be called on. Do you agree that this is happening?

BRAD: I guess so.

TEACHER: Can you tell me why that is a problem?

BRAD: I suppose that doesn't give others a chance.

TEACHER: That's absolutely right. I have to be able to find out whether other students understand what we are discussing.

BRAD: What if they don't know?

TEACHER: You mean, if nobody raises a hand or tries to answer?

BRAD: Yeah, then can I answer?

TEACHER: Do you suppose that some people might need more time to think about what they are going to say?

BRAD: I guess so. But it's boring to just sit and wait for someone to think if I already know it.

TEACHER: It is hard to wait and be patient, but I must be able to teach the whole class and to conduct the discussions for everybody. Can you think of any way that we could handle this so that I can call on others when I want to and you can still have your fair turn?

BRAD: I suppose I could raise my hand.

TEACHER: That would be a big help. I would really appreciate that. I think you have some good ideas and should have plenty of chances to answer. Brad, how often would you like to speak during our discussions?

BRAD: I don't know. (*Pauses.*) Three or four times, I guess.

TEACHER: That would be fine. How about if I guarantee you four times during each discussion? You keep track of the times you answer, and I'll call on you when your hand is raised. If I don't call on you sometimes, you know you'll get your chances later.

BRAD: Okay.

TEACHER: How about our trying this for the rest of the week, and then we'll talk again and see if it solves our problem?

BRAD: Okay.

Dialogue 8.2: Alice and Alicia

TEACHER: Girls, I asked you to stay for this conference because I've been having to take more and more of my time to get you to clean up and to keep work areas neat. I wonder what you both think about this problem.

ALICE: I don't know.

ALICIA: I don't think we're so bad about it.

TEACHER: It has become very frustrating to me. Do you remember that I had to remind you and wait for the jobs to be done?

GIRLS: Yes.

TEACHER: Whose job is it to pick up materials and put things away?

GIRLS: Ours.

TEACHER: Do you think we can find a way for those jobs to get done? (*Girls nod affirmatively.*) Do you have any suggestions?

ALICIA: I could just do it without being asked.

TEACHER: Okay. That is a good idea. Do you have any other suggestions?

ALICE: We could ask someone to help us.

TEACHER: That is an interesting idea. Do you know someone who wants to clean up your things?

ALICE: I don't know. Probably.

TEACHER: Would you like to help someone else clean up or put things away?

ALICIA: Sure, it'd be fun.

TEACHER: How about you, Alice?

ALICE: Okay.

TEACHER: Well, then I have an idea. How about if I let you both be my room helpers this next week. As soon as you finish your own cleanup, you can help me with jobs that I need to have done. How would that be?

GIRLS: Yeah!

TEACHER: Okay. Let's try this out. Tomorrow when you have cleaned up, let me know. Then I'll tell you what you can do to help me. How does that sound?

GIRLS: Sure! Okay.

TEACHER: I'm glad we had a chance to plan this, because now I have two room helpers and we will have our problem solved.

Dialogue 8.3: Terrence

TEACHER: I have noticed that you did not turn in the last three math assignments. What seems to be the matter?

STUDENT: That work is too hard!

TEACHER: You weren't able to do the work.

STUDENT: No. I can't do it.

TEACHER: When I was going around the room during seatwork, I noticed that you were able to do some of the problems, but then you stopped working.

STUDENT: That's 'cause I couldn't do them anymore!

TEACHER: I see. That's pretty frustrating. You know, that happens to other people, too. (*Student shrugs.*) Even teachers. Did you know that even teachers sometimes don't know what to do next?

STUDENT: No.

TEACHER: Even me. (*Student smiles.*) Do you know what I do when I can't figure out how to do something?

STUDENT: You ask somebody?

TEACHER: Right! Does that give you any ideas about what to do when you don't know what to do?

STUDENT: Ask somebody.

TEACHER: Sure. If you get stuck, ask. Do you know whom you can ask?

STUDENT: You.

TEACHER: That's right. And you can also ask anyone at your table if I am busy and you need help right away.

STUDENT: Okay.

TEACHER: Did you finish your math problems today?

STUDENT: No. I need some help.

TEACHER: Why don't you get your paper from your desk and let's see what the problem is. . . .

9

Managing Problem Behaviors

In this chapter, we describe a series of strategies for dealing with problem behaviors that you may encounter as you teach. Although previous chapters have
described preventive measures as well as tactics that can be used to manage inappropriate behavior, we think that it will be helpful to consider the full range of
approaches that can be used. We hope that you will not encounter problems, especially serious ones, in large numbers. But as you work with adolescents, you will
undoubtedly face difficult situations that must be dealt with to preserve the climate
for learning or to assist a student in developing behaviors more compatible with
group life and learning. The aim of this chapter is to pull together and organize a
wide array of possible strategies from which you can select. By having a number
of approaches to draw on, you will be better able to choose one that fits specific
conditions. Having some alternatives in mind is very useful, too, in case your first
plan doesn't work.

We hope that this chapter's concern with behavior problems will not be taken
as a grim comment on the teacher's role. In particular, the extensive list of strategies in this chapter should be considered within the context of the other chapters
in this book. We have advocated generally a positive, supportive climate with major
reliance on preventive measures. Within that framework, however, we must be
ready to deal with problems when they arise. With a variety of strategies at hand,
we can tailor our approach to fit the situation, keep interruptions to the instructional program to a minimum, and at the same time promote student adjustment
and productive behavior.

This chapter's focus is on problem behaviors rather than problem students.
Only a small percentage of students exhibit maladaptive behaviors with such consistency and to such a degree that they warrant being labeled emotionally disturbed
or behaviorally disordered. Adolescents do, however, behave inappropriately on occasion; we think that it is much more constructive in the long run to deal with
the student's behaviors and help the student learn how to behave rather than im-
pute internal causes for the behavior and assume that the student's capacity to make
good choices is impaired.

On occasion, problem behaviors result from substance abuse or stressors
(e.g., abuse, a death in the family, parental unemployment, serious illness, or di-
vorce) the student is experiencing at home or elsewhere. If a student's behavior
changes or if inappropriate behavior persists after reasonable attempts to deal
with it have been made, a discussion of the situation with a school counselor,
assistant principal, parent, or guardian is in order. Often, the student's current
or previous teachers can provide additional insights. When you talk with the student about what is happening, use listening skills (see Chapter 8) to try to understand the situation. Be empathic, but help the student understand that acting
out (or whatever the problem behavior is) will not help the problem. If you discover that a situation outside the classroom is affecting the student's behavior,
discuss what next steps would be appropriate with the student's counselor or assistant principal.

What Is Problem Behavior?

The concept of problem behavior is very broad. Rather than enumerate all of the possible misbehaviors that might occur in classrooms, it is more manageable to think of some categories.

Nonproblem

Brief inattention, some talk during a transition between activities, small periods of woolgathering, and a short pause while working on an assignment are examples of common behaviors that are not really problems for anyone because they are of brief duration and don't interfere with learning or instruction. Everyone is the better for their being ignored. To react to them would consume too much energy, interrupt lessons constantly, and detract from a positive classroom climate.

Minor Problem

This includes behaviors that run counter to class procedures or rules but do not, when occurring infrequently, disrupt class activities nor seriously interfere with student learning. Examples are students calling out or leaving seats without permission, doing unrelated work during class time, passing notes, eating candy, scattering trash around, and talking excessively during independent or group-work activities. These behaviors are minor irritants as long as they are brief in duration and are limited to one or a few students; we would not give them much thought except for two reasons. Unattended, they might persist and spread; further, if the behaviors have an audience, not to respond might cause a perception of inconsistency and potentially undermine an important aspect of the overall management system. Moreover, if students engage in such behavior for an extended period of time, their learning is likely to be adversely affected.

Major Problem, but Limited in Scope and Effects

This category includes behaviors that disrupt an activity or interfere with learning, but whose occurrence is limited to a single student or perhaps to a few students not acting in concert. For example, a student may be chronically off-task. Another student may rarely complete assignments. Or a student may frequently fail to follow class rules for talk or movement around the room or may refuse to do any work. This category also includes a more serious, but isolated, violation of class or school rules—for example, an act of vandalism or cheating on a test.

Escalating or Spreading Problem

In this category, we include any minor or major problem that has become commonplace and constitutes a threat to order and to the learning environment. For example, many students roaming around the room at will and continually calling out irrelevant comments make content development activities suffer; social talking that continues unabated even when the teacher repeatedly asks for quiet is distracting to others; and talking back and refusing to cooperate with the teacher are frustrating and may lead quickly to a poor classroom climate. Frequent violations of class guidelines for behavior cause the management and instructional system to break down and interfere with the momentum of class activities.

Goals for Managing Problem Behavior

To begin to address problem behaviors, several types of goals must be considered. We need to judge short-term and long-term effects of any management strategy we choose. In the short term, the desired results are that the inappropriate behaviors cease and the students resume or begin appropriate behaviors. In the long run, it is important to prevent the problem from recurring. At the same time, we must be watchful for potential negative side effects and take steps to minimize them. Effects on the individual student or students causing the problem as well as the effect on the whole class should also be considered.

> Joel is talking and showing off to a group of students during seatwork. The teacher could squelch Joel by using a sarcastic put-down or a strong desist but chooses instead to redirect Joel's behavior and stand close by until he is working on the assignment. The put-down or strong desist might get quicker results in the short run, but it may lead to resentment or even conflict if Joel tries a rejoinder. Redirection and proximity control take a little more effort but do not have negative side effects. In addition, they offer more support for appropriate behavior.

The ideal strategy is one that maintains or restores order in the class immediately without adversely affecting the learning environment; in addition, such a strategy should prevent a repetition of the problem. In reality, classrooms are very busy places, and we rarely have sufficient time to mull over the various options and their effects whenever a problem arises, especially in the midst of a crisis. If only there were a "pause" button for classroom events! The need for prompt reaction should not, however, deter us from evaluating the results of our efforts and from seeking alternative approaches, especially when our initial efforts do not meet with success. It is, therefore, useful to have a repertoire of strategies to apply to various problem situations.

Management Strategies

In this section, we present useful strategies for dealing with a variety of classroom behavior problems. The first several strategies can be utilized during instruction without much difficulty, require little teacher time, and have the great virtue of being relatively unobtrusive. Thus, they have much to recommend them because they do not give undue attention to the misbehavior, and they do not interfere with the flow of instructional activity. As we move down the list, we encounter strategies that are more direct attempts to stop the behaviors and to do so quickly; these strategies, however, have more negative features: They demand more teacher time, they may have unintended consequences on students, or they interrupt class activities. A general principle that is helpful in selecting a strategy is to use an approach that will be effective in stopping the inappropriate behavior promptly and that has the least negative impact. A corollary is that minor problems should usually be dealt with by the use of limited interventions. As problems become more serious, the limited interventions may be ineffective in quickly ending the disruptive behavior; thus, a more time-consuming or intrusive intervention may be required.

It should be emphasized that most secondary schools have prescribed procedures to deal with certain types of major problems and sometimes even minor ones. For example, teacher responses to events such as fighting, obscene language, stealing, vandalism, and unexcused absence are likely to be directed by school (or district) policies. Therefore, the beginning teacher must learn what policies are in force and follow them. When no specific policy is established for particular problems or when teachers are given latitude in their response, the following alternatives will be helpful in guiding teacher action.

It is a given that preventive measures are more desirable than reactive ones. Thus, the contents of earlier chapters have been devoted mainly to establishing a classroom environment that greatly reduces the need for frequent recourse to major interventions. Notwithstanding such efforts, reactive strategies are needed at times. However, when teachers find themselves frequently using major interventions to deal with problems, it is time to reevaluate the overall management and instructional plan and make needed modifications. To this end, reviewing suggestions for management presented in prior chapters and perhaps using the checklists from those chapters to provide focus may result in changes that can help reduce the problems. Teachers should also be sensitive to the possibility that the source of the problem lies in frustration with content that the student does not grasp or with tasks that the student lacks skills to perform. When the problem is one of a poor fit between student capabilities and academic demands, the teacher must address the source by developing more appropriate class activities and assignments or by giving the student more assistance.

If you have a special education student whose behavior is causing a problem, you may find it helpful to discuss the situation with a special education teacher and ask for suggestions. In particular, ask the teacher whether the student has a special discipline program as part of an individualized education plan (IEP). Sometimes such a plan specifies particular ways to respond to the student or presents some useful alternative strategies. Even if no specific discipline plan is included in the IEP, you may be able to obtain some helpful ideas for working with the student.

In the pages that follow, we describe classroom strategies that have a wide range of application, but the list is certainly not exhaustive. Readers interested in additional sources for ways of coping with behavior problems will find articles by

Shukla-Mehta and Albin (2003) and by Myles and Simpson (1994) helpful. Books that contain good descriptions of strategies for dealing with specific problems or with crisis management include Poland and McCormick (1999), Cohen and Fish (1993), and Stoner, Shinn, and Walker (1991). Many of the recommendations in these books are for school administrators or school psychologists, but there is much of value for teachers as well. Finally, the *Handbook of Classroom Management* (Evertson & Weinstein 2005) has many excellent chapters that describe strategies for managing problems.

Minor Interventions

USE NONVERBAL CUES

Make eye contact with the student and give a signal such as a finger to the lips, a head shake (no-no!), or hand signal to issue a desist. Sometimes lightly touching a student on the arm or shoulder helps signal your presence and has a calming effect. Never touch a student when you are angry, though, and avoid touching students when they are angry. Touch in these cases may cause the situation to escalate.

GET THE ACTIVITY MOVING

Often, student behavior deteriorates during transition times between activities or during dead time when no apparent focus for attention is present. Students leave their seats, talk, shuffle restlessly, and amuse themselves and each other waiting for something to do. The remedy is obvious: Move through the transition quickly and reduce or eliminate the dead time. This entails planning activities so that all materials are ready and adhering to a well-conceived lesson plan. Trying to catch and correct inappropriate behaviors during such times is usually futile and misdirected. Just get the next activity underway and cue students to the desired behaviors.

USE PROXIMITY

Move closer to students. Combine proximity with nonverbal cues to stop inappropriate behavior without interrupting instruction. Be sure to continue monitoring the students at least until they have begun an appropriate activity.

USE GROUP FOCUS

Use group alerting, accountability, or a higher participation format (see discussion in Chapter 5) to draw students back into a lesson when attention has begun to wane or when students have been in a passive mode for too long and you observe off-task behavior spreading.

REDIRECT THE BEHAVIOR

When students are off-task, remind them of appropriate behavior. "Everyone should be writing answers to the chapter questions," "Be sure that your group is discussing your project plan," "Everyone should be seated and quiet unless you have been given permission to leave your seat or talk." To avoid giving attention to inappropriate behavior, it is best to redirect behavior by stating what should be done. If only one or two students are engaged in inappropriate behavior, a private redirection will be less likely to interrupt the activity or to direct attention toward the incorrect behavior.

PROVIDE NEEDED INSTRUCTION

Especially during individual or group work, off-task behavior may reflect poor comprehension of the task. Check student work or ask brief questions to assess understanding; give necessary assistance so that students can work independently. If many students can't proceed, stop the activity and provide whole-class instruction. Next time be sure to check comprehension before starting the independent work activity.

ISSUE A BRIEF DESIST

Tell the student(s) to stop the undesirable behavior. Make direct eye contact and be assertive (see Chapter 8). Keep your comments brief and then monitor the situation until the student complies. Combine this strategy with redirection to encourage desirable behavior.

GIVE THE STUDENT A CHOICE

Tell the student that he or she has a choice: either to behave appropriately (be sure to state the desired behavior) or to continue the problem behavior and receive a consequence. For example, suppose a student has refused to clean up properly after completing a project: "You may choose to clean up now; if not, you are choosing to stay after class until your area is clean." To a student who continues to distract nearby students: "You may choose to work quietly on your assignment at your seat, or you will have to sit by yourself to do your work." The purpose of stating the consequence as a choice is to emphasize the student's responsibility for his or her behavior. Also, making the consequence clear increases the chance of the student's choosing to self-regulate.

USE AN "I-MESSAGE"

An I-message is a statement that describes the problem and its effects on the teacher, the student, or the class; it may also include a description of the feelings produced by the problem. The formula for an I-message is as follows:

- When you (state the problem)
- Then (describe the effect)
- And it makes me feel (state the emotion)

For example, to a student who constantly calls out comments, the teacher might say, "When you talk without permission, it interrupts the lesson, and I get frustrated and resentful." It isn't necessary, of course, to follow the formula exactly; the main idea is to communicate clearly what the problem is and why it's a problem (e.g., "It's very distracting to me and to others when you wander around the room during seatwork."). The I-message can be combined with a brief desist or with redirection. A rationale for using an I-message is that students often act without much awareness of the effects their behavior has on others, and they will change if they realize that they are causing someone a problem. Also, by communicating directly with the student about the effects of the behavior, the teacher implies that the student is capable of controlling the behavior if he or she understands its effects. These messages need to be delivered assertively. A whiney, pleading I-message will be ineffective.

Moderate Interventions

These strategies are more confrontational than the limited interventions just described and thus have greater potential for eliciting resistance. In cases in which the student's behavior has not become especially disruptive, it is desirable to use a minor intervention first or issue a warning to the student before using these interventions. Doing so permits the student to exercise self-control and may save teacher time and effort.

WITHHOLD A PRIVILEGE OR DESIRED ACTIVITY

Students who abuse a privilege (e.g., being allowed to work together on a project, sitting near friends, or moving freely around the classroom without permission) can lose the privilege and be required to earn it back with appropriate behavior. Sometimes teachers allow quiet talking during seatwork activities, and removing this privilege can be an effective way to limit unproductive behavior. Other teachers allow a class to choose a favorite activity or a short period of free time on one or more days each week as an incentive. Time lost from such activities can then be a strong deterrent to inappropriate behavior at other times. Although withholding a privilege is a form of punishment, it usually has fewer side effects than punishment that requires directly applying an aversive consequence.

ISOLATE OR REMOVE STUDENTS

Students who disrupt an activity can be removed to some other area of the room, away from other students. It is helpful to have a carrel with sides or at least a desk at the back of the room facing away from other students to discourage eye contact from the time-out area. If no suitable place is available, the student may need to have time out in the hall outside the door, although not if your school has a policy prohibiting this because of the problem of adequately supervising the student.

Time out is a variation on the preceding consequence, in that it takes away the student's privilege of participating in the classroom activity. It is a good idea to allow excluded students to return to the activity in a short time, as long as their behavior during time out is acceptable. Some teachers prefer to let the student retain some control over the return, using a direction such as, "You may come back to the activity in five minutes if you decide that you can follow our class rules." Other teachers prohibit the student from returning until the activity is completed or until they have a brief conference with the student.

A problem with time out is that some students may find it rewarding. They receive attention when it is administered, and it allows them to avoid an activity they dislike. When this occurs, you should switch to another strategy. Another problem is that a student may refuse to go to the time-out area. Usually, this is a temporary problem; if you are firm, ignoring the student's protests and continuing with the activity, the student will go eventually. One way to move a recalcitrant body is to offer a choice: "You can either take time out or you can take a walk to the principal's office. It's your decision."

Time out has another risk. Its use clearly identifies a student as someone who is excludable, and it may result in implicit labeling by the teacher, by other students, or by the excluded student. If used frequently with an individual student, it may cause resentment and anger. Therefore, be sure to provide opportunities for the student to resume full participation in the class, and use other strategies to promote appropriate behavior at the same time.

USE A FINE OR PENALTY

Sometimes a small amount of repetitious work is required as payment for inappropriate behavior. For example, in physical education, students may be required to run an extra lap or do some push-ups. In math, students may have to write multiplication tables or work some extra problems. In a language class, students can write verb conjugations. The advantage of this type of consequence is that it can usually be administered quickly with a minimum of teacher time and effort. A disadvantage is that the task is being defined as punishing, and therefore, the student's attitude toward the content may be negatively affected. Another problem with the use of fines or penalties is that their ease of use can lead to overuse, detracting from the overall climate.

ASSIGN DETENTION

Another commonly used penalty is detention, either at lunch or before or after school. Because of the logical relationship between the problem and the consequence, this penalty is often used for misbehaviors that involve time (e.g., tardiness, extended goofing off and time-wasting; behavior that interferes with instruction or student work time). Other common uses of the penalty are for repeated rule violations and for frequent failure to complete assignments. You may need to supervise the detention in your room, or your school might have a D-Hall with an assigned monitor. The time in detention need not be lengthy, especially for misbehaviors that are not severe or frequent; a ten- or fifteen-minute detention is often sufficient to make the point.

An advantage of detention as a penalty is that it is disliked by most students and they want to avoid it; at the same time, it is administered away from other students in the class and thus does not give undue attention to the behavior. Also, it is a common punishment, so extensive explanations and unusual procedures aren't needed. Finally, the teacher can sometimes use a little of the detention time to hold a conference with the student and perhaps work out a plan for improving the situation.

A disadvantage of detention is that it does take teacher time, especially when the teacher must supervise it. Even when the school has a D-Hall, the teacher still will have to write a referral. Another disadvantage is that students might be able to avoid detention, at least in the short run, simply by not showing up. Thus, the teacher or the school must have a backup plan, such as doubling the time; moreover, records must be kept and often additional time will be required to deal with such students.

USE A SCHOOL-BASED CONSEQUENCE

If your school has a prescribed consequence for particular problem behaviors and you are allowed some latitude in its administration, you should consider utilizing it after you have not had desired results with other strategies. For example, some schools have a system of referral to an assistant principal, who then deals with the student. Often, a first referral consequence is limited to detention or to a warning, with subsequent referrals resulting in a parent conference. It is necessary to apprise the administrator of the basis for the referral and, if time permits, to discuss the desirable outcome. Advantages of this approach are that it does not require

"About this time of year, I start thinking of them in the past tense."
© Martha F. Campbell. Reprinted by permission of Martha F. Campbell.

much teacher time and it is often an effective limit for students who do not respond to other consequences. A disadvantage is that the usefulness of this strategy is dependent on others for its effectiveness. Also, extensive and frequent external support for handling in-class problems is not a realistic option in most schools.

> ## ◎ FOR REFLECTION
>
> Teachers' reactions to problem behaviors such as those described in this chapter are often affected by the adult models they observed and the type of discipline they received as children, both at home and at school. Recall your early experiences in this area and consider their implications. To what extent do these earlier models provide a positive guide for managing problems of varying severity? Would the strategies that were effective for you be equally appropriate or effective for the varied kinds of students you may teach? Where do you need to add to or modify your approach?

More Extensive Interventions

When students do not respond to minor or moderate interventions and their behavior continues to disrupt classroom activities and interfere with their own and others' learning, one or more of the following strategies can be helpful in reducing the inappropriate behaviors and allowing the teacher to reestablish a focus on learning.

DESIGN AN INDIVIDUAL CONTRACT WITH THE STUDENT

When a student's inappropriate behavior has become chronic or a problem is severe and must stop immediately, try an individual contract. You will have to discuss the problem with the student and try to understand the student's perspective. Then you and the student can identify appropriate solutions and agree on which course of action to take. Typically, the contract specifies changes the student will make, but it might also call for the teacher to alter some behavior or activity. You should also make clear the consequences that will occur if the plan is not followed, and you can identify some incentive to encourage the student to follow through with the contract. The plan and consequences are written down and signed by the student. Contracts can also be used with other strategies (see the five-step plan and the reality therapy sections below).

HOLD A CONFERENCE WITH A PARENT

Sometimes a telephone call to a parent can have a marked effect on a student's behavior, signaling to the student that accountability for behavior extends beyond the classroom. Parents react best if they don't feel that they are being held responsible for their child's behavior in school (after all, they aren't there), so don't put the parent on the defensive. Describe the situation briefly and say that you would appreciate whatever support the parent can give in helping you understand and resolve the problem.

Acknowledge the difficulty of rearing adolescents as well as teaching them. Be sure to use listening skills (see Chapter 8) during the conversation, and be alert for information that might help you determine an appropriate strategy for dealing with the student. Have your grade book handy so that you can give the parent specific information about the student's progress if the information is requested or needed.

Rather than a phone conference, you might need to schedule a face-to-face conference with a parent. Sometimes, but by no means always, when such conferences are arranged, it is because a problem has become quite severe, and other school personnel (e.g., a counselor or principal) may have to be present. If you have initiated the meeting, you should try to brief the others and plan your approach ahead of time; also, inform parents about who will attend the meeting.

The chief drawback to parent conferences is the time and energy they require. The effort is frequently worth it; although not every conference is successful, many times the student's behavior will improve. Another potential problem is identifying ahead of time the best strategy to follow with the parent. Occasionally, parents overreact and punish children excessively; other parents may be defensive and unable to provide support. As the year progresses, you will get to know parents better and be able to gauge the probable effects of your call or conference.

USE A CHECK OR A DEMERIT SYSTEM

This approach is used with the entire class; it requires that the teacher give a check or demerit when a student violates some rule or rules. If a student persists in the misbehavior, additional checks are given. A specific penalty is attached to receiving one or more checks—for example, fifteen minutes of detention. An example of this approach is the "name-on-the-board" system suggested by Canter and Canter (1976, 1989). The teacher provides a list of rules to the students and informs them of the consequences of violations. A typical plan would be for the teacher to write the student's name on the board after the first violation, put a check mark after the second infraction, and so on. Associated consequences could be a warning for the name-on-the-board, followed by fifteen minutes of detention after each check. More severe penalties are added after the third check (e.g., call the parents or send the student to the principal). The student starts with a clean slate each day. More recently, Canter has suggested using a clipboard instead of the chalkboard to record student names. A clipboard avoids the public display of student names and thus reduces the risk of giving them undue attention. It also preserves a record of problem behaviors and perhaps makes follow-up more effective.

A variation on this procedure is a demerit system in which rule violations (e.g., tardiness, failure to bring text or other materials, excessive talking) are recorded on a form that the teacher retains in a file folder for each class. In this approach, a record is maintained by the teacher, and the student is required to sign the form, acknowledging responsibility for the behavior. Consequences initially are mild, but after several infractions in a given period of time, detention, a parent conference, or a behavior contract is used. Students can be allowed to erase demerits with good behavior—for example, no rule violations for a week.

An advantage of these systems is that they can help teachers set and maintain limits consistently. In addition, they make the consequences of rule violations clear to students and thus increase the predictability of the classroom environment. There are, however, several potential disadvantages. Probably the chief problem is the emphasis on catching students being bad. Whether the student's name goes on the chalkboard, clipboard, or a piece of paper, attention is directed at the misbehavior. This may not be a major drawback if checks or demerits aren't given frequently and if the teacher is careful also to give students positive attention. If, however, many checks or demerits are given, not only are misbehaviors receiving attention, but also the flow of the lesson will be impeded, compounding classroom management problems. Finally, if the inappropriate behaviors are not easy to observe accurately, it will be very difficult to appear consistent in the use of these systems. For example, trying to manage side talk during seatwork would be impossible in many classrooms because it is too hard to detect each time it occurs.

Teachers sometimes adopt the name-on-the-board strategy as a last resort when student misbehaviors have become frequent and they believe they are in danger of losing control of a class. Unfortunately, this is the situation in which this type of consequence system is most likely to break down because the teacher spends excessive time attending to inappropriate behavior and to punishing students. If a class has become unruly, we suggest choosing one activity (e.g., seatwork or content development) and targeting for this system only one or two easily observable but problematic behaviors (e.g., being out of seat without permission, continuing to talk after being asked by the teacher to stop). Students should know exactly what behaviors are not allowed and also what behaviors are desired. To avoid the teacher's having to play the role of "sheriff" continuously, the system should be used only in that specific activity (i.e., not for the entire period). The activity should be kept short and briskly paced during the first several days of implementation to increase the chances of success. The teacher should provide attention and appreciation for appropriate behaviors and for students' greater maturity and improved behavior. When student behavior is under reasonable control in the selected activity, the system can be used in another activity if necessary.

USE PROBLEM SOLVING

Because problem solving was described extensively in Chapter 8, it is not discussed in this chapter. However, the next three strategies, which share some features with problem solving, are sufficiently unique to warrant a separate presentation.

USE A FIVE-STEP INTERVENTION PROCEDURE

Jones and Jones (2004) recommend following five steps (Figure 9.1) when dealing with disruptive student behavior.

STEP 1: Use a nonverbal signal to cue the student to stop.

STEP 2: If the behavior continues, ask the student to follow the desired rule.

Figure 9.1 Steps in Responding to Students' Violation of Rules and Procedures

Step	Procedure	Example
1.	Nonverbal cue.	Raised index finger.
2.	Verbal cue.	"John, please follow our classroom rules."
3.	Indicate choice student is making.	"John, if you continue to talk while I am talking, you will be choosing to develop a plan."
4.	Student moves to a designated area in the room to develop a plan.	"John, you have chosen to take time to develop a plan."
5.	Student is required to go somewhere else to develop a plan.	"John, I really wish we could solve this here. If we cannot, you will have to see Mrs. Johnson to develop your plan."

From Vernon F. Jones and Louise S. Jones, *Comprehensive Classroom Management: Creating Communities of Support for Solving Problems,* Seventh Edition. Copyright © 2004 by Allyn and Bacon. Reprinted/Adapted by permission.

STEP 3: If the disruption continues, give the student a choice of stopping the behavior or choosing to develop a plan.

STEP 4: If the student still does not stop, require that the student move to a designated area in the room to write a plan.

STEP 5: If the student refuses to comply with Step 4, send the student to another location (e.g., the school office) to complete the plan.

The use of the five-step intervention process requires a form for the plan (Figure 9.2). When the approach is introduced to the students, preferably at the beginning of the year, the teacher explains its purpose and how to fill out the form. Role-playing the use of the five steps is recommended, both to teach the procedures as well as to provide a positive model of their application. It is also helpful to laminate a couple of examples of appropriate plans so that students have models.

Advantages of this approach include its emphasis on student responsibility and choice. Also, a graduated response to the problem allows the teacher to intervene nonpunitively at first and thus provides a means of settling the matter quickly with a minimum of disturbance to the ongoing activity. The steps are simple and straightforward, which promotes consistency in their use by the teacher; students in turn are aided by the structure and predictability of the approach.

A disadvantage of the system is that movement from Step 1 to Step 5 can occur very rapidly and some intermediate strategies may be necessary to avoid excessive reliance on sending students out. In addition, some students will have difficulty writing an acceptable plan by themselves. Finally, setting up the system,

Figure 9.2 Problem-Solving Form

Choose to Be Responsible

Name _____ Date _____

Rules we agreed on:

1. Speak politely to others.
2. Treat each other kindly.
3. Follow teacher requests.
4. Be prepared for class.
5. Make a good effort at your work and request help if you need it.
6. Obey all school rules.

Please answer the following questions:

1. What rule did you violate? _____

   _____

2. What did you do that violated this rule? _____

   _____

3. What problem did this cause for you, your teacher, or classmates? _____

   _____

4. What plan can you develop that will help you be more responsible and follow this class-

   room rule? _____

   _____

5. How can the teacher or other students help you? _____

   _____

I, _____, will try my best to follow the plan I have written and to follow all

other rules and procedures that we created to make the classroom a good place to learn.

From Vernon F. Jones and Louise S. Jones, *Comprehensive Classroom Management: Creating Communities of Support for Solving Problems,* Seventh Edition. Copyright © 2004 by Allyn and Bacon. Reprinted/Adapted by permission.

meeting with students to discuss their plans, and monitoring implementation require at least a moderate investment of time.

USE THE "THINK TIME" STRATEGY

Designed to help students learn self-control and to prevent a reciprocally escalating sequence of student noncompliance–teacher warnings and reprimands, the think time strategy removes a noncompliant student to another teacher's classroom to provide time for the student to gain focus and reenter the classroom later after making a commitment to change the behavior (Nelson & Carr 2000). Using the think time strategy requires the cooperation of another teacher whose classroom is in close proximity. The partner teacher reserves a location in the room that is not in a high traffic area and that will minimize attention to the entering student. After arriving at the receiving classroom, the student waits quietly in the designated area and thinks about what happened. As soon as is practicable (e.g., three to five minutes), the receiving teacher makes contact with the student and gives him or her a debriefing form to fill out that asks, "What was your behavior?" and "What behavior do you need to display when you go back to your classroom?" The student is asked if he or she can do it or if a conference is needed with the teacher. If the student completes the form acceptably, the receiving teacher sends the student back to the original class.

If you use this strategy, you'll partner with another teacher. After preparing a location in your rooms to receive think time students, you'll each need to teach your students about think time. Nelson recommends treating this task as you would any other complex procedure. You'll need to explain the purpose of the strategy (e.g., to help students learn self-control and to minimize disruption to learning) and what behaviors might result in think time. You'll also need to describe the signal you'll use to send someone to think time (e.g., hand them a pass card) and model how students will be expected to leave the room and enter the other teacher's room. The students should also be shown an example of the debriefing form with examples of appropriate responses. For high school applications, Nelson recommends having a backup administrative sanction, such as an office referral, if a student becomes disruptive. Likewise, if a student is required to use think time more than once in a class period or after the third time in a semester, then an office referral or In-School Suspension (ISS) assignment is used along with a parent contact.

One advantage of think time is that it gives the teacher a way to manage students who don't respond to simpler desist techniques and at the same time it short-circuits the reciprocal escalation of hostile interaction that can develop when a student resists a teacher's attempt to stop misbehavior. Another advantage is that think time provides a "cease-fire" opportunity in which students acknowledge their part in the problem and identify a solution. In this respect, it is similar to other problem-solving strategies. Limitations in the use of the strategy are that it takes the cooperation and commitment of another teacher, and it requires planning and systematic application to be successful. A training videotape is available through the publisher, Sopris West (www.sopriswest.com).

USE THE REALITY THERAPY MODEL

William Glasser's (1975, 1977, 1986) ideas have been widely applied in education. Some of his recommendations for dealing with disruptive or maladaptive behaviors in a classroom setting are presented next.

The essential features of using a reality therapy strategy when working with an individual student include establishing a caring relationship with the student, focusing on the present behaviors, getting the student to accept responsibility, developing a plan for change, obtaining a commitment to follow the plan, and following up. Glasser believes strongly that students choose behavior depending on their perceptions of its consequences. Most students choose appropriate behaviors when they believe these will lead to desirable outcomes, and they avoid behaviors that they perceive will lead to undesirable consequences. Glasser's plan can be put into effect by following these steps.

STEP 1: Establish involvement with the students. If students believe the teacher cares for them and has their best interests in mind, they will be more likely to follow the teacher's guidance when evaluating and changing their behavior. Teachers can show commitment to and caring for students in numerous ways: commenting favorably to the students about their work; being friendly; and showing an interest in students' activities, families, likes and dislikes, and hobbies. Teachers can also get involved by demonstrating school spirit, joking, being good listeners, and taking time to talk with students about their concerns. The best time to establish involvement is before a student becomes disruptive, but even if a student has begun to exhibit problem behavior, it is not too late to begin. When a teacher makes a special effort to have two or three friendly contacts a day with such a student, it can be helpful in creating a more positive climate for change.

STEP 2: Focus on behavior. When a problem has occurred, Glasser recommends that a brief conference be held with the student. The initial concern should be to determine what the problem is. To this end, the teacher should ask only questions about "what happened" or "what's going on" and avoid trying to fix blame. Even if the teacher knows exactly what the problem is, it is wise to obtain the student's perspective.

STEP 3: The student must accept responsibility for the behavior. This means that the student acknowledges that he or she did engage in the behavior. No excuses are accepted. Admitting responsibility is difficult, especially when there are so many other handy things to blame. Of course, it is possible that more than one individual is responsible for the problem, but that should not be an excuse for irresponsibility or denial.

STEP 4: The student should evaluate the behavior. If students have difficulty perceiving their part or if they minimize it, Glasser suggests asking, "Has the behavior helped or hurt you? Has it helped or hurt others?" The teacher may have to point out the negative consequences of continuing the behavior. Unless the student sees that it will lead to negative consequences and that changing it will produce desirable consequences, there isn't much reason to expect a change.

STEP 5: Develop a plan. The teacher and student must identify ways to prevent the problem from recurring and the new behaviors that are needed. The plan can be written as a contract.

STEP 6: The student must make a commitment to follow the plan.
Progress will be limited at best if students do not seriously intend to make a
change. It may help if the teacher makes clear the positive and negative consequences of following or not following the plan. The plan must be doable
in a reasonable time.

STEP 7: Follow up and follow through. If the plan doesn't work, it should
be modified with the student; if a negative consequence was called for in the
plan, it should be used. Glasser also proposes several additional steps beyond
the classroom if a student continues to be a problem. For example, use of in-
school suspension could be a consequence of continuing misbehavior; before
the student is allowed to return to the classroom, an acceptable plan would
have to be agreed on. Only after several attempts to obtain a change have
failed should the teacher refer the student to an assistant principal.

The reality therapy approach to dealing with individual discipline problems
has much to recommend it. It is a systematic way for teachers to deal with many
kinds of individual student problems, and it provides a simple, yet effective, process
for getting right at the issues and avoiding being sidetracked by fault finding, con-
ning, or excuse making. Research on the effects of this aspect of reality therapy supports its effectiveness when used with individual students (Emmer & Aussiker
1990).

USE PEER MEDIATION

Conflicts between students can be disruptive and engender resentments that spill
over into the classroom. At some schools, conflicts between students in the community, sometimes resulting from gang affiliation, contribute to tension, ill will,
and fighting at school. In response to such problems, some schools and teachers
have implemented peer-mediation programs. The goal of these programs is to resolve conflicts peacefully, enabling all students to learn constructive approaches to
handling problems and engendering acceptance of responsibility.

Mediation utilizes a process in which the parties in conflict are assisted by a
mediator to negotiate a solution to the problem. David and Roger Johnson, leaders in the development of school mediation training, list four steps in the procedure: (1) stop the hostilities, (2) obtain a commitment from both parties in the
conflict to participate in the mediation process, (3) help them negotiate a solution, and (4) formalize the agreement (Johnson & Johnson 1995). The negotiation
process itself involves the participants in deciding what they want to accomplish,
describing their feelings, and explaining the basis for both. They must also understand the other party's point of view and help generate alternative solutions that
will be acceptable to all individuals involved in the conflict. Finally, they must
choose a particular solution to implement.

The role of the mediator is to listen to each side in the dispute, to clarify issues, to help generate and negotiate possible solutions, and to write up the agreed-
on solution. If an agreement is not reached, the mediator helps the participants

decide on the next step in resolving the dispute (Cutrona & Guerin 1994; Stomfay-Stitz 1994). The mediator is not an arbitrator who passes judgment on the merits of the sides and who imposes a solution. Instead, the mediator attempts to facilitate an understanding of the problem and the development of a solution by the parties involved in the dispute.

Becoming a mediator requires learning the goals and rationale for the approach and receiving systematic training in each of the steps in the process. When peer mediation has been adopted as a schoolwide strategy, such training is typically provided to students by a school counselor or by a teacher who has received such training. If you would like to use peer mediation in your classroom and it is not being used schoolwide, you might start by reading the references on mediation cited earlier and listed at the end of this chapter; additional information about training activities and materials is included in these references.

Special Problems

In addition to the general types of problems described at the beginning of this chapter, some specific types occur commonly enough and are severe enough that it is worthwhile to describe additional strategies for managing them. Previously described approaches can also be applied to these behaviors.

Rudeness toward the Teacher

Rudeness may take the form of sassy back talk, arguing, or crude remarks and gestures. Although such behavior may trigger anger in you, it is best that you maintain a low-keyed, calm, and respectful manner when you respond, because you will be modeling the kind of behavior that you expect from students, and you will be more effective when interacting with the student in question. Frequently, the student is using such behavior as a means of getting attention from you or from peers or avoiding an assignment that he or she does not feel able to complete successfully. (Adolescents would often rather appear "bad" than "dumb.") Therefore, avoiding sarcasm, overreaction, argument, or a power struggle is essential. To some extent, your response will depend on the degree of rudeness and on how public it was. In borderline cases, a student may not even realize that a comment was offensive, or the student may be impulsively reacting to frustration from instruction or a task that may be unclear or too difficult. A reasonable first reaction is to inform the student that he or she must find a more acceptable way to express frustration. Possibly refer to a general classroom rule such as "respect others" or "be polite," and offer to work with the student individually as soon as you have finished giving instructions to the class. If the incident is repeated or if the original comment was intentionally rude, a conference should be held with the student to find out, if possible, the reason for this behavior, and/or some type of penalty should be used. Should persistent and disruptive obnoxious behavior occur, the student should be isolated from other students or sent to the school office and not be allowed to return until he or she agrees to behave appropriately. Most schools have a standard policy for dealing with extreme cases, and you will be able to rely on whatever procedures have been established.

Chronic Avoidance of Work

You may have students who frequently do not complete assigned work. Sometimes they fail to complete assignments early in the school year; more often a student will begin to skip assignments occasionally and then with increasing regularity, until he or she is habitually failing to do the work. This behavior can be minimized by an accountability system that clearly ties student work to grades (review Chapter 3 for details). However, even in classrooms with a strong accountability system, some students still may try to avoid work.

It is much easier (and much better for the student) if you deal with this problem before the student gets so far behind that failure is almost certain. By catching the problem early, you will still be able to provide some incentive (i.e., passing the course) for the student to get back on track. To be in a position to take early action, you must collect and check student work frequently and also maintain good records. Then, when you note a student who has begun to skip assignments, you can talk with him or her to identify the problem. It is possible that the student is simply unable to do the work. If so, you may be able to arrange appropriate assistance or modify the assignments for that student. It is also possible that the student feels overwhelmed by the assignments. In this case, break the assignments into parts whenever possible. Have the student complete the first part of the assignment within a specified period of time (e.g., five or ten minutes); then check to see that

"Pi what squared? Long John, you should be able to get this."

it has been done. A bonus of a few minutes of free time at the end of the period (e.g., to sit quietly, read, do an enrichment activity, or help with a classroom chore) can be offered for completion of the portion within the time limit or for working steadily without prodding.

If ability is not the problem, the following procedures can be used in addition to talking with the student. Call the student's parents or guardian and discuss the situation. Often, the home can supply the extra support needed to help motivate the student. Also, if the student participates in athletics or other extracurricular activities, the coaches or other supervising faculty may be able to support your efforts. Many schools have a system (e.g., a weekly checklist) for monitoring academic progress of students involved in certain extracurricular activities. Finally, apply the consequence, usually a failing grade, for repeated neglect of work. There is no purpose served in softening the penalty because the student promises to do the work during the next grading period or because you think that he or she could do better by just working harder. Such leniency teaches the student to avoid responsibility.

Fighting

This is rarely a classroom problem; usually, it occurs in hallways or in other areas of the school. Whether or not to intervene directly depends on your judgment as to whether you can do so without undue risk of injury. If you do not intervene directly, you should of course alert other teachers and administrators so that action can be taken. If you do intervene, try to do so with the assistance of one or several adults. It is hard for one adult to stop a fight, and attempting to do so may be dangerous. The difficulty increases particularly when a large crowd has gathered. Dispersing the crowd and instructing a student to summon an administrator or another teacher may be the wisest first step. Your school will undoubtedly have a procedure to deal with fighting, so you should familiarize yourself with your responsibility (e.g., to file a report with the office). Typically, students are questioned by an assistant principal who will contact the parent, perhaps call the police, arrange a conference, and mete out any prescribed penalty, such as suspension.

Other Aggressive Behavior

Students engage in other types of aggressive behavior besides fighting, and it may occur in the classroom. Examples include name-calling, overbearing bossiness, bullying, or rudeness toward other students, and physically aggressive—but "playful"—pushing, shoving, or slapping. Offending students should be told that such behavior is not acceptable, even if it is just "fooling around." It can easily escalate. Refer to whatever class rule fits the situation, such as "Respect others." Give no more than one warning, and then assess an appropriate penalty. Students engaged in such behavior should be separated and seated apart if they give any indication of intending to persist.

Once you are aware of aggressive tendencies in a student, you will need to be especially alert in your monitoring to anticipate when the student is becoming agitated. Intervene with a quiet talk or allow the student to sit away from the group if that might help him or her to stay calm. Seat the student away from others who tend to provoke anger. Assume that the student wants to maintain self-control, and communicate that in words and actions. When having a conference with such a student, point out how it is in his or her best interest to control this behavior, and when appropriate, help the student set up a time to meet with a school counselor.

Bullying

Bullying has been identified as a serious problem in many schools and communities. It is an unacceptable pattern of behavior characterized by harassment or domination of one student through a pattern of threats, constant teasing, or physical abuse. Bullying is learned from peer groups, the home, or through the media. Because of its damaging effects on students, some schools have a zero tolerance policy for bullying.

Bullying is certainly contrary to a climate of respect and caring, and it can lead to serious and long-term emotional consequences for both the victim and the bully. When bullying occurs inside the classroom, teachers don't always recognize it (Hyman et al., 2005), and bullying outside the classroom isn't usually observed by teachers. It's important, therefore, that students learn that bullying is not acceptable and should be reported. Victims may be reluctant to report it for fear of retaliation, and victimizers are often popular but socially manipulative individuals, so teachers need to be vigilant if there is a suspicion that bullying is occurring in the classroom, hallways, cafeteria, school buses, or other building areas.

The most effective programs aimed at decreasing bullying are schoolwide; see Olweus Bullying Prevention Program at www.stopbullyingnow.com. In your classroom, you can utilize social skills training; see www.cfchildren.org. Students also can learn ways to respond if they are bullied or if they are bystanders to bullying behavior. In addition to group discussions on bullying and learning to recognize feelings generated in both the victim and victimizer, lessons on friendship skills, assertiveness, and problem solving are useful.

If you encounter bullying, you will need to evaluate the seriousness of the behavior. For instance, persistent teasing because of racial differences, disability, or physical disfigurement is not acceptable and should always be addressed. After meeting with the individual students involved, you will have to determine whether or not to contact school administrators, counselors, and/or parents. If your school has a peer-mediation program, it may be helpful in dealing with the problem. Stopping pervasive bullying needs coordinated efforts, and changing individual and group perception of the behavior is critical to dealing with it.

Defiance or Hostility toward the Teacher

This type of behavior is understandably very threatening, particularly when it occurs in front of other students. The teacher feels, and rightfully so, that if the student is allowed to get away with it, such behavior may continue and other students will be more likely to react this way. The student, however, has provoked the confrontation, usually publicly, and backing down would cause a loss of face in front of peers. The best way to deal with such an event is to try to defuse it. This can be done by keeping it private and handling it individually with the student if possible. If it occurs during a lesson and is not really extreme, deal with it by trying to depersonalize the event and avoid a power struggle. "This is taking time away from the lesson. I will discuss it with you in a few minutes when I have time." Then leave the student alone and give him or her a chance to calm down. Later, when you have time, have a private talk with the student and assess a penalty if it seems warranted. Should the student not accept the opportunity you have provided but rather press the confrontation further, you can instruct the student to leave the room and wait in the hall. After the student has had time to cool off, you can give your class something to do and discuss the problem privately with the student.

When presented with this type of behavior, you should try to stay objective. Don't engage in arguments with the student. Point out that the behavior was not acceptable, and state the penalty clearly. Listen to the student's point of view; if you are not sure how to respond, say that you will think about it and discuss it later.

In an extreme (and rare) case, the student may be totally uncooperative and refuse to keep quiet or to leave the room. If this happens, you can call the office or send another student for assistance. In almost all cases, however, as long as you stay calm and refuse to get into a power struggle with the student, the student will take the opportunity to cool down.

A Final Reminder: Think and Act Positively

In this chapter, many of the strategies for dealing with problem behaviors involve some form of punishment. This is especially the case for the strategies in the moderate and extensive categories. A drawback to punishment is that, by itself, it doesn't teach students the behaviors that should be practiced. Consequently, it is important also to communicate clearly what behaviors are desired. That is, the focus should remain on teaching appropriate behaviors. Furthermore, a classroom in which the main consequences are negative does not have a very good climate. Thus, teachers using strategies in the moderate and extensive categories more than occasionally may wish to incorporate some additional incentives or a reward system into their overall classroom management to help mitigate the negative effects of using punishment. Finally, after correcting student behavior, the teacher who supplies a generous measure of warmth and support reassures students that they have been restored to good grace.

 Further Reading

Cutrona, C., & Guerin, D. (1994). Confronting conflict peacefully: Peer mediation in schools. *Educational Horizons, 72*(2), 95–104.

Problem behaviors that pit student against student can escalate to threaten schoolwide climate and safety. They often frustrate teachers and are difficult to resolve through adult intervention alone.

This article describes the use of peer mediation to resolve conflicts. Examples of such programs are also presented along with an analysis of their benefits.

Kottler, J. A. (1997). *Succeeding with difficult students.* Thousand Oaks, CA: Corwin Press.

This brief book provides insightful suggestions about dealing with challenging students. The author emphasizes the importance of the teacher's understanding of the source of the conflict with the student, as well as his or her reactions. Alternative strategies to create a climate for change are described.

Myles, B. B., & Simpson, R. L. (1994). Prevention and management considerations for aggressive and violent children and youth. *Education and Treatment of Children, 17,* 370–384.

Aggression is typically preceded by warning signs and follows a sequence of stages. This article describes prevention and intervention strategies keyed to these stages. Many of the suggested strategies are also useful for nonaggressive inappropriate behaviors.

Shrigley, R. L. (1985). Curbing disruption in the classroom—Teachers need intervention skills. *NASSP Bulletin, 69*(479), 26–32.

A sequence of strategies is set forth for dealing with various mild and moderate disruptions. The strategies, which are consistent with many of those presented in this chapter, are easily applied in classroom settings, providing useful alternatives for handling problem behaviors.

Shukla-Mehta, S., & Albin, R. W. (2003). Twelve practical strategies to prevent behavioral escalation in classroom settings. *Preventing School Failure, 47,* 156–172.

The authors describe ways to avoid or deescalate confrontations with students. For example, the teacher should reinforce calm and on-task behavior, recognize what sets off a student, avoid responses that add to the escalation, and intervene early.

Suggested Activities

1. Review the descriptions of problem types presented at the beginning of the chapter. Then decide which interventions would be best suited for each type. Given several alternative interventions for a type of problem, how would you decide which to use?

2. Within each type of intervention—minor, moderate, or extensive—are there any that you distinctly prefer? Do you reject any? Discuss your reasons for liking or disliking particular approaches.

3. Listed below are several problem situations. Decide on a strategy for dealing with each and also an alternative response if your first approach does not produce good results. Indicate any assumptions you are making about the teaching context as you choose your strategy.
   - *Situation 1.* Ardyth and Melissa talk and pass notes as you conduct a class discussion. Several other students whisper or daydream.
   - *Situation 2.* Desi and Bryce talk constantly. They refuse to get to work and argue with you when you ask them to open their books.
   - *Situation 3.* Joe manages to get most of his work done, but in the process, he is constantly disruptive. He teases the girls sitting around him, keeping

them constantly laughing and competing for his attention. Joe makes wise-cracks in response to almost anything you say. When confronted, he grins charmingly and responds with exaggerated courtesy, much to the delight of the rest of the class.

■ *Situation 4.* When someone bumped into Marc at the drinking fountain, he turned around and spit water at the other student. Later, Marc ordered a boy who was standing near his desk to get away, and he then shoved the boy. On the way back from the cafeteria, Marc got into a name-calling contest with another boy.

■ *Situation 5.* Behavior in your third-period class has been deteriorating. Class discussions are interrupted by irrelevant comments, and an under-current of talking makes it difficult to conduct activities. Students write notes as you teach, talk during seatwork assignments, and complain about having to do any work. Many students do no work during the last ten minutes of the period as they get ready to leave and spend the time chatting.

4. Make a list of student behaviors including defiance, rudeness, aggression, and unresponsiveness that are the most likely to embarrass you or make you uncomfortable. Write down how you might handle the behaviors. For a group activity, compare notes and see if the members can agree on a preferred approach to common problems.

5. Find out if your school has a policy regarding bullying and how that policy is communicated to students and parents. What is the teacher's role in implementing and enforcing the policy?

10

Managing
Special Groups

Although the management principles and guidelines discussed in previous chapters are applicable to most classroom settings, classroom management is, of course, affected by the characteristics of the students making up a class. The ages, academic ability levels, goals, interests, and home backgrounds of students have an impact on their classroom behavior. Consequently, effective teachers adjust their managerial and instructional practices to meet the needs of different groups of students. Two groups that frequently present some special challenges are very heterogeneous classes and remedial-level classes.

Types of students for whom some adjustment in teaching and management is usually necessary include students who are working substantially below grade level, students who are academically or physically disabled, and students whose English language skills are limited. Often, a classroom includes several such students, requiring careful planning to be sure that the needs of both the identified and the other students are met. Accommodating such diverse needs and abilities requires extra effort. This chapter presents information and suggestions that, combined with the principles in previous chapters, will help you organize and manage classes with a range of student achievement or ability levels, groups of students with low skill levels, and students with special needs.

Teaching Heterogeneous Classes

Many secondary school classrooms contain students with a very wide range of entering achievement levels. For example, a very heterogeneous eighth-grade English class may include some students who score at fourth-grade levels on reading and language usage achievement tests and other students with grade-equivalent scores of eleventh grade or higher. In middle school mathematics classes, students' entering achievement levels may be spread across five or more grade levels. Required science and social studies courses often present extremes of student heterogeneity, with students' entering achievement levels in reading comprehension, mathematical reasoning, and content knowledge varying greatly. Of course, any class is to some extent heterogeneous: No two students are alike. Ideally, every individual student should receive instruction tailored to his or her needs, abilities, interests, and learning style. In practice, the pupil/teacher ratio in most secondary schools makes large-group instruction the most common and efficient means of teaching the standard curriculum. However, in very heterogeneous classes, a whole-class assignment may be unchallenging or repetitious for some students and too difficult for others. Students who are bored or frustrated are not likely to stay involved in activities, and inappropriate or disruptive behavior may result. Extreme heterogeneity may, therefore, have an impact on the management of student behavior as well as on instruction. Attempting to cope with heterogeneity by using many different assignments, providing an individualized, self-paced program, or using small-group instruction extensively in secondary classrooms increases the complexity of classroom management, requires a great deal of planning and preparation, and may require instructional materials that are not readily available. Rather than completely altering their instructional approach, many effective teachers provide for different levels of student ability by supplementing their whole-class instruction with limited use of special materials, activities, assignments, and small-group work. The following instructional procedures will help you cope with very heterogeneous classes.

Assessing Entering Achievement

The first step in planning for instruction in a heterogeneous class is to gather information about students' entering achievement levels and skills in areas that will affect their ability to succeed in your classroom. You can get this information by investigating existing test scores, administering pretests, and carefully assessing student performance on classwork in the first weeks of school. Results of achievement or aptitude testing from the previous school year may be available through the counselor's office. Examining these scores will give you an idea of the extent of differences in your classes and will identify students whose aptitudes are sufficiently extreme to require instructional adaptations. Although the variation in scores provides an indication of the heterogeneity of your class, be careful not to place too much reliance on a single test score to assess an individual student. Instead, supplement formal test information with observations of student performance on several assignments of different types to gauge the degree to which a particular student has special instruction needs. Other ways to obtain preliminary assessments of students may be found in teacher's editions of your course texts and from other teachers in your field. Often, departmental chairpersons have a file of classroom assessment materials. As you gather such information, be aware of the potential for developing and communicating a low performance expectation to students whom your early assessments identify as needing remediation. Also, be wary of bias resulting from an initial assessment, which might cause you to discount subsequent information that does not support the initial evaluation.

In addition to the information available from student performance on assignments, you can gain valuable insights from performance on specially designed classroom exercises. For example, in many courses, the ability to follow a lecture and take good notes is important. It is a good idea, therefore, to present a short lecture at the beginning of the year, telling students ahead of time that you will be collecting and checking their notes. This assessment will help you identify students who are likely to need special assistance and monitoring during content development activities. Similarly, requiring that students read a short section of the text, outline it, and answer some comprehension questions in class will give you an idea of the range of students' abilities to learn from the textbook you will be using.

Information on student needs and other characteristics, such as student interests and backgrounds, can also affect learning and instruction and should be considered whenever possible as you plan instructional activities and set goals. For instance, such information can be used to plan extra-credit projects and alternative assignments, as well as to identify small groups for instruction, pair students for peer tutoring, or create cooperative groups for learning activities.

Modifying Whole-Group Instruction

When you have information about how heterogeneous your classes are, you can plan appropriate adjustments of your instruction. First, consider ways that you can accommodate varying student needs simply by modifying your whole-class activities.

PARTICIPATION

During class discussions, recitations, or content development activities, be careful to include all students. Use some system (e.g., write each student's name on a three-by-five card, shuffle, and then systematically go through the stack) to be sure that each student has opportunities to participate frequently. Guard against the tendency to focus only on the higher (or lower) achieving students, allowing them to set the pace for the lesson.

PROCEDURES FOR MANAGING STUDENT WORK

In very heterogeneous classes, carefully planned and implemented student work procedures become especially important. You need to get information daily about how all students are performing, and students benefit from frequent individual feedback. Your accountability system should accommodate extra-credit or enrichment assignments, and it must also be designed so that lower achieving students who work diligently and make progress can make a satisfactory grade.

SEATING ARRANGEMENT

If you have one or two students who are especially likely to have trouble with whole-class assignments, place these students where you can easily keep an eye on them during instruction and seatwork. As soon as you have given seatwork instructions to the whole class and have monitored to ensure that students have begun work, check with the identified student(s) privately either to go over instructions again or to modify the assignment as needed. If there are more than two such students, it may be more efficient to treat them as a small group when giving supplemental instructions. Naturally, you will avoid labeling these students as remedial or slow.

FLEXIBLE ASSIGNMENTS

Include some classroom activities that can be done in a whole-class format but at different levels by different students. Use a grading or credit system that emphasizes individual student progress rather than competition among students. Examples of such activities include projects or reports, reading assignments of varying difficulty, and fluency-writing exercises in which students write for a specified period of time on an assigned topic, trying to increase the number of words they can generate each day. Other assignments that can be challenging to students at many different achievement levels include various composition and creative thinking assignments with open-ended directions such as "List all the Spanish -*ar* verbs you can think of; name as many protein foods (or mammals, or nations, or words with EAT in them, etc.) as you can." When assigning research papers or projects, provide a choice of topics or assign topics to students individually, adjusting the difficulty of the topic and the amount of structure you provide according to student ability.

SUPPLEMENTARY MATERIALS

Supplement whole-group instruction by providing enrichment materials for high-achieving students and remedial (review or practice) materials for lower achieving students. These materials can be used as the basis for regular, differentiated assignments or as extra-credit options. To differentiate class or homework assignments, plan a core or basic assignment that all students must complete. Then provide an additional part or parts that are either optional (e.g., for those seeking an A grade) or required of different groups (e.g., different spelling groups). Begin building a collection of supplementary materials by examining workbooks and texts from other grade levels, borrowing from other teachers and your curriculum coordinator, and reading from professional journals and magazines in your content area.

Enrichment or extra-credit material for students who finish classwork early should be work related and should not distract other students. Avoid free-time activities that are so attractive that slower working students feel deprived or are tempted to stop or rush through their work. Provide supplementary reading materials at a variety of reading levels. Set up a system for giving credit, feedback, or recognition for completion of enrichment activities.

PEER TUTORING

Peer tutoring provides an opportunity for one or more students to receive one-on-one assistance, particularly when the teacher is unavailable. It can be done during class by pairing students at similar levels to work together or by asking a student who has achieved a certain level or learned a concept to work with another student who has not. The student who receives assistance benefits from individualized instruction. The helper, or peer tutor, benefits from planning for and providing instruction.

Effective peer tutoring requires that certain management issues be addressed. You must decide when tutoring is and is not acceptable. There may be some topics for which peer tutoring is not appropriate. Also, peer tutors should have sufficiently learned the content to be able to provide assistance.

You will also want to decide where tutoring will occur. Some teachers provide a special location within the classroom where peer interactions are less likely to interrupt other classroom activities or disturb students who are working unassisted. Others may allow students to work quietly side by side at their desks or tables.

If you are going to use peer tutors frequently, it is a good idea to discuss with them the behaviors their role requires. Potential peer tutors should be shown how to model desired behaviors (e.g., demonstrate a skill or explain a concept), instructed in how to ask questions to assess the other student's understanding, and counseled on interpersonal behaviors. For long-term peer tutors, you may be able to provide brief training during class or before or after school. Other directions can be given as part of the overall instructions for an activity.

Cooperative Work Groups

For many activities, using small work groups or learning teams with mixed ability levels and/or diverse backgrounds provides a good opportunity for all students to help and learn from each other. Often, such groups are used as an alternative to individual seatwork after the teacher has provided whole-class instruction. Sometimes groups are used very extensively to organize instructional activities in a class. Researchers such as Robert Slavin (1990) have shown that working in mixed-ability teams can benefit both higher and lower achieving students in many subject areas. Benefits of cooperative groups can include increased student achievement, positive race relations, and increased student self-esteem. Not all researchers or educators agree that learning teams are as effective as their proponents have argued. We believe, however, that the weight of the evidence supports the use of cooperative groups as helpful in addressing the problem of heterogeneity. Because Chapter 6 presents guidelines for managing cooperative groups, we do not repeat that content here, but instead suggest that you review it before attempting to introduce this instructional method into your classes.

Small-Group Instruction

In some classes or in some content areas, the preceding suggestions for modifying or supplementing whole-class instruction may not be adequate to solve the heterogeneity problem. In these classes, teachers might need to use small-group instruction, forming relatively homogeneous subgroups. This commonly occurs in reading courses, in English classes for spelling instruction, or in mathematics classes, where some students lack skills in basic operations necessary to go on to more advanced work. In many subjects, small-group instruction might be used as a temporary measure with a group of students who have failed to pass a criterion-referenced test covering material that is prerequisite to subsequent units. The following are some examples of how small-group instruction might be conducted in secondary classes.

> Once per week, the teacher of an eighth-grade English class uses small-group instruction for spelling only. She has three groups: six students using spelling materials at the fourth-grade level, sixteen at the eighth-grade level, and five using advanced materials to prepare them for interscholastic competition. After opening class, the teacher goes over general seatwork directions with the whole class. Seat-

work directions are written on the board. They include one or two assignments (e.g., journal writing) that students can do without any further explanation from the teacher. Groups one and three begin seatwork while the teacher meets with the middle spelling group for content development and more seatwork directions. The teacher then meets with the first group for checking and content development and gives them another assignment. She checks on the middle group again before moving to content development with group three. In the time remaining in the period, after she finishes with the last group, she gives individual help to students and monitors seatwork.

In eighth-grade math, the teacher uses whole-class instruction for approximately the first half of the lessons in each chapter. Then students are divided into two groups: one containing six students and one with twenty-two students. The smaller group, which has students who are very deficient in math skills, uses a supplementary workbook covering essentially the same content and receives a second sequence of presentation, review, and practice similar to that for the material previously covered. The larger group continues in the textbook chapter until it has been completed.

Although small-group instruction can help cope with extreme heterogeneity, it presents more problems than modifying whole-class instruction. Small-group instruction makes classroom management and organization more difficult. It also requires more extensive planning and more materials—important considerations when you must prepare for five or six different class sections. Monitoring student behavior and work is more difficult because you are instructing the groups most of the period. Another important consideration is that when small-group instruction is used, students frequently spend relatively shorter periods of time interacting with you in content development and longer periods of time in seatwork. Consequently, seatwork assignments have to be planned so that students can do them with little assistance from the teacher. Despite all these problems, small-group instruction may sometimes be necessary to meet your students' needs, and it can be managed well with careful attention to instructional planning and classroom procedures. Some of the procedures you will have to decide on and explain to your students, if you use small-group instruction, follow.

LOCATION OF GROUP

Wherever you plan to meet, be sure the location allows you to watch the rest of the class while you are working with the small group. Other considerations include minimizing distractions and making efficient use of classroom space and time.

Decide whether to rearrange student seating according to group or, if you have space in your room, whether you wish to set up a group instruction area. Rearranging seats by group has the advantage of eliminating student movement when you change groups; you move from one group to the other—the students need not leave their desks. Also, you may be able to plan small-group seating so that each group is close to a different board, screen, or display area for assignments and to different storage areas (e.g., bookshelves) for materials. A disadvantage of rearranging seats according to small-group assignment is that it may have the effect of segregating students by achievement level and emphasizing differences among students. A good alternative, if you have the classroom space and workable numbers of students in each of your small groups, is to set up a table for small-group instruction at one end of your room.

MATERIALS

You must plan for and obtain materials and supplies for each group and set up files or other storage facilities.

STUDENT MOVEMENT

If you are able to set up a small-group instruction area to which you can call students, you will have to decide what procedures, rules, and signals you will use for student movement into and out of the group. Smooth and efficient transitions will depend on your explaining these procedures clearly and seeing that students follow them.

OUT-OF-GROUP PROCEDURES

Before using group work, you must communicate your expectations for students not in the group. For example,

- Will students be allowed to whisper or talk, or must they maintain silence?
- Under what circumstances may they leave their seats?
- What should they do if they need assistance on the assignment and you are not available?
- What should they do when they finish their work?

Mastery Learning

Teachers sometimes adopt a "mastery learning" approach when teaching heterogeneous classes. (Note, though, that the approach may also be used in other types of classes.) In a mastery learning approach, students receive instruction, complete assignments, and take tests just as they do in traditional classroom instruction, but if they do not reach some predetermined level of proficiency, they have the opportunity to repeat assignments and tests until they reach a mastery level of performance. In most mastery systems, grades are determined differently than in traditional classrooms. When students have mastered a particular objective, they receive full credit for that component (e.g., an A or all of the designated points). Students who do not demonstrate mastery do not pass that objective or receive any points. Teachers sometimes modify this grading system to include two levels of mastery (e.g., A or B), or they award partial credit or points when a retaken test or redone assignment indicates that performance is "passing" but not at a mastery level.

The goal of mastery learning is to improve achievement by providing increased feedback to students about their performance and an opportunity to revisit content not previously mastered in order to receive corrective instruction. Students are permitted to redo assignments and to retake tests until mastery is achieved (although such opportunities are constrained by available time and resources). In a heterogeneous class, this approach might permit students who require more learning time or assistance to reach an acceptable level of achievement on course objectives rather than be left behind early in the year or semester.

Establishing a mastery learning program entails a good deal of managerial planning. Areas needing attention include (1) arranging constructive feedback and supplementary instruction to aid students whose initial work is unsatisfactory; (2) finding time to develop and grade alternative forms of tests for retakes and to grade redone assignments; (3) scheduling retakes of tests; (4) developing enrichment activities and assignments to challenge students who reach mastery early; (5) managing paper flow and recordkeeping; and (6) communicating with students, their parents, and other teachers and administrators.

Ways to deal with these concerns include combining several short assignments into longer ones to reduce the frequency of paper transfer and recordkeeping. When more than a few students encounter similar problems on a test or assignment, reteaching in a large-group format can be an efficient feedback and instructional tool. Students who reach mastery earlier than other students can help with feedback and review by tutoring as an enrichment activity. Such students can also work on self-selected extension assignments or group projects for enrichment. Repeat tests can be scheduled for particular days of the week; students not taking the tests can work on other tasks at that time. Teachers usually specify due dates for redone assignments and establish a particular location for leaving and returning them so that reasonable organization of grading is possible. A handout describing the grading system is a must to assist both students and their parents in understanding the system (Kahn 1995). If possible, the teacher should include with the handout a statement of the purpose and underlying rationale for mastery learning.

Developing a mastery learning program incrementally might be a better strategy than attempting to implement it all at once. For example, a teacher could start with one class, allowing students a second opportunity to bring assignments or other performances up to the designated mastery criterion, or he or she might design one unit of instruction, including tests and assignments, on a mastery basis. The following semester, additional units might be added. A gradual approach permits the teacher to develop more efficient systems for managing paper flow and for providing feedback, supplemental instruction, and enrichment.

Teachers wishing to use a mastery learning approach will find it profitable to do some reading about it. Descriptions of mastery learning can be found in Block, Efthim, and Burns (1989) and Guskey (1994). Summaries of research on the approach are presented in Kulik, Kulik, and Bangert-Downs (1990) and Slavin (1987). A review of Case Study 4.3, illustrating the introduction of a mastery learning system at the beginning of the year, should also provide some helpful ideas.

Teaching Remedial Classes

In many secondary schools, especially in core academic subjects, students are assigned to classes on the basis of standardized test scores, academic record, teacher recommendations, diagnostic placement tests, or some combination of these factors. This process of homogeneous ability grouping or tracking results in the formation of several sections of a subject (e.g., high, average, and low sections) or, at least, in special remedial classes for students deficient in basic skills. Such grouping practices are carried out on the assumption that they help schools provide instruction that meets the needs of all students. Whether homogeneous grouping accomplishes this putative goal or instead actually results in harmful segregation of lower achieving secondary students is a topic that has been debated and researched for some time (Loveless 1999; Slavin 1990; Hallinan 1990; Oakes 1985). As can be inferred from this chapter's extensive presentation of strategies for managing heterogeneous classes, we believe that it is possible to accommodate substantial individual differences in a regular classroom setting. It is also the case that many teachers, other educators, and the communities they serve believe that teaching and learning at the secondary level can be accomplished more efficiently when the range of achievement in a class is not too great. The practice of grouping by "ability" is therefore likely to continue, even where there is an emphasis on accommodating diversity.

Concentrating lower achieving students in homogeneous groups can exacerbate management problems. Poor classroom management and organization in a remedial class can result in a classroom climate in which any student would have difficulty learning. It is possible, however, to manage such classes effectively and to maintain student involvement in learning activities with little disruption. When such classes are effectively managed, students can make progress in the subject and complete the course with positive attitudes. Most of these students will do their work if they have a reasonable chance of success, and they will pay attention and cooperate with the teacher. Obtaining good results with a lower track class requires extra effort both in managing behavior and in organizing instruction. The following sections describe how to use that effort efficiently.

Learner Characteristics

Students in remedial classes usually are achieving two or more grade levels below average students at their grade and age levels. Their grades in the subject usually have been low in the past, and some may have failed the subject in a previous year. These students bring with them more than their share of problems, some resulting from their lower achievement and some contributing to lower achievement. For example, absence and tardiness are often higher in such classes. The completion rate for assignments, particularly for homework, is probably lower than in other classes. Many low-achieving students are likely to view grades as arbitrary, failing to see a connection between their classwork and homework and the grades they receive in a course. Frequent failure in school in the past has caused some of these students to become very discouraged, and they may react by giving up easily or by fighting back. Teachers may encounter these reactions in the extremes of apathy, belligerence, or clowning around in class. Some of these students are very poor readers, which causes them problems in all subject areas. Others may have poor memory abilities. Most have poor study skills (e.g., in taking notes, outlining, being organized and methodical, and pacing efforts on long-term assignments). Maintaining attention for long periods of time is often difficult, particularly when they encounter a demanding or frustrating task.

When considering these general characteristics, keep two important points in mind. First, a homogeneous low-level class is not, of course, homogeneous at all. Such a class contains students with a range of achievement levels, academic aptitudes, other talents, learning disabilities, goals and aspirations, attitudes toward school, and family backgrounds. Avoid making assumptions about individual students just because they have been placed in a remedial class. Second, the preceding description of general characteristics of students at low academic levels might be interpreted as a list of reasons that teaching such classes effectively is difficult (or impossible). It is not intended as such. Instead, it is intended as a description of needs that should be addressed by the management and organization plan for such a class. These general characteristics suggest some special considerations with regard to monitoring student behavior and work; establishing classroom procedures, rules, and grading and accountability procedures; and organizing and presenting instruction.

Establishing Your Management System

In low-track classes, particularly in the early secondary grades, extra class time and attention may be required to teach students classroom procedures, rules, and routines at the beginning of the year. There may be more absences, shorter student attention spans, less ability to remember, and more testing of limits in such classes than in other class sections. Consequently, give extra attention to explaining, demonstrating, reviewing, and reminding students about your expectations; do not limit presentation, review, and feedback to only the first day or two of school. Plan to introduce and reinforce classroom procedures and routines gradually and methodically. Do not assume that students understand everything the first time you explain it. Question them, provide practice, and give them feedback. A "fun" written quiz on classroom procedures, routines, and requirements at the end of the first week of classes might be helpful. The following example illustrates how one middle school teacher devoted part of class time throughout the first two weeks of school to establishing her management system in a lower track English class. After the first several weeks of school, the class was task oriented and functioned smoothly.

> On the first day of school, a Monday, Ms. Evans spent about twenty minutes discussing school and class rules with students. She described the rationale for each

rule and the consequences of breaking rules. She also described a reward system for students who avoided detention hall during each six-week grading period. The discussion the first day was limited to basic school and class rules and procedures. Ms. Evans described the routine to be used by the students at the beginning of class each day. She also told students what materials to bring to class, and she explained procedures they would use to turn in classwork.

On the second day of class, Ms. Evans devoted twenty-one minutes to presenting additional procedures and reviewing some from the first day. As students entered the class, the teacher reminded them of the opening routine. After roll call, she described and demonstrated the correct form for heading the daily assignment paper, and she circulated around the room to check that students were using it. Students then copied the school and class rules discussed on the first day of school onto a piece of paper for their notebooks. When they were finished with the seatwork assignment, the teacher discussed a rule that had not been discussed the first day and described course requirements and the grading system.

On the third day of class, Ms. Evans spent six minutes discussing classroom rules, procedures, and routines with her students. Before the class started, she reminded all students of the beginning routine. At the end of the class, she reviewed some of the school and class rules and procedures and reminded students that beginning the following day, penalties would be assessed for tardiness, failure to bring materials to class, and other rule violations.

On Friday, Ms. Evans devoted ten minutes of class time to a discussion and review of procedures and rules. At the beginning of class, she did not remind students about the beginning routine, but she monitored them closely and reminded two students who were slow to start it. Later, she assigned a demerit to a student who failed to bring a pen or pencil, reviewing the reason for this procedure and penalty aloud to the class. At the end of the period, she conducted an informal oral quiz on class requirements, the grading system, and consequences of not following some rules and procedures. During the quiz, she called on many students rather than only on students who volunteered. After the quiz, she praised the class for their success in completing their first week of school in her class, and she talked with them during the final minutes of the period about their experiences at school during the week.

On the following Monday, the sixth day of school, Ms. Evans closely monitored the beginning class routine and prompted a few students who had forgotten it. She assigned a demerit to a student who failed to bring a pen or pencil. During the class, while students were engaged in a seatwork activity, there was an interruption from an outside visitor. After the visitor had left, the teacher reviewed her expectations for student behavior during interruptions. She also took this opportunity to review several other procedures and rules.

On the tenth day of class, Ms. Evans spent fifteen minutes carefully explaining procedures that students would be using for a new activity: instruction, testing, and seatwork in spelling groups. She assigned students to groups, explained rationales, and provided specific information about what the activity would involve, what she would be doing during group instruction, and what was expected of the students. She told students when spelling books were to be brought and reviewed the system she had set up for reminding students of materials needed for the next class period.

Monitoring Behavior

An absolutely essential ingredient of management is monitoring. You must be aware of what is occurring in your room. Keep your eyes on the students and scan the room frequently. If you see inappropriate behavior, deal with it promptly; when possible, use unobtrusive measures to stop it. Simple interventions, such as eye contact or proximity to the students, are best, as well as those that refocus the students' attention on their academic tasks. For example, "If you have questions about this work, raise your hand and I'll come help you." Or, "You should be working on the first five problems, not talking. When you finish number five, raise your hand and I will check your work." Prompt handling also minimizes the number of students involved and thus avoids creating peer pressure to resist the teacher or show off. Finally, you give the correct impression of fairness and consistency in handling problems.

Managing Student Work

The cornerstone of managing student work in lower level classes is an emphasis on daily and weekly grades. Such a system provides students with frequent feedback; it increases students' chances of success by making it difficult for individuals to fall far behind; it allows you to monitor student progress closely; and it helps develop good student work habits. Receiving some kind of grade or credit for effort and performance each day helps students accept responsibility for their schoolwork, especially if you have them keep a record sheet. You must allow time in class to show them how to follow this procedure. Have each student compute a weekly grade by calculating an average each week. (You may have to teach them how to do this.) Once established as a regular class procedure, it will help your students keep track of their progress. It will also make clear the effects of not completing one or more assignments during the week.

You should also consider making appropriate participation in class a part of your grading system. Participation includes answering when called on, volunteering questions, bringing appropriate materials to class, being on time, raising one's hand before speaking, and not calling out to other students or being out of one's seat. Rewarding participation encourages involvement, learning, and attendance. There are several ways to include participation in your grading system. You can give weekly or daily points for each student to add to his or her daily assignment score. You can minimize bookkeeping time by giving participation scores as a closing activity. If your system is simple (e.g., 3 points = good participation; 2 points = some; 1 point = a little; 0 = none, or disturbed class), you can award, record in your grade book, and call out points to twenty or so students in two or three minutes at the end of class.

You can also help make students accountable by making it clear that everyone is expected to participate in class discussions. To achieve this, use a system that ensures that you call on every student at least once or twice. You might also keep a weekly answer sheet. Put each student's name on it and give checks for good answers during recitation. You can then award points at the end of the week or when figuring weekly averages.

Planning and Presenting Instruction

More student learning and better classroom behavior are likely to result if you (1) organize classroom instruction into short activity segments with frequent assessments of student understanding, (2) pay extra attention to presenting directions and instruction clearly, and (3) build the teaching of study skills into your lessons. When planning classroom activities, avoid activity plans requiring that students attend to a presentation or work continuously for twenty-five or thirty minutes in the same seatwork activity. Instead, use two or more cycles of content development and student seatwork, as described and illustrated in Chapter 5. There are two distinct advantages to using several cycles instead of one in lower ability classes. One advantage is that it is easier to maintain student involvement because of the shorter time segments. Another advantage is that by careful monitoring you can more easily observe the extent to which students are able to complete the assignments. This allows you to pace instruction appropriately and to give corrective feedback and repetition during a later content development activity.

When using several instructional cycles, you must be especially aware of two things: pacing and transitions. You will have to keep track of time to leave enough time for each activity. One way to save enough time for later activities is to plan brief student assignments in the first (or the first and second) instructional cycle (e.g., a few problems, exercises, questions, etc.) and to do one or two with the students to get them started. Thus, these earlier student assignments become somewhat extended work samples. To avoid confusion about the assignment, write it on the chalkboard or display it on the overhead projector, even if it is quite short.

If a period contains more than one activity, it will have several transitions. Consequently, efficient transitions are a must. Rely on simple routines and use them very consistently. You might wish to review the discussion of transitions and pacing in Chapter 5.

Clear communication is important in all classes, but in remedial classes, clear directions and instruction are especially important; careless, overly complex communication is likely to result in student confusion, frustration, and misbehavior. Pay careful attention to the amount of information presented at one time, and use appropriate vocabulary and concrete or specific examples to illustrate new concepts. Check for understanding frequently. Avoid overlapping many procedural directions. Get everyone's attention and then present directions in a step-by-step fashion, waiting for students to complete each step before going on to the next. Finally, as you teach, be especially aware of opportunities to help your students improve their study and school survival skills. For example, assume that you must teach all of your students how to take notes in your class. Provide demonstration, assistance, practice, monitoring, and feedback. Use content presentations or discussions of the text as vehicles for teaching students how to identify main ideas and supporting evidence. Include in your course some instructional activities that will help students build their vocabularies and improve their computation or memorization skills.

Students with Special Needs

This section deals with students who have special needs either because they are physically or cognitively challenged or because they have some characteristic that affects their classroom performance. Students with special needs who are identified as special education students are by law provided instruction in the least restrictive environment. As a result, more and more students with special needs are being served in the regular classroom with some outside help from specialized teachers. Meeting the needs of these students presents special challenges to teachers with a classroom full of other students. Large class sizes and the push to cover prescribed content in regular education greatly limit the amount of individualized planning and instruction for students with special needs. At the secondary level, teacher planning and instruction generally focus on the whole-class and group levels. Research indicates that these factors, along with classroom management concerns, limit the amount of attention teachers give to individual student's knowledge acquisition (Vaughn & Schumm 1994; Schumm, Vaughn, Haager, McDowell, Rothlein, & Saumell 1995). It therefore requires conscious effort to take special needs of students into account and especially to keep abreast of their degree of understanding and progress.

Fortunately, research has provided some specific guidelines to help teachers work with these students in ways that promote their peer acceptance and their self-esteem as well as their academic achievement. Following are some suggestions for planning instruction for students with various types of special needs.

Content Mastery Classroom (CMC)

CMC is a classroom to which students may come from a core subject class for extra help on assignments, new material, or projects, or to have extra time to take or study for tests. In some school districts, both a general education teacher and a special education teacher are available in CMC to help students; thus, the program serves both special and regular education students who need extra assistance. In other districts, this is solely a special education option. An advantage of CMC, compared to a resource or self-contained class, is that it allows the integration of special education students into regular classes but provides support for them when they need more help. Also, the regular teacher, who may have thirty other students, does not have to provide as much supplemental instruction. Another advantage is that students may be sent as needed or may request to go when they feel they need extra help.

It is important to coordinate with the CMC teacher(s) about the students who may be sent, when they may be sent, and what kind of information and materials they will need to take with them. For example, for younger students, a laminated assignment card may be helpful, with the student's name and grade level printed on it. When a student is to go to CMC, you might write a brief description of the help the student needs, page numbers in the text that the student will take along, and the time the student leaves your room. The CMC teacher may also have some routines for getting information about the students' assignments, work, and so on.

When you have one or more special needs students who use CMC regularly, you must provide assignments ahead of time (e.g., weekly) so that appropriate planning can be done by the CMC teacher. When students take your tests in CMC, be sure you have discussed expectations for assistance with the teacher ahead of time. Because the CMC teacher will have worked with your students individually, he or she may have suggestions for adapting instruction or management that will aid you in teaching the student. Similarly, because CMC teachers have had substantial training and experience in working with students with special needs, you may be able to benefit from their suggestions. The CMC teacher may be reluctant to give unsolicited advice, so be sure to ask if you have questions about how best to work with particular students.

Inclusion

Inclusion programs for special education students provide support that lets them participate in as many general education classes as possible. Typically, a special education teacher works with general education teachers of designated students, both to help modify assignments and written material as specified on the students' individualized education plans (IEPs) and to provide assistance within the classroom itself. Regularly scheduled planning meetings between the special education teacher and general education teachers are crucial to the success of inclusion programs because only by knowing the activities planned by the general education teachers does the special education teacher know how best to provide support. The special education teacher may need to be in the regular classroom at times, such as when students are working on assignments or projects in class. At other times, the special education teacher may give the general education teacher copies of modified assignments needed by certain students and then leave to participate in another class. Both the timing and the nature of the special education teacher's participation in class will have to be specified during planning sessions, as will the extent of lesson modifications needed to accommodate the special students' conditions. Case Study 10.2, at the end of this chapter, illustrates one inclusion program at a middle school.

Students with Emotional and/or Behavioral Problems

It is helpful to remember that students with a diagnosed emotional disturbance are often different from others mainly in the degree of emotionality and their ability to regulate their behavior in response to these emotions rather than in the types of feelings they have. Any psychological report available can be quite informative (it must, of course, be treated confidentially) both in shedding some light on why the students are having such problems and in providing recommendations for working with them. You might also obtain useful information from the school psychologist, the special education teacher, the student's parents, therapists, or anyone else who knows the student well. A behavior management plan may have been developed through the special education department; becoming familiar with it and clear on how to follow it may prevent many problems.

If behavior is a serious issue, be sure you are familiar with the steps laid out in the student's behavior intervention plan. In general, overlook minor inappropriate behavior, reinforce acceptable behavior, and reduce known stressors. This may include lowering your expectations temporarily if the student is having an especially bad day. A positive, supportive, structured, and predictable environment is always a help to these students. They benefit from feeling safe and accepted.

If you have students who sometimes have temper outbursts or become easily frustrated and angry, reinforce all of their attempts toward self-control. Learn to recognize behavioral cues that may precede an outburst so that you can anticipate and intervene to prevent their losing control. Maintain a balanced perspective about such students; for them, getting through the day without an outburst may be more important than following instructions to the letter or completing assignments perfectly. Offering structured choices can be helpful, especially with students who have a strong need to control and who thus often appear noncompliant and oppositional (e.g., "Would you prefer to do the odd-numbered problems or the even-numbered?" "Would it be helpful for you to work awhile in the study carrel, or do you think you can concentrate well enough at your own desk?").

Work with the principal and special education staff to devise a plan to carry out if students with emotional problems become angry or aggressive in your classroom and no plan has been developed. These students may need to leave the classroom for a while to regain control in a safe time-out area. They will have to be supervised as they cool down. If there is an adult on the grounds who has good rapport with the students (e.g., a special education teacher or aide), try to have that person talk with them.

These students often do not know why they lose control, although they frequently tend to blame something or someone else if required to explain. They do not generally understand how their feelings relate to what has happened and have not yet learned to discern the subtle inner changes that trigger such outbursts. Helping them recognize the signs of increasing tension and suggesting ways to defuse before they have an outburst increases their sense of control and self-esteem. After an incident, a student may be remorseful or embarrassed; when both you and the student have regained your composure, it is important that you reestablish your relationship. Other than attempting to learn from each incident in an effort to prevent future occurrences, it is best if the teacher leaves each incident behind and does not remind the student of past failures.

One crucial reminder: When students lose control and are verbally or phys-ically abusive, the abuse is rarely directed at you personally, even though it may sound and feel as though it is. If you have learned about the backgrounds of these students, logic will tell you that you are merely the convenient target, not the root cause, of their pain or rage. Logic and feelings do not always mesh, however, so you may need a listener who can give you support and feedback when you are dealing with extremely volatile students.

Students who frequently lose self-control are not good candidates for inclu-sion. Their status in a regular education classroom should be reevaluated by the special education multidisciplinary committee that deals with individual education plans and admission, review, and dismissal.

Students with Serious Social Deficits, Often Diagnosed with Asperger's Syndrome

In recent years, increasing numbers of students who have odd or severe social skills problems are being diagnosed as having Asperger's Syndrome, which is technically a mild form of autism (Hodgdon 1995). As very little children, many of these stu-dents appear to be especially bright because of their ability to learn, remember, and recite facts. As they grow older, however, it becomes apparent that they have limited understanding of these facts and cannot generalize or apply any of the things they relate so accurately. Another severe deficiency becomes apparent: Al-though highly verbal, they have extremely poor communication skills. They tend to stand too close, avoid eye contact, talk too long and loudly in a preaching or robotic manner, and talk in great detail about factual matters that do not interest their peers.

Further, they are quite rigid in their outlook and develop set ways of doing things. They escalate quickly into extreme and visible anxiety when a routine is changed or when their expectations are not met. They may also have an acute sen-sitivity to sounds, with loud noises causing pain to their ears. Frequently, they have concomitant learning disabilities and poor gross and fine motor skills. When emo-tionally aroused, some individuals may engage in repetitive stereotyped movements such as hand flapping.

When students have had such problems to a severe degree, you can be fairly sure that during elementary school various interventions have been tried, possibly including evaluations to determine eligibility for special education services. It is likely that there has been some focus on teaching these students adaptive ways to cope with their strong needs for regularity and predictability and on methods for preventing escalating behavior with anxious verbal or physical aggression. Because most of these students have at least average intellectual abilities, they can usually succeed in general education classes, and they thrive on that intellectual stimula-tion. However, their odd reactions and behavior, despite coping mechanisms they may have learned, require that teachers understand their difficulties and know strategies to use to help them tolerate situations they may find anxiety provoking (e.g., those involving change, movement, or noise). By the time these students reach middle and high school, many of them have been subjected to ridicule by peers and are often confused by the ambiguous nature of interpersonal relationships. The following teaching strategies can help support these students in the regular classroom.

1. Because students with Asperger's Syndrome are visual, rather than verbal, learners, use visual cues and prompts; physically demonstrate how you want things done, and use manipulatives whenever possible.

2. Often, these students cannot process visual and auditory input simultaneously; that is, they are unable to look and listen at the same time. If this is a problem, give them either a visual or an auditory task, not both together.

3. Keep instructions brief. These students often have difficulty remembering sequences, especially in terms of how they are to apply instructions. Write instructions for them, or check to be sure they have written them correctly. Otherwise, give only one or two instructions at a time.

4. Remember that eye contact is extremely difficult and anxiety producing for them. Although you may insist on their attention, do not insist that they maintain direct eye contact with you.

5. The use of "social stories" or "social scripting" has been found to be an effective technique to help these students prepare for new events or experiences or for changes in routine. These are often used extensively in elementary school, but there are situations in which they may be helpful in middle or high school as well. Their purpose is to prevent an escalation of anxiety and facilitate a smooth transition through new experiences or changes in routine. The teacher may write out the story or work with the student to write it before the event. The student should then read it several times so that it will become familiar before time for the change to occur. Example: "On Thursday, I am not going to math class from advisory. Instead I am going with my advisory class to an assembly in the auditorium. After the assembly, I will go to math class."

6. These students may be skilled at computer work or drawing, or they may be fixated on a particular topic, such as maps, weather, trains, and so on. Capitalize on these strengths or interests to reward students for completing assignments, to provide opportunities to contribute positively to the class, and to develop their talents or knowledge and enhance self-esteem.

7. Students with Asperger's Syndrome do not readily learn social skills by observation, so you will have to be alert to awkward situations and be willing to give them specific feedback or step-by-step instruction. If you don't have an opportunity to provide needed instruction in social areas, discuss with the students' special education teacher or counselor any problems you see. When activities within your classroom require extensive peer interactions, consider using the social scripting technique to help such students handle these properly.

Students with Attention Deficit Hyperactivity Disorder (ADHD)

Behavioral characteristics of these students include distractibility, short attention spans, impulsiveness, an inability to organize, and a high level of movement. These symptoms vary in degree as well as combination. Some students with ADHD are mainly distractible, with short attention spans. Others are also very impulsive and disorganized. When the features of the disorder are mild and students' academic skills are average or above average, these students usually manage to compensate and function reasonably well. When academic abilities are weak and/or when impulsive and distractible behaviors are frequent, however, students experience considerable adjustment problems in most classrooms.

It is important to remember that these behaviors are not deliberate and that even highly motivated students can find it very difficult to learn ways to compensate for or control these problems. By the time these students have reached middle or high school, many have experienced much failure and have become discouraged and negative. Fortunately, there are ways of working with these students that increase the likelihood of success.

1. A positive and low-keyed, relaxed approach with much predictability and structure is almost imperative. Simple routines and clear rules and guidelines for behavior, along with friendly but consistent application, help these students.
2. Early in the year, ask other adults who know these students what works best for them. Consider consulting with the students themselves, their parents, and previous teachers or special education teachers.
3. Be sure you have the students' attention when giving oral instructions.
4. Make directions clear and brief.
5. If instructions involve a series of steps, provide them in written as well as oral form, or have the students copy down the steps and mark each one as it is completed.
6. Observe these students as they begin working on any new assignment; be willing to go over directions again individually.
7. Remind the students that accuracy is more important than speed; encourage checking over work before handing it in. Reinforce effort and, when feasible, do not penalize for messy work or errors that are not directly pertinent to the objectives of the activity.
8. Allow students to use a finger or card as a marker for reading to avoid skipping words or lines.

Students who are highly impulsive and distractible may quickly attract your negative attention. If you find yourself frequently correcting such students and are drawn into arguments and power struggles with them, try to refocus your attention on their positive characteristics and behaviors, and try to find things to praise and support. Whenever possible, use redirection, choices, and other unobtrusive interventions to keep the students on task.

Students Who Are Deaf or Hard-of-Hearing

Students with a serious hearing loss may be able to function in regular classes if some crucial modifications are made. If you have such a student, consult with a teacher specializing in auditory disabilities to learn about your particular student's needs and about techniques that might benefit him or her. If adaptive devices are available (e.g., FM auditory systems, caption decoders for videos), the specialist for deaf and hard-of-hearing students can show you how to use them. It is usually best to seat these students near the center of the room, close to the front. Face the students when speaking, and use the overhead projector rather than the chalkboard. This lets students see your face while you are writing. Have the room well lighted so that they can clearly see your lips and face to lip-read. Do not stand in front of windows or a bright doorway while talking; if you do, the glare behind you will make your face difficult to see.

Often, these students miss out on important information, being able to catch only portions of words or phrases. Because understanding is more complex than just hearing or responding to a name and because these students are often reluctant to ask you to repeat, you must make a habit of repeating and rephrasing important information or instructions. When possible, provide written backup as well.

The amount of new content vocabulary introduced routinely may be overwhelming to these students. The support of the specialist in preteaching vocabulary may be necessary to help them succeed in a regular classroom. Content mastery may be used to assist or to reteach, especially with written language assignments.

During classroom discussions, restate other students' questions and responses when feasible because students who are deaf or hard-of-hearing are often unable

"My mom told me to tell you that I am the educational challenge you were told about in college."
Reprinted by permission of Heiser Zedonek.

to lip-read them. Check frequently for understanding during guided practice by asking them questions. They will require close monitoring as they begin written work. If note taking is required, you may be able to provide a copy or enlist the assistance of a good student with legible handwriting who is willing to take notes. Students who are deaf or hard-of-hearing cannot take notes and lip-read at the same time. During films and videos, the narration and placement of actors may make lip-reading impossible. The specialist may be able to help find captioned versions of videos you plan to use. You might also assign buddies to cue these students when it is important to watch the teacher, to locate information in the text being discussed, and so on.

Increasingly, students who are deaf or hard-of-hearing are being assigned interpreters to accompany them to regular classes. Interpreters may serve as oral or sign language interpreters and provide a "communication bridge" between teacher and student. As such, they relay information both from the teacher to the student and vice versa. An interpreter should not function as a teacher's assistant in the classroom, but should support the assigned student. A consultation with the specialist on your campus can be helpful in clarifying the interpreter's role.

Middle and high school students with an auditory impairment may need to have contact with a resource teacher, not only for assistance with written language and content vocabulary, but also to explore the social and emotional impact of being teenagers with a hearing loss. The time spent with a resource person learning coping strategies and/or assistive technology provides important information and skills, allowing older students to gain more independence in managing their hearing loss in light of the changing social contexts of adolescence and adulthood.

Students Who Are Blind or Visually Impaired

Students who are blind or visually impaired may be able to function well in regular classes with your help. Suggestions for adaptations of teaching methods and materials should be available in the students' functional visual assessments, written by a teacher of these students. The following suggestions may provide direction.

1. Remember to read aloud anything that is written on the chalkboard or overhead projector.
2. Allow students to use tape recorders or to have fellow students make copies of their notes for parents to read aloud at home. Large type, dark print, and good contrast are easier to see.
3. When possible, use tactile models and hands-on activities along with oral descriptions to demonstrate concepts. These students often miss gestures, facial expressions, and details in demonstrations.
4. Encourage students to ask for help. If you are in doubt about how you can help, ask them directly, and do not hesitate to discuss their vision problems with them.
5. Remember that students with partial vision may tire more quickly, in part because of the concentration and effort required to perceive material close to their eyes. Frequent changes in the focus of activities may alleviate the strain.

6. Seat these students with their backs to the windows. Glare on materials, on someone who is speaking, or on the chalkboard or displays interferes with their ability to use partial vision.
7. Allow these students to walk up to the chalkboard or other displays as needed.
8. Students with visual impairments may have limited knowledge of spatial relationships and directionality. They may miss social cues and thus need assistance in peer interactions and personal adjustment.

Students Living in Extreme Poverty

Some schools have increasing numbers of students who live in significant poverty, which requires adjustments and understanding on the part of school staff. A key to success for these students is a strong, trusting relationship with a teacher, in an environment in which they feel safe, not threatened or stressed. You may be the one to help them understand how school can ultimately benefit them and why it is worth the trouble for them to attend regularly and work hard. Although by the time they reach secondary schools such students probably understand the kinds of things that get them into trouble and make teachers angry, they may not be able to articulate why they have such difficulty meeting school expectations or the specific differences between the culture of the school and the equally strict but more informal culture of their neighborhood. Talking with them respectfully, finding out what they are thinking, and listening and responding thoughtfully and without criticism will help build this trust and provide insights into their life and perceptions. After you have their confidence, asking questions such as, "What would happen if you did/did not do that in your neighborhood?" or "What would happen if you said that to your mother?" will give you valuable information and provide an opening to help them learn to adjust to the expectations of the school environment.

Adolescents coming from a culture of poverty are likely to present themselves differently from those brought up in a culture more compatible with school expectations. For example, they may talk more loudly than other students and be quicker to defend themselves against any perceived threats. When an adult is talking to them, they are more likely to read the body language and to interpret the tone of voice and facial expressions than to process the words in a lengthy lecture. In impoverished neighborhoods, great emphasis is placed on "saving face." Although this is important to most adolescents, it is of paramount importance to those living in extreme poverty. When being disciplined, therefore, these students may shrug or laugh off a teacher's reprimand, or they may talk back in a manner the teacher interprets as insolent, because they are willing to get into more trouble to keep from appearing weak to their peers. This is understandable because in their neighborhoods, the slow and weak may be exploited and victimized. Take great care not to overreact to or humiliate these students, and whenever possible, discipline them in private. This protects their dignity, reduces their need for defiance, and shows your sensitivity to their well-being, even while requiring that they follow the rules.

Approaches to working with these students can be found in Payne (1998). Because such students are often "at risk" for educational disadvantage, strategies suitable for this population (cf. Hargis 1997) are also applicable. Here are some suggestions for working with students from impoverished backgrounds.

1. Have some extra supplies and materials on hand for these students to use if they don't have them. Determine whether the school or district has a fund for such items or whether there are community organizations that provide assistance.

2. Teach procedures step-by-step. Encourage self-talk that focuses on the steps.

3. Because they are often preoccupied with problems at home, help them "bracket" their anxieties to put off worrying about something until a specific later time. Obviously, you will not do this if the problem needs to be addressed immediately.

4. Assign a peer "buddy," and encourage them to discuss problems and solutions together.

5. These students often need a guide to the underlying assumptions for behavioral expectations. Use a three-step approach: (a) pointing out what they are supposed to do; (b) giving meaning (reasons); and (c) providing a strategy (how to do it).

6. Encourage positive self-talk that will enhance their feelings of self-control: "I do this for myself. Not for the teacher, not for my parents, but for myself."

7. Teach goal setting; have them write down a concrete plan for class today, and at the end of class, see what goals have been met.

8. Allow them to help another student with something they do well.

9. When you meet with a parent of the student, your ability to demonstrate your enjoyment of and caring for her or his child will go a long way toward establishing a cooperative and mutually supportive working relationship. Even if the purpose of the meeting is to discuss a problem, you should set a pleasant and cordial tone. Keep the focus on taking positive steps to address problems.

Students with Limited English Proficiency

English is not the first language of many students in our schools. Some of these students have acquired sufficient English language skills to perform successfully in English-only classes. Other students do not have sufficient skills in speaking, understanding, reading, or writing English; they need additional assistance to participate successfully in school activities.

Some of these students need bilingual classes, where school content is presented in their native language and direct instruction is provided for learning English as a Second Language (ESL). Such classes serve as a support while students make the transition from exclusive use of a first language to the use of English. For many students, learning English occurs in conjunction with learning content in a regular classroom, ideally with the support of an ESL teacher or bilingual aide.

In many classes, including PE and electives such as art, homemaking, and music, bilingual support may not be available. Even in core academic classes, it may be very limited, especially for students whose English acquisition has progressed but who are not yet fluent. If you find that you have some students whose English is limited, here are some suggestions for communicating with them.

1. Find out from the bilingual or ESL teacher the extent of the students' production and understanding of English so that your expectations will be fair and realistic. If there are no bilingual or ESL teachers on your campus, identify the specialist who services your school and ask how to contact that person. Have the specialist evaluate the student and make suggestions.

2. Learn what the students prefer to be called, and be sure to pronounce their names correctly.

3. If their English skills are extremely limited, you will have more success if you learn some key words in their native language (e.g., "listen," "pay attention," "good," "look").

4. Rather than rely on a translator with these students, use your creativity when communicating, speaking naturally and grammatically but not too fast. Use gestures, facial expression, and body language. Point to things when appropriate, and limit your vocabulary when working one-on-one with the student.

5. Reinforce key points with visual aids and demonstration when possible, and restate in clear and concise words. For example, include a simple picture or drawing to illustrate some of the posted classroom rules.

6. Remember that a long receptive period is normal for students with limited proficiency in English, during which time they will respond with gestures, nods, and so on, before they feel confident enough to speak.

7. Keep in mind that even students who appear fairly proficient in day-to-day English may not be able to pick up the nuances of the language easily and thus may misunderstand directions, complex assignments, or difficult content. At times, these students may need after-school help or peer tutoring, when available.

8. If you have several of these students in your classes, ask your administrator to help find and allow you to attend a workshop, perhaps given through your local Education Service Center, focusing on techniques to use with limited English speakers.

9. If you have tried everything and find that the student is not benefiting from instruction because of the language barrier, consult with the school counselor or administrator about making a referral to a specialized program appropriate to meet the needs of the student.

No Child Left Behind

The No Child Left Behind (NCLB) legislation requires extensive testing of students. Although it is designed to have a long-term beneficial effect on educating students, this testing may be particularly stressful for special needs students, for whom any testing can provoke anxiety. For students in special education, teachers must first be familiar with the IEP recommendations regarding special provisions to be made during standardized testing, such as small groups, frequent breaks, different formats, and so forth. If you feel it would help, explain to individual students how their needs will be met (a student with ADHD may be relieved to know he/she may get permission to stand up and stretch during the testing).

Teachers can help relieve students' anxiety by using techniques similar to those they use with all students, although special needs students may require more intensive individualized or small-group training with additional repetition and rehearsal. Relaxation techniques such as deep breathing or visualization can be helpful. Training and practice in taking such tests, and emphasis on the importance of working slowly and checking back over answers, can relieve some fear of the unknown. Teach self-talk about steps to take for answering written questions. Remind students that the testing will be at their own level and that they can have all the time they need. Be sure the desks and chairs fit them and that the room temperature is appropriate to assure maximum comfort; seat them in an area in which they are least likely to be distracted but where you can see them at all times. Also, help students put these tests in perspective (e.g., remind them that the tests are only one part of the school day) to help them think beyond the anxiety of the testing situation and to look forward to more pleasant activities to come later.

Further Reading

Buzzell, J. G., & Piazza, R. (1994). *Case studies for teaching special needs and at-risk students.* Albany, NY: Delmar Publishers.

This book contains more than twenty cases written by teachers chronicling their experiences in teaching students with special needs. The cases cover the full range of physical, mental, and emotional disabilities and provide grounding for analysis and problem solving.

Forness, S. R., Walker, H. M., & Kavale, K. A. (2003). Psychiatric disorders and treatments: A primer for teachers. *Teaching Exceptional Children, 36*(2), 42–49.

The more common psychiatric disorders of adolescents include conduct disorders, ADHD, depression, and anxiety disorders; much less common are schizophrenia and autism. This article describes symptoms and discusses available treatments.

Kronberg, R., Jackson, L., Sheets, G., & Rogers-Connolly, T. (1995). A toolbox for supporting integrated education. *Teaching Exceptional Children, 27*(4), 54–58.

Including special education students requires that special educators, regular educators, and administrators work together to develop new concepts of roles and responsibilities. This article suggests a framework for thinking about how all participants should cooperate, and it also describes some activities and strategies to further the goal.

"Race, Class, and Culture." (1999). *Educational Leadership, 56*(7).

The theme of this issue of the journal addresses challenges that diversity brings to schools and teaching. Articles deal with the nature of effective education for various groups of students, adaptations to cultural differences, and the effects of strategies such as tracking and bilingual education.

"Students with Special Needs." (1996). *Educational Leadership, 53*(5).

This theme issue examines ways in which individual differences can be accommodated in schools and classrooms. Articles consider various approaches to working in regular classroom settings with students who have limited English proficiency, learning disabilities, lower achievement levels, attention deficits, or behavior problems.

 ## Suggested Activities

1. Chapter 2 includes a case study of procedures for small-group work in a science class. In addition to procedures for laboratory activities, the case study describes small-group discussion procedures that will help you in planning for the use of mixed-ability work groups in your class. Reread this case study.

2. Read Case Study 10.1, which details the procedures used by one English teacher for small-group instruction in spelling. As you read the case study, think about ways that these procedures might be adapted to your own classroom.

3. Three scenarios at the end of this chapter describe problems frequently faced by teachers of heterogeneous or lower level classes. After reading each description, review appropriate parts of this and other chapters. Decide what strategies you would recommend to deal with the problems. Discuss each problem scenario with other teachers, and make a brainstorming list of possible solutions and strategies. Afterward, compare your lists with those included in the keys in the Appendix.

CASE STUDY 10.1

USING SMALL GROUPS IN ENGLISH

Ms. Hanson uses small-group instruction during portions of each class period two days a week for instruction and testing in spelling. On Tuesdays, she meets with each of her three spelling groups for content development and introduction to seatwork on the new words for the week. Students in each group are seated together. This facilitates posting assignments, distributing or collecting papers, and group oral work.

The seatwork assignment for each group is posted near its area of the room. Each group's assignment includes at least one simple introductory task that students can do with no help from the teacher (e.g., copying each word five times, looking up words in the dictionary, and/or writing sentences with them). After the general instructions are given, all students begin work. The teacher works first with one group, going to its seating area to preview the words, work on pronunciation, and review the assignment. She then moves to another group. During the group activity with Ms. Hanson, each student is included in some oral recitation.

At the end of the week, Ms. Hanson uses small groups to administer spelling tests. While students are entering the room, she tells them to get out their journals and prepare a sheet of paper for a spelling test. After the bell rings, the teacher introduces two activities that will be proceeding simultaneously: spelling tests for three groups and a composition (journal) assignment. She explains the composition assignment and then reminds the students that she will be going around the room administering spelling tests. When students are not taking the test, they are to work on the journal assignment. Students in each group are seated together. As the students begin work, the teacher begins administering the test to the first spelling group. She stands near the group's desks and uses a low voice. While she gives the test, she also monitors the rest of the class to make sure they remain on-task. After she finishes giving the test (about five minutes), the teacher collects the papers, puts them in a specially marked file folder, and goes to the next group. She begins giving the test to the next group but continues to monitor the remainder of the class and signal for quiet when there is some noise from another area.

When the teacher finishes with the second group, she answers questions for students, files the papers, and then goes to the next group to give the test. She does not allow students to interrupt her while she is working with another group. When she finishes administering the test to the third spelling group, she collects the papers, files them, and lets the students know how much time they have to finish and to proof their journal assignment.

CASE STUDY 10.2

AN INCLUSION PROGRAM IN A MIDDLE SCHOOL

Teachers in this school are on grade-level teams, with a teacher from each of five subject areas at one grade level on each team, along with a special education teacher. Days are divided into seven periods, allowing teachers to have one conference period and one period for team planning. Although this district has a continuum of special education programs, including self-contained classes, resource classes, and Content Mastery, the emphasis is on inclusion to the extent possible. General education teachers make necessary modifications for students who need them, and the special education teacher helps with this. General teachers give the special education teacher their lesson plans so that he or she can make up study guides, do highlighting, and identify areas in which the special students will need supplemental instruction or modification. This teacher determines which class to work in depending on what the general teachers indicate during planning sessions. If a class will be working on a written assignment for most of the period, the special education teacher may modify directions for specific students and give these to the classroom teacher for the designated students to do on their own during class. When more unstructured work will be done in class, the special education teacher usually provides on-the-spot support to some of the students. Often, this teacher assists other students in the class as needed, although the identified students are the first priority.

An example of the way the teachers work together during instruction can be illustrated with a lesson on latitude and longitude in a seventh-grade social studies class. One week, the class worked on a project involving plotting a route for traveling around the world. The social studies teacher introduced the concepts with examples and some initial practice. At the beginning of one period, instructions were provided to students, who were to work in pairs to plan their route. Students had most of one period to complete the assignment, and they had access to a variety of materials including atlases, laminated maps, rulers, string, and so on. The special education teacher entered the room about ten minutes after the class started, shortly before the social studies teacher had finished talking with the students about how they were to work on the assignment. Both teachers monitored the students as they worked, answering questions and offering suggestions. Although the special education teacher's attention was not limited to the identified students, she did provide them with more explanation when it was apparent they had not mastered the concepts needed to perform the assignment.

In this inclusion program, the general education teacher is responsible for planning daily lessons and grading. The special education teacher provides and/or modifies material as appropriate for special students, develops IEPs for the students, and is the main contact person for ARD (Admission, Review, and Dismissal) meetings. On occasion, the special teacher might take students to another area to reteach new or complex material or to give a retest if needed. During planning periods, the teachers work out the details of what is needed and how they will work together on it.

 Problem Scenarios

PROBLEM 10.1: HETEROGENEOUS CLASSES

Never before has Ms. Garcia had to deal with students of such different entering achievement levels in her seventh-grade class. She feels frustrated in her efforts to provide instruction at appropriate levels for some students several years below grade level and others above grade level. The brightest students finish seatwork far ahead of the rest of the class, while the slowest students seldom complete an assignment successfully.

So far, Ms. Garcia has tried two things. She decided to provide extra-credit activities for students who finish work early, and she has begun to help slower students individually more often during class and after school. Both of these steps seem to help, although each has also created some management problems. What else might Ms. Garcia do?

PROBLEM 10.2: TEACHING A REMEDIAL CLASS

Sometimes Ms. Porter feels that the students in her second-period class are either unwilling or unable to learn anything. Many seem apathetic; they won't even try. Many have short attention spans, and some seem to require constant individual assistance.

At the beginning of the year, Ms. Porter assumed that she would teach her remedial section much as she would teach the other classes, except for using a slower pace and allowing more drill and practice for the students. After several weeks of school, she realized that other adjustments would have to be made as well.

She began showing students exactly what to write as notes during teacher presentations, and she began asking more frequent, simple review questions in class to hold students' attention and help them learn. These measures helped, but many students still don't complete their work successfully. What are some other adjustments Ms. Porter might make?

PROBLEM 10.3: STUDENT BEHAVIOR IN A REMEDIAL CLASS

Mr. Oliver is concerned about behavior in his class. Several students are always late, and others frequently forget their books, paper, pencils, or assignments. During content presentations, students call out answers or comments, leave their seats to throw away paper or sharpen their pencils, and often talk or write notes. During seatwork assignments, students work the first problem or two while the teacher is watching but then turn to their neighbors as soon as the teacher turns his back to work with individual students. Mr. Oliver tried to establish order by using a system of penalties, in which students had to write out and turn in definitions of problems if they were caught misbehaving. This system had worked well with his other classes, but in this class, he found he was constantly assigning penalties and was unable to keep track of whether they were turned in. What other ideas could Mr. Oliver try?

Answer Keys
for Chapter Activities

Chapter 1

ACTIVITY 1

The room arrangement shown in Figure 1.2 will contribute to classroom management problems in a number of ways. Specific items include:

- Students at the rear of the row farthest left will have difficulty seeing the overhead projector screen.
- When the teacher stands at the overhead projector, six students will be seated behind her.
- Desks are arranged so that students face other students. Although this formation may be useful during class discussions for encouraging students to respond to each other, it may produce a high level of distraction during other activities.
- Some student desks face windows, which might also be a source of distraction. The same desks face away from a chalkboard.
- The group of four desks on the right side of the room is in front of the bookshelf and impedes movement in that area of the room. Students at those desks are likely to be distracted by students using materials or equipment at that end of the room.
- The wastebasket is not conveniently located; a place nearer the door would be better.
- The table is too near the teacher's desk and crowds several student desks.
- Students working at the table might disturb others nearby. Traffic flow in the area around the teacher's desk and table is poor.
- The major instructional area by the overhead projector has no table, desk, or other storage space to hold materials needed in presentations.

Chapter 3
CASE STUDY 3.4

DIAGNOSIS

Ms. Wood has problems keeping her general mathematics students responsible for their work assignments. In her algebra classes, where students are more motivated, Ms. Wood has fewer problems. Her general mathematics students, however, may need help in learning to assemble a notebook, becoming responsible for doing quality work, and completing it. Because 75 percent of their grade is based on tests, and because their daily work is checked only once a week, students probably think their daily work is not very important. Perhaps this has contributed to their poor sense of responsibility.

SUGGESTIONS

Ms. Wood should review her accountability procedures and her grading system, giving consideration to the following items.

- Make certain that all students know how each assignment contributes to their overall grade and that instructions are clear with respect to completeness, neatness, quality of work, and due dates.
- Monitor progress frequently when standards have been established and students understand them. Students should receive regular feedback.
- Check notebooks periodically for completeness, thus keeping students from getting too far behind.
- Be explicit about what is to be included in the notebooks and how it should be organized. Notebooks should also contain a table of contents and a list of required assignments. Displaying a model notebook would be helpful.
- Allow students to check their own assignments or to exchange papers. This will help provide immediate feedback, and it will allow for more frequent checking of required work.
- Have students keep track of their daily grades, quizzes, and extra-credit work. Spend some class time helping them compute averages on different occasions during the grading period.
- As students work, circulate and monitor student progress rather than remain at the teacher's desk.
- Check promptly with students who fail to turn in assignments. If students need help, provide it; otherwise, require that assignments be completed.
- Do a portion of each assignment orally and question students to check for understanding.

Chapter 4

CASE STUDY 4.4

DIAGNOSIS

Mr. Davis has failed to be specific with his students about his expectations for their behavior. His only rule is too general to serve for all situations. Because he used one general rule, Mr. Davis must constantly interpret concrete instances of infractions as they relate to the rule. Furthermore, he has not been specific about consequences and has mentioned only one penalty, that of going to the office. Mild misbehaviors at the beginning of the year have now escalated into more serious misbehaviors as students test the limits. At this stage, Mr. Davis is receiving poor cooperation both in obtaining written work from students and in the area of class participation.

SUGGESTIONS

Mr. Davis might begin to establish better behavior in his class in the following ways.

- Reevaluate the rules and procedures with the intent of making them more specific, and introduce rules and procedures for areas that were previously not covered.
- Select a time such as a Monday or the day after a vacation period to reintroduce and explain the rules and procedures, providing students with rationales for the desired behaviors and eliciting their cooperation in following them.
- Review procedures for participating in class discussions and for times when whispering and working together is allowed and when it is not.
- Once the rules and procedures are introduced, clear and specific consequences for infractions should be stated. These should be tied to the behaviors themselves; trips to the office should be used only for the most serious offenses. Positive as well as negative consequences should be considered and communicated to students.
- Monitor the class constantly with the goal of anticipating and preventing misbehavior and noting appropriate behavior.
- Make sure students have enough work to do and that they understand it and are able to complete it. Require student attention during presentations, and allow only relevant materials and books to be out on desks. Have students take notes during important parts of the presentation. Be explicit and teach them how to take notes. Require them as part of a notebook.
- Break longer activities into shorter ones, and vary the sequencing and routine for the sixth-period class. Students are tired at this time of the day; maintaining attention is not easy even with well-behaved classes.

- Pace students through their work with statements such as, "You should be halfway through with this assignment by now." Or, "We will check the first part of the assignment in five minutes."
- Reward academic performance and other desirable classroom behavior regularly. For students of this age, extra-credit points or privileges may be more reinforcing than public praise.

Chapter 5
CASE STUDY 5.1

The following suggestions for Ms. Liu would help improve her students' comprehension.

- Outline the lesson sequence, breaking down complex lessons into smaller, easier to understand parts or steps. Be sure to define words that students may not know.
- During presentations, let students know what they are expected to write in their notes by underlining important points as they are written on the chalkboard or by displaying them on an overhead transparency. Another way to structure note taking is to give students an outline with space for additional notes.
- During content development activities, obtain frequent work samples by having students do problems or answer questions. Circulate during these times, checking for areas of confusion, common problems, and students who are not participating. Based on feedback from these samples, adjust instruction by slowing down, increasing the pace of the presentation, or repeating content where necessary.
- Be sure students know the purpose of the lesson. At the end of presentations, always restate major objectives or else quiz students on important points.
- Give students step-by-step instructions for assignments. Check to be sure they understand what they are to do, and then help them pace their work by telling them how long the assignment should take to complete and warning them when there is a short time left.
- Circulate while students are doing seatwork assignments. Check to be sure that they are working on the assignment, that they are doing it correctly, and that they are using their time wisely.
- If it becomes apparent during a seatwork or recitation activity that some students do not understand the material, have them join you in a small group after the general presentation. At this time, you can review the points of the lesson and answer questions.

CASE STUDY 5.2

Mr. Miller could reduce the amount of time wasted by his class by using the following approaches.

- Use an academic warmup as part of the beginning-of-class routine. Have the warmup written on the chalkboard or displayed on an overhead transparency, and require that students complete the task in a set period of time (e.g., five minutes). Be sure that warmup activities are checked and that they count toward the students' grades.
- Use established routines as much as possible for beginning and ending lessons, passing and collecting papers and supplies, and exchanging papers to grade. Monitor to be sure students follow routines.
- Teach students exactly what behaviors are expected during transitions: voice level, pencil sharpener use, procedures for passing papers, and so on.
- Give instructions for what is to be done before beginning transitions, not during them.
- Post assignments where all students can see them. Begin seatwork assignments together as a class, doing the first problems or answering the first question as a group. Then monitor at the beginning of seatwork to be sure that everyone gets off to a good start.

CASE STUDY 5.3

Ms. Kendall could begin organizing her curriculum for the year by taking the following steps.

- Seek out existing curriculum guides. Check with the department chairperson for copies of systemwide curricula, goals, and objectives, as well as anything that is unique to her school. Obtain a copy of the teacher's manual for the text and examine the suggested yearly outline. Seek out the suggestions and aid of a successful teacher who has taught the class for several years and is willing to share ideas and materials. Call the school system's science coordinator for additional information and to find out what resources are available.
- Before preparing lesson plans, gather information on students, texts, facilities, and budget. How many students will be in the class and what are their ability levels and prior science courses? What books will be used; will sufficient quantities be on hand when the school year begins? What facilities, equipment, and materials will be available? What may be purchased and how are requisitions handled?
- Refer to the lesson plan guidelines set forth in Chapter 5. Be sure to include a variety of activities each day—no lesson should be straight lecture or all seatwork. During the first week, allow more time for emphasis on

student learning of rules and procedures. Teach students how to participate appropriately in class, and gear the first week's academic activities to student success. Also, during the first several weeks, be sure to set in place procedures for developing student accountability (refer to Chapter 3).

CASE STUDY 5.4

As his fourth-period class begins, Mr. Case makes eye contact with two students who are exchanging notes; the students quickly get out their class materials. (**Withitness.**) "Let's begin by working some of the exercises at the end of the chapter; you'll need your notebooks." As students begin to get out their materials, Mr. Case calls out, "Oops, I forgot to tell you to bring money tomorrow for the field trip. How many of you will be going?" (**Thrust.**) After a brief discussion, students finish getting out their materials. Mr. Case says, "We'll go through these exercises orally, but I also want you to write the answers in your notebooks as part of today's classwork. I'll come around and check your notebook work later in the period. (**High participation format and accountability.**) Now who can answer the first question? Hands please. Tyrone?" Mr. Case conducts the lesson by calling on various students, some with hands up, others seemingly at random from the nonvolunteers. (**Group alerting.**) About halfway through the exercises, a student enters the room and says that he is new to the school and has been assigned to the class. Mr. Case goes to his desk, sits down, and says, "OK, come here. I'll check out a text to you. (**Absence of overlapping.**) I wish the school office wouldn't send people in the middle of a period. Where are you from anyway?" (**Stimulus-boundedness.**) After giving the student a syllabus and a text, Mr. Case leaves his desk and says to the class, "Now where were we? Oh yes, question seven. Say, where did Kim and Lee go? I didn't give them permission to leave." (**Absence of withitness.**) After several minutes more, Mr. Case calls a halt to the activity and says, "Now I'd like us to discuss the test coming up this Thursday. Let's make sure that you are all clear on what will be on the exam and what you will need to study to get ready for it." After a pause, he adds: "I almost forgot. Get out your questions from before and look at the next to the last one. We need to add an important point that was left out." After finishing the item, Mr. Case turns the topic back to the upcoming test. (**Flip-flop.**) "Now, where were we? Oh yes, I need to show you some items that will be similar to those on the test. Here's one." He writes it on the chalkboard, then pauses: "Well, I don't want to give away the test, do I?" Without discussing the test further, he turns to another topic. (**Dangle.**) "Just wait until you hear about the videotape we will be viewing tomorrow. I borrowed it from another teacher, and she said that her students thought it was one of the most thought-provoking, exciting stories they had ever seen!" (**Group alerting.**)

CASE STUDY 5.5

DIAGNOSIS

Ms. Grant has made a common mistake. She assumes that students will be able to follow her directions with a minimum of structuring or explanation on her part. In this case study, she assigns lab work that requires students to work in groups but does not prepare them for this activity. Group assignments are handed out but not explained clearly, nor do students attend to the directions. When students move to their groups, transitions are disorderly and directions are vague as to how the groups of students are to pursue the question, "What is in the box?" The activity drags, and several groups sit in dead time while others finish. Groups are expected to report their findings, but no directions are given about how to do this. At the end of the activity, Ms. Grant provides no wrap-up or evaluation, and she assigns a textbook reading on a different topic.

SUGGESTIONS

Ms. Grant might achieve more success with her class if she presents information systematically. The following items will help.

- State major goals and objectives, and tell students what they will be responsible for knowing.
- Call for attention; do not proceed without it. Require that students listen to directions and presentations. Have them respond to questions and demonstrations.
- Explain precisely what behaviors are expected when students work together in groups on an assignment. Have each group pick a recorder who will be responsible for presenting the group reports to the rest of the class.
- As groups are working, monitor and circulate to make certain they are on the right track. If widespread problems seem to be occurring, reteach the material. Allow students to begin work only when satisfied that they can complete the tasks satisfactorily.
- Provide additional activities for groups who finish early so that unnecessary dead time is avoided.
- Constructively evaluate the individual reports rather than accepting poor or incomplete answers.
- Follow up the group activity with relevant discussion and a summary of the lesson.

Chapter 8

ACTIVITY 8.2

1. b   2. c   3. d   4. a   5. c

Chapter 10

PROBLEM 10.1

To deal with very diverse ability levels, Ms. Garcia might try the following approaches.

- If one or two students are especially likely to have trouble with whole-class assignments, these students can be seated where the teacher can easily keep an eye on them during instruction and seatwork. As soon as seatwork instructions have been given to the whole class and the teacher has monitored to be sure that they have begun work, she can check with slower students privately to go over instructions again or to modify the assignment as necessary. These instructions and directions can be done as a small-group activity if more than one or two students need the extra assistance.
- Enrichment or extra-credit material for students who finish classwork early should include work-related activities that will not distract other students. Feedback, credit, and recognition for completion of enrichment activities should be a part of the system.
- All students in the class should be involved in discussion or recitation sessions. Systematically calling on each student gives everyone an opportunity to participate.
- If the preceding suggestions are not sufficient for a given class, small-group instruction might be used for part of the coursework. Procedures for group work must be planned and then taught carefully. When two or three work groups are established in a class, instruction and monitoring will be simpler if seatwork assignments are planned so that there is a basic assignment that all students complete, with additional activities at appropriate levels for each group. Some of the instruction can then be with the whole class, with a smaller amount reserved for each group.
- When using differentiated assignments, adjustments in the grading system should be made so that lower ability students can attain satisfactory grades.

PROBLEM 10.2

If she is not already doing so, Ms. Porter should be sure that she is spending adequate class time explaining the material to the whole class. This is preferable to trying to impart the instruction to individuals during seatwork. To avoid long presentations and the attendant problem of maintaining student attention and participation, divide the presentation into two (or more) segments, with short periods of seatwork or classwork in between.

- Frequent work samples, written as well as oral, should be obtained from students during content development activities to keep abreast of student understanding.

- Every student should be included in discussions or recitations to keep them involved in the activity.
- Providing structure for classwork and homework is essential. All assignments in class should begin as a group exercise. Photocopies or worksheets that lead students through tasks in a step-by-step fashion with frequent, short, written responses also are helpful.
- Daily grades should be emphasized, and students should be provided with frequent feedback about their progress to support and encourage their efforts.

PROBLEM 10.3

Mr. Oliver should reconsider his classroom rules and procedures to determine whether they cover the misbehaviors that are causing him a problem. If adjustments are needed, the relevant rule or procedure should be restated and introduced to the students again. Mr. Oliver should also consider whether his monitoring is adequate or whether students are getting away with too much misbehavior before he deals with the problem. In addition, some measures to correct or prevent specific problems described in the scenario are:

- Mr. Oliver may be overrelying on the penalty system to respond to misbehavior. If so, it would be better to use such penalties only for a limited number of situations (e.g., forgetting materials or disturbing the class). Recording penalties can be simplified by keeping a clipboard with a list of students' names and a place for a daily record.
- Compliance with procedures can be rewarded by awarding points toward a participation grade or a favorite activity. Give students daily points or checks for having appropriate materials, being in their seats and ready to work when the bell rings, and staying on-task throughout the period.
- There are several ways to help students remember to bring materials. A supply of pens or pencils may be kept on hand for emergency loans, with some penalty imposed when students have to borrow supplies. Students can be allowed to leave pencils and papers in the classroom so that they will always be available. These can be labeled or kept in a folder with the students' names and class period listed on it. If different materials are needed on different days, Mr. Oliver can have students keep a record of materials and assignments needed for the class so that they can refer to it as necessary. He can also post a list of books and other materials above or next to the door so that students can see it before they enter the room.
- Before content presentations, Mr. Oliver might remind students that he will call on them to answer and that they should not call out except when he signals that it is appropriate.
- Inappropriate behavior during presentations should be stopped by a simple procedure such as eye contact or reminding students of the procedure

or rule, without interfering with the flow of the lesson. If the behavior persists, a penalty can be imposed.

- It is always helpful to move around the room during presentations and while students are engaged in seatwork activities. Mr. Oliver should walk by every student in the room, looking at papers to be sure that students are working on the right assignment and doing it correctly. He should avoid staying too long with any one student, and if a student needs additional help, he or she can come to a table or desk from which Mr. Oliver can monitor all students. Frequent circulating tends to discourage note writers and talkers.

References

Alvermann, D. E., O'Brien, D. G., & Dillon, D. R. (1990). What teachers do when they say they're having discussions of content area reading assignments: A qualitative analysis. *Reading Research Quarterly, 25,* 296–322.

Arlin, M. (1979). Teacher transitions can disrupt time flow in classrooms. *American Educational Research Journal, 16,* 42–56.

Bandura, A. (1986). *Social foundations of thought and action.* Englewood Cliffs, NJ: Prentice-Hall.

Bassin, A., Bratter, E., & Rachin, R. (Eds.) (1976). *The Reality Therapy reader: A survey of the works of William Glasser.* New York: Harper & Row.

Battistich, V., Solomon, D., & Delucchi, K. (1993). Interaction processes and student outcomes in cooperative learning groups. *Elementary School Journal, 94,* 19–32.

Berger, E. H. (2000). *Parents as partners in education: Families and schools working together* (5th ed.). Upper Saddle River, NJ: Merrill.

Bicard, D. F. (2000). Using classroom rules to construct behavior. *Middle School Journal, 31*(5), 37–45.

Block, J. H., Efthim, H., & Burns, R. (1989). *Creating effective mastery learning schools.* New York: Longman.

Boonstrom, R. (1991). The nature and functions of classroom rules. *Curriculum Inquiry, 21,* 193–216.

Bransford, J. B., Brown, A. L., & Cocking, R. R. (Eds.) (1999). *How people learn.* Washington, DC: National Academy Press.

Brophy, J. (1998). *Motivating students to learn.* Boston: McGraw-Hill.

Brophy, J., & Alleman, J. (1991). Activities as instructional tools: A framework for analysis and evaluation. *Educational Researcher, 20*(4), 9–23.

Burns, M. (1995). The 8 most important lessons I've learned about organizing my teaching year. *Instructor, 105*(2), 86–88.

Butin, D. (2000). *Classrooms.* ERIC Report number ED446421. Washington, DC: National Center for Educational Facilities.

Buzzell, J. G., & Piazza, R. (1994). *Case studies for teaching special needs and at-risk students.* Albany, NY: Delmar Publishers.

Cameron, J., & Pierce, W. D. (1994). Reinforcement, reward, and intrinsic motivation: A meta-analysis. *Review of Educational Research, 64,* 363–423.

Canter, L. (1989). *Assertive discipline for secondary educators.* Santa Monica, CA: Canter and Associates.

Canter, L., & Canter, M. (1976). *Assertive discipline.* Santa Monica, CA: Canter and Associates.

Carkhuff, R. R. (1999). *The art of helping in the 21st century* (8th ed.). Amherst, MA: Human Resource Development Press.

Cohen, E. G. (1994). Restructuring the classroom: Conditions for productive small groups. *Review of Educational Research, 64,* 1–36.

Cohen, E. G. (1998). Making cooperative learning equitable. *Educational Leadership, 56,* 18–21.

Cohen, J. J., & Fish, M. C. (Eds.) (1993). *Handbook of school-based interventions.* San Francisco: Jossey-Bass.

Cutrona, C., & Guerin, D. (1994). Confronting conflict peacefully: Peer mediation in schools. *Educational Horizons, 72*(2), 95–104.

Deci, E. L., & Ryan, R. M. (1985). *Intrinsic motivation and self-determination in human behavior.* New York: Plenum Press.

Educational Research Service (1989). *ERS information folio: Cooperative learning.* Arlington, VA.

Edwards, C., & Stout, J. (1990). Cooperative learning: The first year. *Educational Leadership, 47*(4), 38–43.

Egan, G. (1998). *The skilled helper: A problem management approach to helping* (6th ed.). Pacific Grove, CA: Brooks/Cole.

Eilam, B. (2001). Primary strategies for promoting homework performance. *American Educational Research Journal, 38,* 691–725.

Emmer, E. T. (1988). Praise and the instructional process. *Journal of Classroom Interaction, 23,* 32–39.

Emmer, E. T., & Aussiker, A. (1990). School and classroom discipline programs: How well do they work? In O. Moles (Ed.), *Student discipline strategies: Research and practice.* Albany, NY: SUNY Press.

Emmer, E. T., Evertson, C. M., & Anderson, L. M. (1980). Effective classroom management at the beginning of the school year. *Elementary School Journal, 80,* 219–231.

Emmer, E. T., & Gerwels, M. C. (2002). Cooperative learning in elementary classrooms: Teaching practices and lesson characteristics. *Elementary School Journal, 103,* 75–91.

Evertson, C. M. (1994). Classroom rules and routines. *International Encyclopedia of Education* (2nd ed.). Oxford: Pergamon Press.

Evertson, C. M., & Emmer, E. T. (1982). Effective management at the beginning of the school year in junior high classes. *Journal of Educational Psychology, 74,* 485–498.

Evertson, C. M., & Weinstein, C. S. (Eds.) (2005). *Handbook of classroom management: Research, practice and contemporary issues.* Mahwah, NJ: Erlbaum Associates.

Fenwick, D. T. (1998). Managing space, energy, and self: Junior high teachers' experiences of classroom management. *Teaching and Teacher Education, 14,* 619–631.

Fifer, F. L. (1986). Effective classroom management. *Academic Therapy, 21,* 401–410.

Forness, S. R., Walker, H. M., & Kavale, K. A. (2003). Psychiatric disorders and treatments: A primer for teachers. *Teaching Exceptional Children, 36*(2), 42–49.

Fraser, B. J., & Walberg, H. J. (Eds.) (1991). Educational environments: Evaluation, antecedents and consequences. Oxford: Pergamon.

Freiberg, H. J. (1996). From tourists to citizens in the classroom. *Educational Leadership, 54,* 32–36.

Freiberg, H. J. (Ed.) (1999). *Beyond behaviorism: Changing the classroom management paradigm.* Boston: Allyn and Bacon.

Gamoran, A., & Berends, M. (1987). The effects of stratification in secondary schools: Synthesis of survey and ethnographic research. *Review of Educational Research, 57,* 415–437.

Glasser, W. (1975). *Reality therapy: A new approach to psychiatry.* New York: Harper & Row.

Glasser, W. (1977). 10 steps to good discipline. *Today's Education, 66,* 60–63.

Glasser, W. (1986). *Control theory in the classroom.* New York: Harper & Row.

Good, T. L., & Brophy, J. E. (2003). *Looking in classrooms* (9th ed.). New York: Longman.

Gordon, T. (1974). *Teacher effectiveness training.* New York: Peter H. Wyden.

Guskey, T. (1994). Mastery learning. *International Encyclopedia of Education.* New York: Pergamon.

Guskey, T. R. (Ed.) (1996). *Communicating student learning.* Alexandria, VA: Association for Supervision and Curriculum Development.

Hallinan, M. T. (1990). The effects of ability grouping in secondary schools: A response to Slavin's best-evidence synthesis. *Review of Educational Research, 60,* 501–504.

Hargis, C. H. (1997). *Teaching low achieving and disadvantaged students* (2nd ed.). Springfield, IL: Charles C. Thomas Publishers.

Hidi, S., & Harackiewicz, J. M. (2000). Motivating the academically unmotivated: A critical issue for the 21st century. *Review of Educational Research, 70,* 151–179.

Hill, C. E., & O'Brien, K. M. (1999). *Helping skills: Facilitating exploration, insight, and action.* Washington, DC: American Psychological Association.

Hodgdon, L. A. (1995). *Visual strategies for improving communication. Volume I: Practical supports for school and home.* Troy, MI: QuirkRoberts Publishing.

Holubec, E. J. (1992). How do you get there from here? Getting started with cooperative learning. *Contemporary Education, 63*(3), 181–184.

Hyman, I., Kay, B., Tabori, A., Weber, M., Mahon, M., & Cohen, I. (2005). Bullying: Theory, research and interventions about student victimization. In C. E. Evertson & C. S. Weinstein (Eds.), *Handbook of classroom management: Research, practice and contemporary issues.* Mahwah, NJ: Erlbaum Associates.

Johnson, D. W., & Johnson, R. T. (1995). Why violence prevention programs don't work—and what does. *Educational Leadership, 52(5),* 63–68.

Johnson, D. W., & Johnson, R. T. (1999). *Learning together and alone: Cooperative, competitive, and individualistic learning* (5th ed.). Boston: Allyn and Bacon.

Johnson, D. W., Johnson, R. T., & Holubec, E. (1993). *Cooperation in the classroom* (6th ed.). Edina, MN: Interaction Book Co.

Jones, R. A. (1995). *The child-school interface: Environment and behavior.* London: Cassell.

Jones, V. F., & Jones, L. S. (2004). *Comprehensive classroom management: Creating communities of support for solving problems* (7th ed.). Boston: Allyn and Bacon.

Kahn, C. J. (1995). *The implementation of mastery learning in high school English.* Unpublished Master's thesis. The University of Texas, Austin.

Kottler, J. A. (1997). *Succeeding with difficult students.* Thousand Oaks, CA: Corwin Press.

Kottler, J. A. (2002). *Students who drive you crazy: Succeeding with resistant, unmotivated, and otherwise difficult young people.* Thousand Oaks, CA: Sage Publications/Corwin Press.

Kottler, J. A., & Kottler, E. (2000). *Teacher as counselor: Developing the helping skills you need* (2nd ed.). Thousand Oaks, CA: Corwin Press.

Kounin, J. S. (1970). *Discipline and group management in classrooms.* New York: Holt, Rinehart & Winston.

Kounin, J. S., & Gump, P. (1974). Signal systems of lesson settings and the task related behavior of preschool children. *Journal of Educational Psychology, 66,* 554–562.

Kounin, J. S., & Obradovic, S. (1968). Managing emotionally disturbed children in regular classrooms: A replication and extension. *Journal of Special Education, 2,* 129–135.

Kronberg, R., Jackson, L., Sheets, G., & Rogers-Connolly, T. (1995). A toolbox for supporting integrated education. *Teaching Exceptional Children, 27*(4), 54–58.

Kulik, C. C., Kulik, J. A., & Bangert-Downs, R. L. (1990). Effectiveness of mastery learning programs: A meta-analysis. *Review of Educational Research, 60*(2), 265–299.

Lambert, N. M. (1994). Seating arrangements in classrooms. *The International Encyclopedia of Education* (2nd ed.), vol. 9, 5355–5359.

Leinhardt, G., Weidman, C., & Hammond, K. M. (1987). Introduction and integration of classroom routines by expert teachers. *Curriculum Inquiry, 17*(2), 135–176.

Lepper, M. R., & Green, D. (Eds.) (1978). *The hidden costs of reward: New perspectives on the psychology of human motivation.* Hillsdale, NJ: Erlbaum Associates.

Loveless, T. (1999). Will tracking reform promote social equity? *Educational Leadership, 56*(7), 28–32.

Mackenzie, R. J. (1997). Setting limits in the classroom. *American Educator, 21*(3), 32–43.

Malone, B. G., & Tietjens, C. L. (2000). Re-examination of classroom rules: The need for clarity and specified behavior. *Special Services in the Schools, 16,* 159–170.

Marks, L. U., Shaw-Hegwer, J., Schrader, C., Longaker, T., Peters, I., Powers, F., & Levine, M. Instructional management tips for teachers of students with autism-spectrum disorder (ASD). *Teaching Exceptional Children, 35*(4), 50–54.

Marzanno, R. J., Pickering, D. J., & Pollock, J. E. (2001). *Classroom instruction that works: Research based strategies for increasing student achievement.* Alexandria, VA: Association for Supervision and Curriculum Development.

McMillan, J. H. (2001). Secondary teachers' classroom assessment and grading practices. *Educational Measurement, 20,* 20–32.

Mueller, C. M., & Dweck, C. S. (1998). Praise for intelligence can undermine children's motivation for performance. *Journal of Personality and Social Psychology, 75,* 33–52

Myles, B. S., & Simpson, R. L. (1994). Prevention and management considerations for aggressive and violent children and youth. *Education and Treatment of Children, 17,* 370–384.

Nastasi, B. K., & Clements, D. H. (1991). Research on cooperative learning: Implications for practice. *School Psychology Review, 20,* 110–131.

Nattiv, A. (1994). Helping behaviors and math achievement gain of students using cooperative learning. *Elementary School Journal, 94,* 285–297.

Nelson, J. R., & Carr, B. A. (2000). *The think time strategy for schools.* Longmont, CO: Sopris West.

Oakes, J. (1985). *Keeping track: How schools structure inequality.* New Haven, CT: Yale University Press.

Payne, R. K. (1998). *A framework for understanding poverty* (rev. ed.). Highlands, TX: RFT Publishing.

Pederson, J. E., & Digby, A. D. (Eds.) (1995). *Secondary schools and cooperative learning: Theories, models, and strategies.* New York: Garland.

Perron, J., & Downey, P. J. (1997). Management techniques used by high school physical education teachers. *Journal of Teaching in Physical Education, 17,* 72–84.

Poland, S., & McCormick, J. S. (1999). *Coping with crisis: Lessons learned.* Longmont, CO: Sopris West.

Positive School Climate. (1998). *Educational Leadership, 56*(1), 1–85.

Putnam, J. W. (Ed.) (1998). *Cooperative learning and strategies for inclusion* (2nd ed.). Baltimore: Brookes.

Race, Class, and Culture. (1999). *Educational Leadership, 56*(7).

Raffini, J. P. (1996). *150 ways to increase intrinsic motivation in the classroom.* Boston: Allyn and Bacon.

Rosenfield, P., Lambert, N. M., & Black, A. (1985). Desk arrangement effects on pupil classroom behavior. *Journal of Educational Psychology, 77,* 101–108.

Shrigley, R. L. (1985). Curbing disruption in the classroom—Teachers need intervention skills. *NASSP Bulletin, 69*(479), 26–32.

Shukla-Mehta, S., & Albin, R. W. (2003). Twelve practical strategies to prevent behavioral escalation in classroom settings. *Preventing School Failure, 47,* 156–172.

Slavin, R. E. (1987). Mastery learning reconsidered. *Review of Educational Research, 57,* 175–214.

Slavin, R. E. (1990). Achievement effects of ability grouping in secondary schools: A best evidence synthesis. *Review of Educational Research, 60,* 471–500.

Slavin, R. E. (1995). *Cooperative learning: Theory, research, and practice* (2nd ed.). Boston: Allyn and Bacon.

Slavin, R. E., Karweit, N. L., & Wasik, B. A. (1994). *Preventing early school failures: Research on effective strategies.* Boston: Allyn and Bacon.

Stigler, J. W., & Stevenson, H. W. (1991). How Asian teachers polish each lesson to perfection. *American Educator, 15*(1), 12–20, 43–47.

Stomfay-Stitz, A. M. (1994). Pathways to safer schools. *Childhood Education, 70*(5), 279–282.

Stoner, G., Shinn, M., & Walker, H. (1991). *Interventions for achievement and behavior problems.* Silver Spring, MD: National Association of School Psychologists.

Students with Special Needs (1996). *Educational Leadership, 53*(5).

Thorson, S. A. (2003). *Listening to students: Reflections on secondary classroom management.* Boston: Allyn and Bacon.

Tudge, J. R. H. (1992). Processes and consequences of peer collaboration: A Vygotskian analysis. *Child Development, 63,* 1364–1379.

Vaughn, L., & Schumm, J. S. (1994). Middle school teachers' planning for students with learning disabilities. *Remedial and Special Education, 15,* 152–161.

Wade, A., Abrami, P., Poulsen, C., & Chambers, B. (1995). *Current resources in cooperative learning.* Lanham, MD: University Press of America.

Webb, N. M., & Farivar, S. (1994). Promoting helping behavior in cooperative small groups in middle school mathematics. *American Educational Research Journal, 31,* 369–397.

Whicker, K. M., Bol, L., & Nunnery, J. A. (1997). Cooperative learning in the secondary mathematics classroom. *Journal of Educational Research, 91,* 42–48.

Zuker, E. (1983). *Mastering assertiveness skills: Power and positive influence at work.* New York: AMACOM.

Index

Notes and Reminders

Ideas for Room Arrangements

Ideas for Procedures and Routines

_____

_____

_____

_____

_____

_____

_____

_____

_____

_____

_____

_____

_____

_____

_____

_____

_____

_____

_____

_____

_____

Beginning of the Year Notes